THE SECRETS OF

Songwriting

THE SECRETS OF

Songwriting

LEADING SONGWRITERS

REVEAL HOW TO FIND

INSPIRATION & SUCCESS

SUSAN TUCKER

07   06   05   04   03   5   4   3   2   1

Published by Allworth Press
An imprint of Allworth Communications, Inc.
10 East 23rd Street, New York, NY 10010

Cover design by Mary Ann Smith, New York, NY

Page composition/typography by Integra Software Services Pvt. Ltd., Pondicherry, India

ISBN: 1–58115–278–7

Library of Congress Cataloging-in-Publication Data:
Tucker, Susan, 1952-
The secrets of songwriting : leading songwriters reveal how to find inspiration and success / Susan Tucker.
    p. cm.
Includes index.

ISBN 1–58115–278–7

1. Popular music—Writing and publishing. 2. Composers—Interviews. I. Title.
MT67.T83 2003
782.42′13—dc21
                    2003007526

Printed in Canada

I wish to dedicate this book to Harlan Howard.

I never had the opportunity to interview Harlan, but I find that his words have lived on through everyone he ever mentored and all who have appreciated his music.

He is missed.

TABLE OF CONTENTS

ACKNOWLEDGMENTS

I want to acknowledge the many people who helped make this book a reality. First and foremost, this whole project would not have been possible without the wonderful thoughts and experiences of the hit songwriters who agreed to be a part of this book. I had a great time talking with you about how you became successful in developing your talents for songwriting. You are all magnificent, caring people, and I know that anyone reading this book will benefit immensely from your insights.

I wish to send a huge thanks to Kim Copeland, my business partner in this endeavor. You were my sounding board and I could not have done this without you.

Special thanks to Tracy Tucker, Scott Milford, and Greg Stoff for your transcribing. Thanks for jumping on board and working those long hours.

To my attorney, Steven Gladstone, you have always believed in me. I appreciate your guidance in all of my endeavors.

Thank you to John Dotson and Kim Copeland for helping me take my books into seminar form. Songwriters from all over the world will now be able to experience the magic of hearing hit songwriters speak live about their creative process and songwriting success.

And last, but certainly not least, to Tad Crawford, Nicole Potter, and all the fine folks at Allworth Press. Thanks for helping me share these inspirational words with songwriters all over the world.

FOREWORD

BY RENEE BELL*

It all begins with a song. To me, this phrase says it all. I'm a song groupie. Years ago, when I was working for MCA Records in Atlanta, I remember sitting in my car playing Emory Gordy, Jr. a song off one of my favorite records for him to consider for Nicolette Larson, whom he was producing at the time. I'd never heard of A&R, but Emory said, "You need to meet Tony Brown," who was the head of A&R at that time for MCA. He said, "We need to get you to Nashville to work in A&R." I always loved country music. It always felt like it was such a part of me, but I really never knew why until I moved to Nashville to work for Tony Brown in A&R; it was the songs.

My first several years in Nashville I worked 24/7. I lived at the Bluebird Cafe. I couldn't get enough of the songwriters and songs. I think the time I spent at the Bluebird made me a better A&R person. There is nothing like hearing a song in its rawest form, right after it's been written, and totally being blown away by it. I'm in constant awe of songwriters and how they can write exactly what I am feeling.

Great songs can cause any emotion in a person, just as long as they cause an emotion. I love funny songs that make me laugh, story songs that paint an incredible picture, and sad songs that make me cry. We need them all in our crazy lives.

Songs define moments in our lives, as Hugh Prestwood said in "The Song Remembers When." Other songs that have totally moved me over the last few years, and started artists' careers or taken them to new levels, are: "Don't Laugh at Me," by Allen Shamblin (The first time I heard it I started bawling—I've never made it through the song without crying), and "I Can't Make You Love Me," by Mike Reid and Allen Shamblin. Every word was so perfect; Tia Sillers, "I Hope You Dance"—once again, a perfect song. Every word killed me; Chuck Cannon's "I Love The Way You Love Me"; Craig Wiseman's "The Good Stuff"; and Gretchen Peters' "Independence Day." I remember where I was when I heard each one for the first time.

I am so happy to see so many of my favorite songwriters included in Susan's new book and to hear them discussing, with great intimacy, the inspiration for these wonderful songs—these songs that define moments in time for me.

We (record labels) spend a lot of money signing artists and making records, but if we don't have a great song, the chances of us breaking an act are very slim. An artist is an interpreter of a song, so once again, "it all begins with a song." And the song begins in the heart and soul of the songwriter.

This book offers an amazingly candid, insightful look into the hearts and souls of some of the most gifted songwriters of our time!

Renee Bell
Senior VP and Head of A&R for RCA Label Group
RCA Label Group, Nashville, TN

* Harlan Howard was one of my dearest friends. Everything that came out of his mouth was a song. He was so full of knowledge. He taught me so much about writers and songs. To be able to have called Harlan my friend is just one more blessing in my life. We miss him so very much!

INTRODUCTION

You have picked up a book titled *The Secrets of Songwriting*. I think I can make two basic assumptions about you. You are writing songs, and you would love to hear your songs on the radio.

While conducting workshops and seminars over the last several years, I have had occasion to talk with hundreds of songwriters. I think that, on a very elemental level, all songwriters are the same. We all love music and words. We all dream about writing a song that is going reach an audience of millions of people.

For my first book, *The Soul of a Writer*, I interviewed thirty songwriters. In that group there were writers with number one hits, and some that were just on the verge of breaking in. There were singer/songwriters, as well as writers that were far from mainstream commercial writing. There was one who wrote themes for movies, some who were pop writers, and several country songwriters. My goal was to find the similarities in the creative process, for this diverse group of writers. It was quite a learning experience to see the ways in which everyone's process is the same, as well as the ways in which the process is totally individualistic.

This book, *The Secrets of Songwriting*, contains interviews with only thirteen writers. But they are *all* hit songwriters, and you will see some of the most notable songs of the last several years represented here. This time, I was trying to find that mysterious ingredient that takes a songwriter from being good, to being great.

If you will read not only all the lines of text written here, but also read between the lines, I know you will find that piece of the puzzle. In addition, you will find validation and inspiration, two qualities that nurture creative souls. For example, when you sit down to write a song, do these kinds of thoughts ever cross your mind?

- "That sucks. What do you think, you've got something to say?"
- "I've written the last song that I'm ever going to write in my life."
- "Well that's that; you're a has-been."
- "I don't know how I ever wrote a song before, I'll never write again."

- "This is the time that the world is going to find out that I don't know how to do this."
- "This is a piece of crap."

Would it make you feel better to know that these are quotes from the writers of such great songs as, "I Love The Way You Love Me," "No One Else On Earth," "I Hope You Dance," "The Good Stuff," "Independence Day," and "The Song Remembers When?"

Whatever stage of learning you are at in your songwriting—and we never stop learning—you surely have felt that invisible wall that separates good songwriters from great songwriters. What is that missing ingredient or quality that is needed to break through that wall and plant your self firmly on the other side? Is it something that you have to be born with? Is it something that you can learn? I think it can happen both ways.

So, assuming you are not someone who has been born with that magic something, how do you go about learning it? We learn from people who are successful. We study, observe, and question them and learn from their mistakes and accomplishments. That is the basic premise for my two books on songwriting.

I know that when you reach the last page of this book, you will be in a whole new place with your writing. Enjoy!

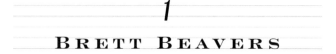

1

BRETT BEAVERS

Brett moved from Texas to Nashville in 1991 to play in a trio at the Opryland Hotel with long time friend Deryl Dodd. Within the year, he became a part of Martina McBride's band and toured with her for four years. It was also during this time that his songwriting efforts began to pay off. Having started his own publishing company with good friend Alex Torrez, the pair of Texans began getting Brett's songs recorded with acts such as Tim McGraw, Billy Ray Cyrus, Ricky Van Shelton, Deryl Dodd, Chris LeDoux, and others.

In 1997, Brett helped put together Lee Ann Womack's first band. He spent the rest of that year writing songs and touring and the follow year secured a publishing deal with Sony/ATV Tree Music Publishing. Some recent cuts include: "Out Go The Lights" (Lonestar), "The Great Divide" (Tim McGraw), and "A Heart With Your Name On It" (Billy Ray Cyrus). Brooks & Dunn took Brett's song "My Heart Is Lost To You" to number 5 on the charts in 2002. Lee Ann Womack recorded "Something Worth Leaving Behind," which became a Top 20 hit and the basis for a book Brett wrote for Rutledge Hill Press with co-writer Tom Douglas. Brett is also producing Capitol Records artist Dierks Bently.

How did you get into songwriting?

I started when I was fifteen, as soon I could play guitar. I never made a conscious decision to write; it just seemed like the thing to do. It was already in there, that creative juice or whatever it was. Having that musical instrument in your hand is so expressive that, if you're a creative person anyway, you're just bent to fall that way.

Through my teenage years I just, basically, wrote what was personal to me. When I was picking with my brothers on the back porch, we wrote bluegrass. When I was sick in love, I wrote sappy love songs to a girlfriend. When I was thinking about God, I wrote something spiritual. It was just an extension. I did that all through high school.

When I got to college, I played in a contemporary Christian band and a couple of country bands. I also wrote songs for them. The week after I graduated college, I answered an ad at a music store, and got in a country band. Of course, it wasn't long before I was showing the guys the songs I'd written.

That went on for about four years, until I just got really burned out on the club circuit, four or five nights a week, four or five hours a night. I was burned out, and I was engaged. My wife got a good job in another town, so I put my guitars under the bed and we moved.

For a year I tried teaching school, selling fishing tackle, and stuff that wasn't musical. But actually, I wrote six or seven songs that year, so I've always done it. I've never been able to not write.

And then, I got a fateful phone call from a buddy of mine, in the summer of 1991. Deryl Dodd, who had a record deal here and had been around Nashville for a while, called and said that he had a chance to play in a trio, here in Nashville, and he needed a bass player. That was all it took. We came up and I auditioned, and I called my principle from here and said, "I know it's a month before school starts, but I'm not coming back." My wife quit her job and we had a big garage sale. A U-Haul trip later we were here.

So, the first nine months I was here, I was playing the Opryland Hotel several nights a week, working a day job at a video store, and writing whenever I could. I'll never forget that first fall we were here. I picked up a book on how to be a Nashville songwriter. One of the things it said was, "Look at the charts, look at the publishers on the charts, call them up, see if they'll take a meeting." So, I did that. I popped open a *Billboard* magazine, and wrote down twenty or thirty of the biggest-name publishers from the singles charts. I called every one of them, and maybe six of them took a meeting with me.

They all passed on the songs, so I got my first little taste of disappointment and rejection then. Looking back, that was just a sampling of the many years of disappointment and rejection to come. Fortunately, I got that in small doses right up front. But, as always, I kept on writing.

Within a year I had an audition with Martina McBride. I joined her band when she was first getting started, and we went on the road that summer of 1992, opening for Garth Brooks. So, within a year of me moving to town from the school-teaching job, I was opening for Garth. It was surreal. But it was nice, because the father-in-law, and the parents, and everybody who told me I was crazy, all of a sudden now, wanted free tickets. So, it was sweet.

I continued to write, on the bus, in the hotel room, in parking lots. I'd take a lawn chair and sit up by the creek. It's very difficult to write on the road. I'd wait till everybody left and went to the hotel rooms, and I'd go back on the bus and sit there late at night and write. I don't remember consciously having a game plan or anything, but I am just absolutely in love with my guitar and writing.

Looking back, if I had gotten a publishing deal, and had written in the decade I had been here, I may have had more big hits up to this point. But I feel like I've had a pretty good little roll, especially since I have been on the road working with platinum acts for nine of the eleven years I have been here. I was never really in town full time writing, which is extremely important for the competition level here. I was with Martina for four and a half years, and I've been with Lee Ann Womack, as bandleader, for five years.

I was in a demo session, probably in 1992, when I met a guy named Alex Torres. I guess I was playing bass on it. We hit it off and he said, "What do you do?" I said, "I play with Martina, but I want to be a songwriter." And he said, "I play with Tracy Lawrence, but I kind of want to get into publishing." We said, "You know, what the heck? Why don't we start our own company?"

So, too stupid to know any better, we started our own little company called Homesick Cowboy Music. Of course, we had no money, but I wrote them, he helped demo them, and then he pitched them because he had good contacts; very political, loved rubbing elbows, that whole deal, you know.

And I was dynamically involved in this community. I was not just holed up in my apartment writing songs, calling myself a songwriter. The fact that I now had a guy who was playing them for people he knew, it was like that was the real deal for me. I was pitching my songs to Martina, who I was working with at the time. She gave me good listens. She actually sang one of my demos. And Paul Worley heard a couple things early on, so I felt like things were happening. I think the first cut I got was in 1994 or 1995, maybe after I'd written fifty or sixty songs.

Somewhere along the way, somebody hooked me up with Philip Douglas, who had a publishing deal, which was huge to me. I had this thing I'd been working on, and I brought it in, and we wrote it. The song ended up being recorded on Billy Ray Cyrus, so, that was neat, a little income stream. Within the same year, Tim McGraw recorded a song I'd written by myself, and so that was a 100-percenter. And Alex and I owned the publishing, so that was pretty nice.

It made a lot of money, for me and for our little company. It gave me a lot of confidence, because I had written it by myself. And it opened a lot of doors for me. After that, people would say, "You know, this guy wrote this song on Tim McGraw's record by himself, I want to write with him."

I've heard it said that if you come to Nashville and want to become a writer, it takes five years before anything really positive's going to happen, like a hold or a cut, but it's going to take ten years for you really to have a foot in. That's pretty close for me. I may have had a couple cuts early, but it took five full years for anything to really lock up. I can look back over a decade and I can see how, after ten, you kind of figure it out.

There are over a hundred songs that Alex and I had, as partners. I think we ended up getting eight or nine cuts out of that catalog by ourselves.

How much of your encouragement comes from within?

The first thing is, I couldn't *not* write, especially in the early years. I did it purely for the love of it. It wasn't until I got to Nashville that the business part became a reality for me. Meaning, that there are perimeters, and games, and lots of things that go on here that will threaten to seep into that process that you grew up loving.

Secondly, I have a gift of being creative. I don't know how gifted I am at being a craftsman, but I have a gift to think, and be quiet, and to ponder. To me that's a very important part of the creative process.

When any disappointments came, my wife was very supportive. She came here, left her family, took a job she didn't really like, but she never thought twice. I never really, consciously, sit around and think about, "I could have never done this without my wife," because, all you young songwriters out there listening, if you think you can't do this without your wife, or a buddy, or your dad, then you probably can't. Never, was it consciously in my mind, "I can't do this without my wife here to support me," because I could have, I would have, and I can.

I'll tell you one way every songwriter finds encouragement to keep on going, is knowing that you won't find another songwriter in this town that has not experienced the same thing, probably worse. For every heartbreak story I had for the first five or six years, I had heard one worse.

A second thing is a positive mental attitude. If you get down on yourself and you think too much about it, you will drive yourself crazy, and make yourself miserable. And you'll lose wives, and kids, and kidneys.

"Opportunity is missed by most people because it's dressed in overalls and looks like work."

I'm well rooted, well rounded. I'm a Christian. I have faith. I believe in self-improvement, and positive thought. I'm a collector of thoughts, and when someone like Winston Churchill says, "Never, never, never, never give up," there's a reason for it, and that has validity in songwriting. When Thomas Edison says something like, "Opportunity is missed by most people because it's dressed in overalls and looks like work." I believe that too. You need to learn from other songwriter's that you're not alone, and you've got to have the heart of a poet and the hide of a rhino.

What is creativity?

To me, creativity is a reflection of God, whether it's singing, writing a song, or designing the Golden Gate Bridge. To me, when the mind goes in motion, and reaches, and strives to bring something out of nothing, that's creativity. Obviously, to me, that reflects the nature of God.

Do you have a writing room or special place where you feel the creativity flows more easily?

I have written everywhere. I've written in parking lots, on the road, on a bus. I've written in my bunk in the bus.

I do have a little place that I go to regularly. It's a building right across the parking lot. We have several writers' rooms there. I've written songs in every room in that building. I think it's just that the building's familiar to me. Also I've written songs in my co-writer's office, which is lined with gold records and, maybe the first time you walk in, can be very intimidating.

I've been able to write good songs everywhere. I understand the benefits of having a comfortable work area, especially free from distractions. Maybe it's not so much where I do it, just so there's not music blaring, not any distractions, no people coming in and coming out.

I like windows. I like being able to see outside. To me, writing also, metaphorically, involves windows. Sometimes they're open; sometimes they're shut, even in the process of writing a song for three hours. There's another room over there, with no windows, and it kind of closes in quick.

Are specific activities such as driving, showering, or mowing the lawn catalysts for creativity?

Early on, it was driving. Especially long trips. That always stirred me, just because it was my moment of solitude. I think it's primarily the solitude, the quietness, and getting rid of the clutter. And then, when you add to it, the world in front of you, in the windows passing by, that's icing on the cake. I can go outside, let the clutter go and ponder about something, and that too will be inspiring.

So, it's not really all-important where I am. It's not really all-important to me who I'm with. I don't have to have my coffee in this cup. I don't have to have this window open and this pen. There might have been a time when those things were positive to me, but I've fallen deeper in love with songwriting. It's like a woman to me. As I know her more, I trust myself with her more. Sometimes she's going to be in a bad mood and not want to talk. Sometimes she's going to open her arms, and we're going to make love.

When I pick up a guitar and people ask me, "What are you going to do today, Beav?" I always hate to say, "Well, I've got a songwriting appointment," or "I've got to go write." What I really want to say is, "I'm going to go pick up my guitar and see if she talks. See if she wants to make love today."

I'm learning to trust my instincts, understanding how the process happens. There are days—call it what you want, call it God's will, biorhythms, planets lining up—there are days when I pick up a guitar and a song drops out of nowhere. And there are days I sit there for hours, and

I feel like the worst writer in the world. I cannot write my way out of a bag, and I feel like I've got everybody fooled.

I know that my identity is not wrapped up in whether or not I write a song. I think, as I've matured, I have learned how to dance with whatever music is coming at that moment. If I pick up my guitar and it just doesn't happen, I don't force it. I don't beat myself up. I understand that there are other factors involved in the inspirational process.

Now, when I pick up a guitar and I feel it happen, I'm there in the moment. I don't edit. I don't write much down. I may write, just to scribble, to keep my phrasing right, but I won't fix a line, because I'm more a musical guy. I'm going to let the music come first. And if the music's coming, I'll start a tape recorder, and I'll just let it roll. I'll play, but I will not edit. Like Quincy Jones said, "The faucet opens, and I've got to fill my bucket as long as it's running," because it may turn off after lunch, or when the phone rings. It's not something to be afraid of, it's something be cherished.

Talk about the role of your subconscious mind in songwriting.

I love that question, that's an excellent question. I'm not going to address it based on how I think the subconscious plays into the writing of a song. I would rather address it based on how I think the subconscious plays into the making of a songwriter.

I believe, very much, in the power of the mind. "As a man thinketh, so he will be." For whatever reason, I had to write songs as early as I began playing music, and I consider myself a songwriter. I have had a hit or two, but I haven't had a number one song yet. But I've rehearsed my acceptance speech for Songwriter of the Year. I've seen myself standing behind the podium getting the award. It's on my list of things to do before I die; have a number one song, be a BMI Songwriter of the Year, and have a hundred of my songs recorded. I've written my speech down, so I could see what it looks like on paper. It sounds different now than it did six years ago.

I don't think this necessarily makes me write a better song. I think it subconsciously makes me live in such a way, and keep my work ethic as sharp as I should, to achieve what I can. Subconsciously, it spurs me on.

And I'm lucky because I love it. If I had, subconsciously, been telling myself, "I want to be a jet pilot," then I may not be walking on that path. But I've seen it. I know what I want to be. I'm not talking about goals, I'm talking about plowing ahead, doing everyday or every week, the things it takes to be successful, and letting success come to me when it's ready. But, all along, knowing I'm a songwriter and, "This is who I am."

Have you ever experienced a period when the flow of your creativity seemed endless?

Yep. Now, I'm talking about songwriting from a real personal, inspirational standpoint. I don't want to get too esoteric, but there are writers in this town, who I write with, who do it as a job. To them, it's a numbers game. If they write a hundred songs per year, percentages go up. A lot of them are going to be crappy. That's just the way it works. Once in a while, one of them pops out and is going to be great.

I love those kinds of songwriters. I wish I could be one. But I've never had the time to be one, because I've always been on the road supporting my habit.

I'm not the kind of guy that says, "I'm going to write exactly what I want to write and, if nobody likes it, I don't care because I've got to follow my heart." I'm not that way either. I believe I'm a good marriage of the two, because I want to be successful, I want to have number ones, I want to pay for my family's retirement, my kid's college. I want success. I want to be the best.

There are times when I'll complain to my wife, "I haven't been able to write for weeks. I sit there everyday with a guitar and nothing's happening." She always says what I hate for her to say, which is "You say that all the time and then, a few months later, the sky's going to open. You're going to hit a lick, and you're just going to boom, boom, boom, write them up. Then you'll come back home and tell me how, 'God, it's just flowing, and I'm writing these great songs, and how great it feels.'" It happens every year.

So, during the times when I really feel inspired, I just try to write as much as I can. I try to get musical nuggets on tape, a verse, a chorus, or a groove. Another day, I'm going to go back and work on that, and hone it down, and sharpen it up.

Do you meditate?

I do. It's deep thinking, to me. It's not prayer. When I pray, I pray to God. When I meditate, I try to push everything else out. It's trying to be as much, *in the moment*, as possible. Getting the distractions out of your mind, and the business of the day out of the way, just so you can develop a keener sense of self. For me, it's being quiet.

What I do regularly is drift off, daydream. To me, daydreaming is not wasteful time. It's washing the crap out. When you get to be a father, a car owner, a homeowner, you live, and the world will get its hooks in you. Whatever your passions are come last. You have to fight everyday to water those passions.

Like I said, it's daydreaming. But it's also like, if I want to meditate on the decade I've been here, everything that's happened, why it's happened, where it leads from here.

Anybody that reads your book needs to get ready for an adventure. It could be an adventure that leads to a dead-end road, but it will be an adventure. It could also lead to a yellow brick road.

Is there a certain time of day that you feel you write better?

I'm creative when I have my guitar in my hands and I'm alone. The mornings though, are when I'm most alive. If I can get up before the kids, and have that first cup of coffee, sit outside and maybe meditate, it's an awakening.

How many songs do you generally have going at one time?

No limit. I always have more than one, because I have a really short attention span. I'll get three chapters into a book, and I'll see another book that interests me more, so I'd rather start it.

I tend to be the same way with songs, even co-writers. "Let's roll this thing along, guys," or "Man, let's get it going." If it starts clicking, that's great. And if we're really excited about it, I don't mind coming back and working on it two or three more times. But, if we're not just falling in love with it, I'd rather start over from scratch.

I have six to ten pieces of different melodies going at a time. To me, the discipline comes in going back, listening to them asking, "Is there something here?" Why that is beneficial also, is that I have made some good decisions by writing with guys who are more lyrically oriented.

I would rather just write the music, although I do both. I trust my instincts on music more, and it comes quicker for me.

Do you keep notebooks or idea books?

Yes I do, I keep titles, I do all that stuff. I think like a songwriter, believe me. Before I ever drove to Nashville, I would listen to country radio, and I had it broken down.

I knew, before I did my first demo sessions, that intros where about ten seconds long on hits. I knew that, most times, it's nice to get to the chorus within a minute. And that three minutes was about that magic number. I knew all of that before I got here.

I wanted to get my songs on country radio, and that's what it takes. After a while, this is in my subconscious. I'm just collecting all the data. I'm not writing it down, but I'm collecting it.

I analyze every song I hear. On the one side of my brain, I'm completely listening for the lyric. I'm not analyzing it. I'm not judging it, but I'm just listening to how it's written, how it flows. Every now and then, a line will jump out I go, "God, did you hear that line?"

"I don't know if you are going to ask about sacrifices in the songwriting business, but if you're not careful, one thing you'll sacrifice is your love of music."

And then, the other side of my brain is listening to the music, the grooves, the sounds, and the structure. That, partially, comes from being in bands and being a player.

I don't know if you are going to ask about sacrifices in the songwriting business, but if you're not careful, one thing you'll sacrifice is your love of music. It becomes such a business to you that it can be difficult to enjoy. Even in movies, listening to soundtracks, even when it moves me, I catch myself going, "What is that? That would be great on a country record."

A blank sheet of paper—now what?

Totally exciting to me. It doesn't intimidate me. I don't see a blank sheet of paper. I see the next song coming.

I write on pads of paper, and also in books, the ones that are bound. If I've been working on a song with a guy for a couple days, then a lot of pages are filled, and every nook and cranny, because I tend to write down everything.

I've just got my baby in my arms, and I open it up to new pages, and its like, "Oh, my gosh, I can put anything on here I want to." It's exciting to me.

Do you think of yourself as disciplined?

I think of myself as extremely disciplined. But my songwriting regimen might not show it, purely because of my schedule. Take a look at the last year. I had two big singles on the charts this summer, my best year, as far as radio play. I'm also producing an album with a guy, and I finished my book (*Something Worth Leaving Behind*, Rutledge Hill Press).

It's probably the worst year yet, as far as being with my mistress, songwriting. I'm still traveling this year, with Lee Ann Womack. In between that, working on this record, and the book, in the first part of the year, out of sheer necessity, something had to be pushed aside for a while. It happened to be my songwriting.

So, as a writer, I haven't been disciplined this year. Obviously, if I was disciplined, I would be getting up at 4:30 A.M. and writing for two hours every day.

I believe in destiny, and I kind of believe there is a reason for my schedule this year. Maybe I'm going to move more into producing and writing. I'm writing a lot of the project with the artist, so I'm still involved, and it's still a creative process.

How important is the opening line?

I've never consciously thought of it as being that important. It's not on my list of the top ten important things to remember in a song.

There might have been a time in country music songwriting when the opening line was really, really important. I don't think so much today. To me, every line is important today, as competitive as it is, and with the shrinking playlists on radio. It's not like it was in '92. There are half as many artists, and they take twice as long to cut a record. I've seen a lot of people lose their deals and go away. Even guys I've written with, who have over ten number one songs, would be the first to admit it is damn hard to get a cut these days.

Which verse is hardest to write?

The first verse seems hardest to write, for me.

Do you ever come up with the second verse first?

No, unless we just, by accident, write it as the first verse. To me, the first verse is more difficult because this is your introduction, to your listener. "Hey, I want to tell you a story." Or, "I want to tell you how I feel about this woman." Or, "I want to tell you what this woman did to me." This is where you've got to get them, in the first verse.

So, in response to your other question, yeah, the first line is important, because the first verse is important. And then, when you get to the chorus, explain it, or take it up a notch. The second verse is, a lot of times, a continuation, unless you want to turn it or twist it.

What are the basic songwriting skills? What makes a person a good lyricist or melody writer?

Read a lot. And, if my son said he wanted to be a songwriter, I'd teach him to play an instrument. Piano or guitar, something he could accompany himself with. If you can sit down and accompany yourself, I think that's better. For me, being able to sit down and play an instrument opens windows to the melody, the phrase, and the song. To me, the music is where it is. And hopefully somebody else will have a better answer for you, for the lyricists out there, but I would say, learn to play an instrument.

What are the advantages and disadvantages to co-writing?

The main thing is, don't let your publisher hook you up with everyone they want to hook you up with, unless they really, really know you. The dynamics of co-writing are such that you'll get with guys where you're going to be the alpha in the room. You're going to do the driving. Then there's going to be times when you get in there and you can't get a word in edgewise. And, times when the person will not shut up. For me, who likes to think, that's difficult.

I've always gone in there and said, "Let's just knock it around, and see what happens, and after a couple hours, if nothing happens, let's just call it." I would much rather call a songwriting session after an hour, than force myself to write a song that I don't want to write, or do it long enough where I start hating doing it. There are times, even now, when I'm like, "I'm hating what I'm doing right now. I'm writing a song. It's what I do for a living, and I'm hating it."

One of the benefits is that your co-writer can fill in where you have some weaknesses. I like to try writing with really good lyric people. I have a lyric guy I have written a bunch of songs with. There's not a day gone by that he and I have not been able to write a lyric together. We get a song every time, and we've gotten cuts together. So, they can pick you up where you may have some weakness, plus they bring an energy to the room.

When I'm writing by myself, if I'm knocking my head against the wall, it's easy to quit. But if I'm writing with a guy, and we've both carved out our time, I have a motivation to stick it out, to deliver something good to the table, to impress him, to come out on the back end of it with a finished song.

What about that "editor voice" that we all have in our head?

I tend to edit myself a whole lot more on lyrics than I do on music. That's because I know my guitar so well. I trust my instincts with music so much more than I do with lyrics. When I'm coming up with a melody, I will, instinctively, with a hair trigger, be able to edit my melodies.

I don't trust my instincts as much to go, "I know exactly how this lyric has to work out." Sometimes I doubt myself, and I don't know when they're right. They could sound right to me, and my publisher might not think they are right, or my wife might not get the song. So I don't really know if they are right.

I edit my lyrics hard because it's hard for me to ever know when they are really right or really done. When I sing them, and they get into place in my phrasing, they feel good and they sound good to me playing them, and it's hard for me to pull myself out and listen.

Define "writer's block."

I think writer's block is in between those cycles of your creativity. I have it at times. I've heard of people going through two or three years of writer's block, couldn't write a song all year. That wouldn't happen to me. I would write. I'd write music. It might not be a song, or it may not be any good. But I'd write a song, because that's what I love to do. I've never experienced writer's block where I was like, "Six months, I just cannot write a song."

Who are three or four people you'd love to co-write with?

If I did have a wish list, it would be so that I could watch, and learn more about the craft from people I look up to. I love Sting's use of melody, mood, and beautiful musical changes. He also writes great lyrics, ranging from the deep, to the commercial pop, and he does so much of it alone. He's very versatile.

And Willie Nelson, the man who has crossed all musical boundaries and transcends categorization, for more reasons than this chapter would hold. Irving Berlin, a prolific writer of so many standards, also very focused on the commercial and business ends of songwriting, truly dedicated and "street smart" in his day. I'd write with them to watch and learn.

What do you think is the most intimidating thing about songwriting?

Knowing there's a chance you may never get another cut, or have another hit. Never fully understanding the complete process of writing a great song enough to be able to do it at will.

If you build fences for a living, what you do is dig a hole, set a post, put up your rails or barbed wire, stand back and admire a job well done, pick up your check, and go to the next project, knowing you can repeat what you just did. Songwriting has never been like that for me. She has always been the woman I must try to make fall in love with me, over and over again. But it's the chase that makes me feel most alive.

> **"Songwriting has always been the woman I must try to make fall in love with me, over and over again. But it's the chase that makes me feel most alive."**

What are the advantages of having a staff writing deal?

Being in a community of like-minded, creative people. Being part of a team. Also, having someone pay the bills so you don't get bogged down running your own business, You, Inc., so you can just focus on writing great songs.

The right staff deal can open all kinds of opportunities for you as a writer, as well as ways to exploit your songs. The best song pluggers are also your agent, your fan, your cheerleader, your motivator, etc.

What are the disadvantages?

Competing with the sometimes huge catalog of songs in your company. Plus, you have to share ownership of something you create. And, when you leave a publishing company, the songs you write while you were there may fall into a black hole and be forgotten.

Give us some tips on surviving the ups and downs of the songwriting business.

This is possibly more important than talent or knowledge. Here are some things to know before entering the field.

Know the ups and downs are coming. Get ready for rejection, and learn how to let it motivate you to forge ahead with more tenacity.

Live and write in the present. Live in the present moment of the songwriting process. You should strive for excellence and originality, letting the song be the star. Don't let your mind wander anywhere from there. Don't begin thinking about how soon this song will get cut (the future), or about how this song stacks up with other songs you've written (the past). Write the best song you can, in the moment.

Make the best demo you can. Do your part to see that the song gets heard by the right people, and then move on!

Always be willing to learn from every other writer you come in contact with. Sitting around and complaining about why certain songs in your catalog have never been cut (we all do it) will bury you in negativity and cynicism, if you let it.

Don't listen to hype of any kind, ever! When you can buy a record in Tower Records that has one of your songs on it, then and only then, are you allowed to celebrate. I've been told so many times, as all of us have, that such and such was going to happen with a song of mine. Don't believe it. Don't have a bad attitude or think, "Woe is me," but just guard yourself, and remind yourself that the most important thing, the thing that you live for most, is the process of writing. Remember the odds are tremendously stacked against you, so make sure you love what you're doing.

My songs are like my children. I conceive them (an idea or melody), raise them the best I can, with my focus on them (the writing process), prepare them for the cold cruel world (re-write, polish, demo, etc.), then I let them go. I always stay in touch with them to see how they are doing, but most of my job has been done, and I don't let my life revolve around them anymore because I've got more kids to raise, and they need my immediate attention. And, who knows, one of them may grow up to be in the movies, win major awards, and make lots of money. Still, I love them all.

2
JASON BLUME

A staff writer for Zomba Music since 1991, Jason Blume is one of those rare individuals who has achieved the distinction of having songs on the Country, Pop, and R & B charts—all at the same time. *Blume's songs are on albums that have sold more than 45 million copies in the past three years, and he is the author of critically acclaimed* 6 Steps to Songwriting Success: The Comprehensive Guide to Writing and Marketing Hit Songs *(Billboard Books), the nation's #1 best-selling songwriting book.*

His song "Back to Your Heart" is included on the Backstreet Boys' Grammy nominated Millennium *album, which received Gold or Platinum awards in forty-five countries and was named Billboard's "Album of the Year." "Dear Diary" (co-written with Britney Spears) is included on Grammy-nominated* Oops, I Did it Again, *and is Blume's second cut with the pop superstar. Upcoming releases include his fifth cut with country star Collin Raye, as well as songs in Japan and Australia.*

This multitalented writer's hits include John Berry's Top 5 country single, "Change My Mind" (certified Gold and included on John Berry's Greatest Hits), Steve Azar's country hit "I Never Stopped Lovin' You," and Bobbi Smith's Canadian single, "I'm So Sorry." Blume's composition, "I'll Never Stop Loving You," was a #1 video in the U.S. and an international hit for fifteen-year-old J'Son, garnering an NSAI Award for being among the "Favorite Pop Songs of the Year." Additional recent releases include cuts with LMNT, 3 of Hearts, and Boyz 'N Girlz United.

Jason's upcoming book, Inside Songwriting: Getting to the Heart of Creativity, *will be published by Billboard Books in Spring 2003. He produced* Writing Hit Melodies with Jason Blume, *the first in a series of instructional CDs, as well as* The Way I Heard It, *a CD featuring Jason's versions of his own songs that have been recorded by artists including the Backstreet Boys, John Berry, Collin Raye, the Oak Ridge Boys, and more. Additional information can be found at* www.jasonblume.com.

How did you get into songwriting?

I wrote my first song when I was twelve years old. I strummed the three chords that I knew on my father's mandolin, and thought nothing about trying to make sense lyrically. Just whatever came out of my mouth, that was the lyric. I had no clue about anything like song structure. It was pure, joyful, wonderful catharsis, just singing my angst out to the universe. That started when I was twelve, and it hasn't stopped yet.

Music was such an important part of my life and my world. I just loved listening. I went to virtually every single pop or rock concert that came to Philadelphia, where I grew up. It didn't matter who the artist was, I was going to be there. I listened constantly and I had a lot of different influences.

To a certain extent, that still defines me, in that I don't write one kind of music. I've had success on the pop, country, and R&B charts. Probably, by the time I was about sixteen, I was writing pretty regularly. I was never a strong player, but I did learn a few more chords.

There was a long period, say from the time I was twelve up until my early twenties, where I was writing, but really in a vacuum, with no input in terms of how one would do this professionally, or how one would do this successfully. It was all about catharsis. It was all about writing from my heart, putting on candles, sipping my wine, and just writing. It was an opportunity for me to express myself; I didn't imagine that I could earn a living doing this.

My parents had drilled into me that I had to have something to fall back on. So, I went to college and I got a degree in psychology, which certainly prepared me for the insanity of the music business. By then, I had picked up guitar. I was really a dreadful player and, to this day, I would say I'm a worse guitarist than probably 98 percent of the people that I teach, or that I deal with in Nashville. But I learned enough that I could help support myself, going through college by playing in coffee houses.

At one point, I was a strolling mandolinist in an Italian restaurant on the waterfront of Philadelphia, where, twelve times a night, I played the theme from *The Godfather*, and "Feelings," which I sang in several languages. I really enjoyed it.

Then, after about a year of working in a psychiatric hospital, after college graduation, I went on a vacation. It's amazing sometimes, how you can get a whole different perspective on life when you are in a whole different environment. There I was, walking for miles along the beach, in the Caribbean, and I knew in my heart that I was not going to be happy unless I at least gave it a 100-percent try to become a successful songwriter. At that point in time I also wanted to be an artist.

> **"I knew in my heart that I was not going to be happy unless I at least gave it a 100-percent try to become a successful songwriter."**

I came back from my vacation and, Monday morning, I gave notice at my job. It was a very scary thing to do because they were offering to put me through a graduate program, all paid for, and I could see my life and my career mapped out ahead of me.

The decision to walk away from that involved leaving not just financial security, but my family, a relationship, and the sense of security. I will never forget driving away from Philadelphia with everything I owned in my Datsun. I had $400, and I drove away sobbing, knowing that my life had changed forever. I knew in my heart that I would never be back again. I also knew in my heart that, in one year, I would be tremendously successful, a Mercedes in the driveway, and fame and fortune. That is not exactly the time frame that things developed with.

I headed to Los Angeles, and when I hit Colorado, I saw a double rainbow in the sky. I took as the sign that I was on the right journey, that I was on the right path, and that I would have the success that I dreamed of.

When I still was several hours away from Los Angeles, but at the California border, I picked up an *L.A. Times* newspaper. I was looking through the want ads, and I called and inquired about a job opening. I didn't know that I would get the job, but I had the appointment set up before my car even arrived in Los Angeles. That was a job that I wound up taking. I was, essentially, a gopher for a group of incredibly wealthy real estate developers.

The reason it was the perfect job for me was that it required no thought whatsoever. I had given everything up to go to Los Angeles and focus on writing songs, and becoming a superstar. I had no interest in working eight hours a day, and zapping all my energy and strength, so I took this job.

I would take their Mercedes to the car wash. I would pick up their dry cleaning. Sometimes I would pick up their food at the supermarket, and I would water the plants at the office. I worked about three or four hours a day, and made very little money, just enough to survive in this horrible place where I lived, which was one room in Hollywood.

Growing up in Philadelphia, I knew what ghettos looked like. Well, where I lived in Hollywood looked fine to me. It looked great, actually looked pretty, and there were palm trees. But, like so much in Hollywood, it was a façade.

The first day that I arrived, there was a SWAT team on the roof of my building, shooting at robbers who were in the middle of a robbery across the street. That pretty much set the tone. I lived in a building, which had twelve rooms that the landlord rented out, and we all shared one bathroom, including a shower and a toilet. There was no kitchen. I was not permitted to cook in my room but, of course, I bought a little toaster oven and did the basics there. Every person in that building was a junkie, a prostitute, or a songwriter. That might be redundant, but that's the truth.

There is the famous story about me eating cat food. I had no other money. I got the coins out from behind the couch and had twelve cents. Pretty much all it was going to buy was a can of cat food. I was hungry enough that, that's indeed how that happened.

But what's interesting is, this was a very happy time in my life. I was so alive, and excited, and filled with the knowledge that I was pursuing my dreams, and they were right around the corner. So while it might sound so terrible, and I did live with mice and cockroaches in this one little tiny room, I genuinely was very happy. During this time, I worked about three or four hours a day, and the rest of my time was spent studying the craft.

I took a songwriter workshop almost the moment I arrived in L.A. It really set me on the road that eventually allowed me to become a professional songwriter, in that it exposed me to the craft. I didn't know there was such a thing as song structure. I didn't know that the title was supposed to be inside the song. Up to that point, I wrote exclusively whatever poured out of my heart. There was no consideration of a listener, or structure, or commercial writing. That didn't enter my mind. Suddenly, I was exposed to writers who were serious about this, who were using tools and techniques, not just writing whatever they felt like.

After a couple of years, I couldn't handle the way I was living. It was no longer fun and exciting. I was getting a dose of reality and, by then, realizing that the Mercedes was not about to pull up in my driveway within the following year. So I started taking more serious jobs. Temp jobs, so that I had flexibility, but I was working full-time a lot of the time. But I was still writing almost every single night when I got home.

I think it's so important that we find a way for our creativity to have a chance to express itself, even though we all have responsibilities, or day jobs, or families, or a hundred obstacles in our way. If

> **"I think it's so important that we find a way for our creativity to have a chance to express itself, even though we all have responsibilities, or day jobs, or families, or a hundred obstacles in our way."**

you focus on the obstacles, that's what you're going to see. If, instead, you make up your mind to say, "Okay, this obstacle exists, I will get around it. Let's just decide what I need to do to get around it," you'll get around it.

I would come home from my day job depressed, exhausted, and feeling like the creativity was being smothered inside of me every time I put on a jacket and tie and had to pretend to be this person that I wasn't.

But, at the end of the day, I could come home, take a nap, wake up, shower, and suddenly, that day felt no longer connected to me. It was a million miles away. I could now write, from 7:00 P.M. until 10:00 or 11:00 P.M., and feel that I could be devoting the time that I wanted to my creativity. Later, I found that I could do it better by doing it in the morning, before I went to work. I sort of shifted into becoming a morning person. What I'm really saying is that we have to find the ways that work for us.

Interestingly enough, somewhere along the line, a temp agency sent me out to a management and public relations firm that handled a lot of major artists. The artists they had on their roster included Engelbert Humperdinck, The 5th Dimension, and several others. The people who ran this company were certifiably insane, and I tolerated a level of abuse from them that I would never tolerate at this point in my life.

But in exchange for that, I made some incredible contacts and, even more importantly, got a phenomenal education about being inside the music industry. I started out as a temp, it was supposed to be three days that I would be there. The person I was supposed to be assisting was in the midst of a drug-related nervous breakdown, and I wound up doing her entire job for her. Before long, I had her job.

At the age of twenty-three, I found myself handling Engelbert, the 5th Dimension, and Patrick Duffy, from the TV show *Dallas*. It was an incredible amount of responsibility. I hated it, but I was suddenly making a lot of money. I went, practically overnight, from living in the one-room with roaches and mice and sharing a bathroom, to living in Beverly Hills and having limousines pick me up.

I did that for two years that were seriously, without a doubt, the most miserable two years of my life, proving beyond a question of a doubt, that money does not equal happiness. What I was doing was suffocating my own dream, and my own writing, and my own creativity. I was working fourteen hours a day or more. I was on call twenty-four hours a day. I was traveling, and was no longer pursuing what I wanted. I woke up one day, and just walked in and said, "I quit."

With my next job, I lied about what my previous experience was. I knew I would never get hired if they knew I had been a director of public relations for big artists. Instead, I said I had been a secretary at a public relations firm. They didn't check, and I got hired at an educational film production company as the receptionist. I thought, "What could be more mindless than answering telephones all day?"

I actually worked a ten-hour workday, four days a week. That gave me three full days for my creativity. I could come home, take a nap, and write every night, and I was back on track now. I was recording demos at a studio from midnight to 6:00 A.M., at a dirt-cheap rate. It was just unbelievably cheap because, otherwise, the studio would just be empty. So I'd be up all night, and at 6:00 A.M. I'd leave the studio, go to McDonalds, drink as much coffee as I could, and start my workday at 7:00 A.M.

One of the filmmakers, one day, came out and said, "I noticed you're always carrying cassettes around. We're having a screening of a rough cut of one of my new films and I'm desperate for music, something that would be like Pat Benatar. Do you have anything like that in your case?"

Well, little did she know, I had been demoing a song the night before that I hoped to pitch to Pat Benatar. I gave her the song, and it was almost weird, almost creepy and hard to explain. I don't know if it's God, fate, or coincidence, but my song worked so perfectly as the opening music of her film that it was almost as if the edits had intentionally been cut to the changes in my music. Well, the song, of course, stayed in the film, which won major awards in the educational film arena. And I became the in-house composer for this film company, and went on to score, and write, theme songs for television, and quite a few of their other educational films. I won an Area Emmy Award for a film I scored.

To me, what this shows, beyond a question of a doubt, is that impossible things really can happen. Just because you're not where you want to be doesn't preclude the possibility of getting there, at some point in the future. After I left that job at Churchill Films, I got another job through a temp agency. Part of me says, "I must be the luckiest songwriter on earth." But another part of me says, "Yes, there was an element of luck involved, but I would not have had this opportunity if I had not picked up my butt, and moved it from Philadelphia, where these opportunities did not exist." I put myself in a place where it was possible to get these opportunities.

The opportunity I'm referring to is, I went out through a temp agency and I specifically said to them, "I would very much like any placements in the entertainment industry, particularly music." They sent me out, as a temp, to RCA Records. This was beyond my wildest dreams and expectations. I had been pounding on those doors for years, and trying to pitch songs, trying to get my foot through those doors that were locked, closed to me. And now, someone was going to pay me to be inside RCA Records.

That was the good part. The bad part was, it was in the country promotion department and I detested country music. I thought it was garbage, and decided that this must be some cruel punishment for something I had done in a previous life, that I was going to have to sit and listen to this hideous music for eight hours a day.

I was supposed to work two days a week in country promotion, stuffing envelopes, helping with filing, doing whatever was required. My very first hour on the job, the first thing they asked me to do was to stuff envelopes with the first single by a brand new act on the label called The Judds. And that changed my life, because I fell in love with the music.

I had had this total misconception of what country music is. I think my idea of country music was somewhere back in the fifties or sixties. I didn't know that country music had changed somewhere along the line. Suddenly, I was hearing songs that sounded like the best-written, most well-crafted songs I had ever heard in my life.

Harmonies that just sent chills through me, and Wynonna's voice was just incredible. And the production on the records, I thought, was just amazing. I loved it, and I wanted to do that.

That really set me on a path. I wound up staying for quite a long time in that position, probably about two years. It was the absolute golden era of country music at RCA. I was interacting with all the artists, and I was immersed in their music, not to mention the invaluable information I was learning about how a record label worked, in terms of music promotion.

I had decided I would write a song for the Judds. I wrote my very first country song and it was called "I Had a Heart". I knew I had this brilliant twist that had to make a perfect country song. I re-wrote the song seven times, and brought in a collaborator, Bryan Cumming. Because I had made connections from working at RCA Records, I was able to take it to a publisher, and he sent the song to Nashville. The next day, we had a single. It was recorded the next day. Of course, it took a little while before the single came out.

This was on a little, tiny independent label, on a new artist. It didn't matter to me. As far as I cared, this was the big time. I could never have imagined that I could earn eighty-seven dollars from that record, but it changed my entire life. It was clearly the turning point, because the producer of that record had written six number one country singles, and loved the song, and wanted to write with me. Little did he know, I had written one country song in my entire life, up to that point. I was beyond intimidated.

His name was Don Goodman and he was in Nashville. At the moment, as we're doing this interview, he's on the charts with *Ol' Red*. I had never been to Nashville but I booked my trip as soon as he said he wanted to write with me. I borrowed money on my credit card and arranged to come here, specifically to write with him.

Then I spent two weeks desperately trying to come up with brilliant ideas, snippets of melodies, song starts, just a phrase, a title, maybe a half of a chorus, and in some instances, I would even write out pretty much a whole lyric. That way, I knew that if I showed up to write with him and was petrified, or had a headache, that I still could contribute because I had already done my homework.

Don never showed up for our writing appointment. His publisher felt terrible about it and went down the hall looking for someone else for me to write with. She came back and said, "Jason, this is A.J. Masters. A.J., this is Jason. Y'all go write a hit now."

And we did. We had taken a lyric that I had started in LA and turned it into "Change My Mind." That song changed both of our lives. That night, when A.J. played it for his wife, Stephanie, she cried and said, "Our kids are going to college!"

Three and a half years later, the Oak Ridge Boys, who were huge at that time, recorded it. They were coming off a number one single and they'd had Grammys.

Thank God, when I wrote that song, I had an attorney who had far more sense and knowledge than I did, because A.J.'s publishers asked to publish my share of the song. My attorney said, "Look, you already have to pitch this song because A.J. is your staff writer. Jason has nothing to gain by giving you his publishing share, so we're not giving it to you. However, if you pay for his share of the demo, and you are the one responsible for getting a major label release on this cut then, as a bonus 'thank you,' we'll give you one-third of Jason's publishing."

So, I had not just an Oak Ridge Boys cut, but also one that was slated to be a single. And I owned two-thirds of my publishing, which I could then dangle as a carrot, and use to secure that staff writing deal that had eluded me for eleven and a half years. What it took for me to get that deal was having something concrete to bring to the table.

There was no way they could lose money on an Oak Ridge Boys single by offering me a staff writing deal. I had a huge decision to make. Do I want to parlay this into that staff writing deal that I wanted so desperately, or do I keep my publishing and figure that, if this is a number one single like their last single was, I could be looking at $100,000? What do I want?

I didn't have a crystal ball, but I basically reviewed all the information available to me, and decided that I would rather have a staff writing deal that could conceivably turn into so much more than just this one cut, than just having the money from one cut. I had actually had six offers of staff writing deals at that point, and decided to go with Zomba because they owned a pop and R&B record label, and I wanted the opportunity to be able to write, not just country songs, but to be able to get plugged into pop and R&B projects.

In addition to actually owning the record label, they had very successful offices in New York, London, L.A., and other countries around the world. Zomba actually offered me five thousand dollars less than another company to sign that deal, and that was an astronomical amount of money to me at that point in time. Gratefully, I went for the lower money, but what seemed to be a place where I would have more of a future.

I could never have imagined, when I signed with Zomba in 1991, that there were little kids in elementary school, who would grow up and record my songs specifically because of the Zomba connection. Of course, their names are Britney Spears and the Backstreet Boys.

So, I was a combination of incredibly lucky, or blessed, to have made the decision that I made. But, at the same time, I'll give myself a little bit of credit and say I was willing to forego the immediate extra money, in the hopes that things would develop the way that they actually did.

Are there specific things that are inspirational to you?

There are a lot of different things that have sparked inspiration for me. Before I had moved here full-time, but was spending a lot of time here, I would go to the Bluebird a lot, probably at least two or three nights a week, and just study the songs that were being performed. Stripped down by the writers, I could really study what they were doing, lyrically and melodically. I would be so inspired by what I would hear, that virtually every single time I left the Bluebird, I was working on a song before I got home. I would stay up, sometimes for hours into the night, because I was so inspired.

For me, nature is also a very important part of my life. Weather permitting, I walk outside almost every morning. I tend to come up with a lot of my ideas while walking. I'm not sure what it is, but the combination of walking, and knowing that I have a co-writing session coming up in an hour and that the pressure is on, that's very often when I come up with my ideas. I also have come up with some of my best ideas in the car, driving to my co-writing session.

What is creativity?

For me, creativity is an extension of a spiritual process. I feel like, while I'm not a religious person in any organized religious sense, I'm a very spiritual person. To me, the very act of creation, right from the very beginning, when life began, began a chain of events that eventually led to my creation.

I believe that we are literally born creative beings. At every moment we are interpreting and, in a sense, creating our perception.

It's virtually impossible for us, as humans, as part of the definition of being human, to not be creating. Even thoughts, thinking things, new ideas. For me, that's almost a sacred component to the creative process.

So, whether it's an idea, a song, a poem, a painting, or even simply a new perspective on how to see something, it's just all part of how we've been created to continue the process of creation.

Are you aware of the cycles of creativity?

I'm not a person who has ever experienced so-called writer's block. I've heard it said that the problem with writer's block is, there's somebody down the block who doesn't have it, and if you're going to compete, you'd better get through it.

I've never had a period where I would say, "I cannot write," but there's no doubt that I can look back and say, "Oh, that was a period where my best work came out, and I don't know why." Whereas, there might have been another period, following that, where I was just as productive in terms of the number of songs that I wrote, but the quality, the special factor, the uniqueness of them wasn't nearly as strong. So yes, I would have to say that that kind of creativity that I most value, and most hope for, seems to indeed come in spurts.

> "I cannot teach anybody how to access a brand-new thought, or a new angle on a love song that has never been done before. I can encourage them to create an environment in their life that is hospitable for those thoughts to emerge."

Talk about the role of your subconscious mind in songwriting.

Oh, I think that's who deserves the writer's credit, the subconscious mind. But I also feel like there's a combination that's crucial. I cannot teach anybody how to access a brand-new thought, or a new angle on a love song that has never been done before. I can encourage them to create an environment in their life that is hospitable for those thoughts to emerge.

The ways we could create those environments would include things like allowing time for them to come in, special time, whether it's a walk in the woods or just an hour of quiet time with a notebook. You're much more likely to access a deep level of creativity at that period of time, than if you're under stress at a job that you hate during that same hour. You need to create that environment, where the subconscious mind can be heard and can have an opportunity to bubble forth.

One of the biggest turning points for me, as a writer, came when I grasped that the cathartic way of writing, that was simply self-expression, was only one part of the equation of successful songwriting. I needed to learn a lot of craft to successfully use that subconscious gift, that thought that bubbled up, that angle, that new way to look at a song, that melody, and take it, and package it, and deliver it in such a way that my listeners could receive it.

Then it was no longer a one-sided equation of being all about me. Now it was about taking something that was important to me—that started as a spark in my heart—and imposing conscious mind onto it to express it in such a way that it could be received, so that it could move more than just me. So it could move you.

If you ever find yourself in a rut, how do you shake things up?

I am a confirmed travelaholic, and nothing works better for me than getting out of the environment. Not just if I'm in a creative rut, but also if I'm in a rut in any other area of my life. Remember, I told you that the whole shift where I decided to quit my job and become a songwriter came while I was on vacation in a totally different environment.

I do an enormous amount of traveling. I return from it changed, and refreshed, and with all new perspectives. So, there's my rationalization for why I should get to take vacations all the time and write them off.

Do you like to read?

I think reading is a lyric writer's best secret weapon. I love to read. There is never a time when I'm not in the midst of a book.

It's very rare for me to read a well-written book without coming out with song ideas. I've gotten many song ideas from books, and also from movies.

> **"I think reading is a lyric writer's best secret weapon."**

I love to read any genre that is extremely well-written, including great detail. I want to feel that I'm in the story, which is essentially what we want to do as songwriters also. I don't really care if it's a murder mystery, science fiction, historical, or a biography. If the writing is rich, and textured, and detailed, I tend to love it. For me, it's almost the telling of the story as much, if not more, than the plot.

Do you think of yourself as disciplined?

I don't. However, other people looking at me might say that I am a disciplined writer. I would probably be a more successful writer if I were able to be a little bit more disciplined, and do all the things that I teach other people how to do.

I'd say that other people would call me disciplined in that, on average, I probably am working on at least three songs a week, in my office with co-writers, and I'm regularly working on demos and on pitching songs, and that kind of thing. Where I would like to have a little bit more discipline, is to take more time on my own to really put each and every line under that microscope, the way I tell everyone else to.

Is your writing style altered by writing on a different instrument?

I do think that it has a big impact. I believe very strongly that some of the best writing happens when you write on the instrument that I use, which is the tape recorder. I write my melodies a cappella, by singing into a tape recorder, so that I am not constrained by going to the next predictable chord, the chord that I'm comfortable playing, and the chord that I recently learned. I feel strongly that melody has to rule, and that melody is what we sing in the shower, on the interstate, walking down the street when we don't have a guitar or a piano. It's the melody that I want to stick in somebody's brain.

In no way am I implying that the chords are not important. They're very, very important. But their job is to support the melody, and I believe the number one pitfall that developing songwriters fall into, is allowing their chord changes to dictate their melody. Coming out with predictable, boring, perfectly good melodies that work with the chord changes, but lack freshness and the originality that will make a listener go, "Wow." If I'm not touching an instrument, I'm much more likely to be 100 percent focused on the rhythm, and the actual note choices of my melody.

That's what I do when I write. Afterwards, I figure out my chords.

Is there any one part of songwriting that you could label as the most intimidating part?

It's hard for me to imagine any other answer than the blank page at the beginning of the day. I will confess that I am nervous, anxious, maybe even frightened, every single time that I start a new song, because I can't control what will come out of me. I want it so desperately to be incredible and there is a fear, when I'm just beginning. "Will it flow? Will it be powerful? Will it be special? Will it be unique?"

I deal with that fear by reminding myself that, no matter how much I want it to be, nine times out of ten, it's not going to be the incredible, special song. By virtue of definition, each thing we do cannot be the best. Only one gets to be the best this year or this month, and the rest, no matter how badly I want them to be the best, can only be the best I can do that day.

I admit it's frightening for me to start each new song. Especially if there's a lot riding on it, if I'm writing with a major artist, or I'm writing with a producer, or with a high-level writer that my publisher has hooked me up with, and I want to show that I can come through in one of these situations. Not to mention, financially there can be a lot riding on it. It's very intimidating. I've had to learn that everything I do will not be successful, and will not be the best, and to just show up anyway.

How important is the opening line?

It's crucial, and the reason I know it's crucial is, when I screened all those songs for RCA Records and had boxloads of tapes, I was pretty much making up my mind in those first twenty seconds. The intro gave me a certain amount of information, in that it told me, "Is this coming from a professional, or an amateur," by the quality of the demo.

Then, the first couple of lines of melody and lyric either gave me a message that said, "Wow, this is special, this is unique, I'm now emotionally and psychologically set up to expect a hit," or those opening two lines have given me a message that said, "You know what, this is just one more well-crafted song, nothing special, nothing unique." As they say, we only get one chance to make a first impression, and your opening lines are your first impressions.

I always suggest that my students go back, when they're finished with their draft, and re-write those opening lines, both melodically and lyrically, three times before they settle, so that they're absolutely sure that they've really focused on that, and done the very best that they can do.

What are the basic songwriting skills?

Persistence, and the ability to function in spite of seemingly endless rejection—I think that without those two qualities, no other skill will get you through. You can be the most extraordinary melody writer, the most incredible lyric writer, and if you can't handle the rejection, and can't hang in long enough, it won't matter.

Of course, there are other skills that we have to have. I think people skills are very important. To be well liked, to be somebody that people want to write with, to be somebody that people want to have meetings with, these are important skills.

Obviously, if you're going to be a melody writer, you'd better know how to write melodies, but I think that goes without saying. Same thing if you're going to write lyrics, you'd better have a way with words. But that won't be enough without the persistence, the ability to handle the rejection, and belief in your self. I think it goes hand and hand with the rejection that is an inevitable part of this career. Virtually, no matter who you are, at any level, you will be rejected far more often than you will get a "yes."

Do you have a philosophy on rejection?

I think it's crucial to separate our self-worth and our self-esteem from whether a song gets recorded, or where it ends up on the chart. There are things that have to do with where that song ends up on the chart that may be political, or may have virtually nothing to do with the quality of our song. The way that the producer produced the song is not in my control; I don't get invited to the studio. The way the singer sang it is not in my control. I can get totally crazy over things that are not in my control, or I can simply focus on what I can control, what can I do.

What I can do is write the best material that I can write, take care of business to the best of my ability, and accept that when these songs are not as successful as I would hope they would be, that does not make me a bad person, or even a bad songwriter.

What about that "editor voice" that we all have in our head?

A lot of times that little voice sounds an awful lot like my father telling me, "What makes you so special? You'll never make it. The chances are one in a million. When are you gonna go back to school and get a real job?" That voice can be a good motivator, if it encourages us to work harder, and acquire skills, and re-write, and keep pushing ourselves. It can also cause a lot of unhappiness if we believe everything that it says. Like so many things in this life, we have to take the message and decide what we do with it.

What advice can you give on dealing with the fear of failure?

There will be failure along the way, and success does not come with a guarantee, ever. I think it's something that simply has to be accepted. No one has a gun to our heads. No one's forcing us to pursue a career that is defined by rejection at every turn in the road. If that is your choice to move forward, then accept that there will be frustration, there will be rejection, and there may not be the reward at the end of the rainbow that you are anticipating.

However, I believe very strongly that there are rewards all along the path. I think the happiest and most successful people are those who can find those rewards along the way. Enjoying the writing process, loving how it feels when you nail that line on the fifth re-write. Loving the process of pitching the songs, embracing the full package, enjoying the interaction with the other writers and being part of the creative community.

Let's face it: Every writer is not going to make it to the top of the charts. Does that mean they are failures? Not in my book. As far as I'm concerned, the failure is the one who was so afraid of failing that they never pursued what was in their heart, and never had a chance.

I wish I could have believed that along the way, because I gave myself a lot of grief, beating myself up over not being successful when, in retrospect, I can see that I was on a path. I was right where I needed to be, and I was on a journey that, indeed, led me to success.

Define "writer's block."

I think that if we slice writer's block very thinly, and put it under the microscope, it's fear, in every cell. There's an actual technique that I teach, that a lot of people have had success using to get through the writer's block. I tell people to set a timer for maybe ten minutes and, while that timer is going, you just write whatever you feel. The only way to do this wrong is to invite that editor into the process. As long as your pen is flowing, and you're writing what you feel, you're doing it right.

I'm not talking about trying to craft a commercial song, or a hit. All I'm talking about is expression. When your ten minutes are up, you're done.

It removes the pressure, the expectation of something *good* coming out of this. I've gotten some of my best lines, or my best concepts for songs, out of that kind of a space. Sometimes, someone might have to do that ten times in a row before the block cracks.

I think it also can help to own and accept that the block is fear, and that we are not machines; that none of us will consistently, day after day, crank out brilliance. We don't have to be afraid of it—just accept it.

3
CHUCK CANNON

Chuck was a solo performer on the South Carolina beach circuit for several years before moving to Nashville in 1984 to attend Belmont University, where he studied Music Business and Finance. In 1988 he met producer Marshall Morgan, who signed him as a staff writer to Taste Auction Music. In 1992, he opened his own publishing company, Wacissa River Music, Inc. He is a member of the Leadership Music Class of '99 and presently serves on Leadership Music's board and the Nashville Songwriters Association International's board, as well as their legislative committee.

Chuck has had songs recorded by Trisha Yearwood ("The Whisper of Your Heart"), Lari White, Roy Rogers, Willie Nelson, Dolly Parton, Randy Travis, Toby Keith ("We Were In Love," "Dream Walking," "How Do You Like Me Now"), John Michael Montgomery, Paul Carrack, Night Ranger, Brooks & Dunn, Boyzone, Lonestar, Mark Wills, Collin Raye, and many others. His credits include several of BMI's prestigious Million-Air Awards as well as BMI's Two-Million-Air award for the Academy of Country Music's 1993 Song of the Year and international hit, John Michael Montgomery's "I Love The Way You Love Me."

He currently resides in Nashville, Tennessee, with his wife, Lari, their daughter, M'Kenzy Rayne, and their son, Jaxon Christian.

www.chuckcannon.com

How did you get started in songwriting?

I started playing guitar the summer I was sixteen. I was real inspired by guys like James Taylor and Bruce Springsteen. I basically taught myself how to play. I was never one of the guys who read the liner notes. I used to just listen to songs. So, I never knew that there was such a thing as songwriting.

I started playing around Myrtle Beach and picked up a pretty good little following down there. All I knew was that I wanted to be a singer. I wanted to be a star. Being the cocky kid that I was, I always thought I sang pretty good.

I just knew that when I got to Nashville they were going to wonder where I'd always been. Instead, they just wondered why I didn't just go on back. Getting into the music scene in Nashville, I started realizing that songwriting was something I needed to bring to the table, as well. I had just, kind of, dabbled in it a little bit; pretty amateurish efforts.

I had lived here for a little over a year and a half, and on New Year's Eve of 1985, I'd had a date, and I had been stood up. I was sitting at this bar, drinking a beer, kind of dejected about the whole thing. This good-looking girl comes over and says, "When are you going to come down here and sweep me off my feet?" I said, "Well, why don't you buy me a drink, and we'll try to get started on that." She laughed and we started dating.

That was Matraca Berg. Young and foolish and falling in love, we ran off and got married. I owe so much to her. I learned so much, even though I didn't write any songs to speak of. While we were married, she wrote a hit for Reba McEntire called "The Last One To Know." She was such a great songwriter. I got an education about what great songs were.

The relationship didn't turn out well. We ended up getting a divorce. A whole lot of that was because we were way too young. But I did learn a whole lot about the business, and a lot about what good songs were and how, at the end of the day, they have to have that little spark of something special.

After she and I broke up, I began songwriting in earnest. That would have been the summer of 1989. With the education I'd gotten, I had such a leg up. I used to go down to the Bluebird and listen to Don Schlitz, Fred Knobloch, and Paul Overstreet, and try to really, honestly assess why I wasn't getting cuts.

I tried to understand what made theirs better. I figured it like this: If somebody had a tape on their desk with my name on it, and one with Don Schlitz's name on it, then my song had to be better than Don's. That was the standard that I had. I knew that was my competition, the best in the business. I tell people who are trying to break into songwriting that you should look at it that way. The very best in the business, that's your competition.

So, I tried to really make an honest assessment of what was better about their work than mine, and what allowed them to have some success at getting recorded. I would listen to a lot of things those guys would say in between their songs. They'd always say stuff like, "Don't try to write stuff that's on the radio, that's what was being written a couple years ago." I'd just try to pick little anecdotal bits of wisdom from these guys.

In 1988 I really started writing in earnest, and really got serious. That was due to a guy named Marshall Morgan. He used to produce Gary Morris and the Nitty Gritty Dirt Band. He got interested in me. He was my champion.

We all need somebody to believe in us. You need someone that isn't just telling you want you want to hear, but believes in your talent, and is urging you to develop your talent. Everyone needs someone like that.

What is creativity?

I think it's 99 percent perspiration, and 1 percent inspiration. You have to say it's 99 percent perspiration because, if you sit around and wait for inspiration to write, I think that you sell yourself really short. There are people that that works for, and I have no issue with them at all. But I've found that some of the very best songs I've ever written have been on those mornings that I've gotten up, and just not felt good, and it's difficult to get to the appointment. You feel like picking up the phone, and calling them up, and saying, "I don't think I want to work today." But I've gone to a lot of those and, honestly, actually, now that's kind of like a sign to me that I'll probably get a good song if I just go on.

I come from a real religious background, and my people would probably say that's the devil trying to keep you from going and doing what you're supposed to do. I do believe in God, and I would hesitate to say that it is all a gift, because there is so much that goes into developing the talent that you are given.

But, at the level of writing a song, I find a lot of times that the song, kind of, has a mind of its own, and will take you where it wants to go. If you try to force it to go somewhere that it doesn't want to go, you may be able to complete the song, but it won't be as good.

Most songwriters that I know would agree that there is a high mystery here, and something going on here that none of us can really put our fingers on, or lay a definition to.

It's that "indefinable" thing that guides a creator, that makes him able to just know how it ought to go, how the melody ought to work, what the lyric ought to say, and makes them just know when that line isn't just right. At some level, you have this sense of it being right, or not being right.

My experience has shown me that from the very beginning. That mystery has never changed. I get the same feeling when I just know. That's the part that I'm so in love with. I feel like I'm tapping into something that holds all this shit together.

I'm a big fan of Keith Jarrett, and he said that he's not creative. He's merely a channel for the creator. That's just another creative guy, trying to explain something about the mystery of all this. There are times when you write a song, and you feel like it's always been there. Those are few and far between but, every now and then, you hook into one. That's scary, because you think, "I must be on top of something." Those are the ones we live for.

Do you have a special writing room that you really feel creative in?

We're in it right now. I like to write here.

What is it about this room?

We're in my control room and studio. Got some pretty good gear, and all my guitars are here. There's my blank page book that I write everything in. Nice, comfortable couch.

But, I can really write anywhere. I just prefer here. My house is a hundred yards up the hill. We're in the middle of the woods. It's quiet, just kind of conducive to the whole thing. I like being able to look outside at the hills. I like the natural light that we have in here. We're secluded and there's no road noise.

Is quiet an important part of it for you?

Yeah, quiet's important. I like to work at night. I get most of my ideas started then. Things that I take to other co-writers, I usually start those late at night. I really like to start writing around nine or ten o'clock, and things start to get interesting around midnight. I always say that's when my editor falls asleep. It's that little guy sitting there going, "That sucks, what do you think, you've got something to say?" It's that guy. He gets tired and goes to sleep.

But, I've written great songs at eight o'clock in the morning too. There's no secret, but there are patterns that I experience. One of my really interesting personal patterns is that, the more I pray and meditate, the more I write, and the better I write.

Another odd thing that I just noticed about four years ago is that I was writing in cycles. I started trying to figure out what was going on in those cycles. I woke up one morning and vividly remembered a dream. I'd been going through a dry spell in writing and that day, I wrote a song. Real fast, and a good one, I think it ended up getting cut. This went on for about a week. I'd remember my dreams, and I would write. Since that time, I've noticed that one of my personal indicators is that, if I start remembering my dreams, there's a high correlation between that time and actual output for me.

Can you relate that to extra time that you might be spending praying or meditating?

Yes, somewhat, but there's a higher correlation with the dream remembering than there is with the praying and meditation. In the final analysis, we're all at the mercy of a great idea. You have to keep your tools sharp, and the way you do that is just by writing, even if you don't get anything but a half a verse, even if you don't get anything but a guitar lick, but writing all the time. Then, when the great idea comes along, you're ready. Writing is not nearly as hard as finding good ideas.

Red Lane told me one time that one of the biggest problems I'd end up with as a songwriter, if I stuck with it for ten years or longer, would be tricking myself into writing, and there's a lot of truth in that.

What do you think that means exactly?

You get to where you start rehashing, covering old material. There's only so many ways you can say "I love you," but the reason love songs keep on working is, there's always a fresh crop of fourteen-year-olds falling in love, and they don't want Big Sister's song, or Momma's song. They want their song.

You hear people bitch about it all the time, saying that you don't ever hear anything fresh on the radio. That's just the way it's always been. That's the way it's always going to be, because there's always a fresh crop of fourteen-year-olds falling in love that need their song.

It's hard to keep your enthusiasm up, as a writer, when you've written so many love songs. Look at the charts. I'd say 90 percent of those songs are something about "how much I love you." It's hard to keep your enthusiasm up for writing when you've gone through that material so many times. But, at the same time, that's our job. If there is drudgery to this job, that would probably be it, the fact that you've got to be fresh on, basically, the same thing.

Actually, I find it to be challenging. I step outside of that box. I write a lot of other stuff. I read an interview once—I think with Bob McDill—they asked him, "What's your advice to songwriters?" He said, "Write something besides love songs."

And that's good advice. I think it's a good exercise to write other things. I think there are other topics that are worthy. Before September 11, it was a period of time in our country when we were kind of oblivious to a lot of those kinds of things. That's why I think the very most important thing, in the eyes, in the hearts, and in the minds of the masses, was simply love. Their relationships, their falling in and out of love.

Now, with this, we'll see a bit more social activism and that will bleed into the arts. The arts have always been a reflection of what's going on. They can't help but be. That's what moves artists, storytellers, and writers, in their souls.

Since the Vietnam War was over, we haven't had anything to hang our collective hat on. Those kinds of emotions, those kinds of things to write about, just haven't been there, not on a massive scale. Basically, for most people, the biggest things going on in their lives were love affairs.

Tell us about some activities that are really good for your creativity.

I watch movies. Other things that I do to spur creativity: I read. I read, and read, and read, and then, I read some more.

I find inspiration in so many things. I like to go boating. I'm a pilot. Driving down the road, I write a lot while driving. I can't get away from it. There's no escape from being a songwriter; I see a song in so many different things.

What kinds of books do you like to read?

Everything, from science fiction, to fantasy, all the way to history, and theology. Theology's probably one of my favorite things to read about. I read a lot on the Internet. I like to read opinions. I'm neither conservative, nor liberal. I think that both of them are equally full of shit. I think what we need to do, is get rid of all the Democrats, and get rid of all the Republicans, and get some Americans up there to run this thing.

Talk about the role of your subconscious mind in songwriting.

I think a lot of things operate on a subconscious level, but it's virtually useless until it perks up into the conscious level. I'm a bit skeptical about a lot of things getting worked out subconsciously. It's a very active thing for me, writing is.

You say you meditate a lot. Isn't that connecting with your subconscious?

I don't meditate as much as I pray. Meditation implies some other things that are not bad; it's just not, necessarily, what I do. I do a lot of listening when I pray. Songwriting is very peripheral to my purposes there. My purposes there are soul stuff. Being a better man, being a better father, being a better husband, being a better songwriter, but that's one of the minor elements that I'm trying to achieve by praying.

"I'm not listening for song ideas; I'm listening for soul ideas."

I'm not listening for song ideas; I'm listening for soul ideas. I'm listening for understanding on a broader level. I think you bring those things into songwriting. But I know plenty of songwriters who don't pray, who don't meditate, and are really successful.

Have you ever experienced a period when the flow of your creativity seemed endless?

I've had years where I've written over a hundred songs. But there is an element of wondering if I'll ever be able to do it again, if I'll ever be able to write another song. At an even deeper place, I know I will.

I am in a place of endless flow. It never goes away. I'm quoting something Red Lane told me once: "I don't believe in writer's block. I ain't had writer's block since 1963." The way he did that, was that he always had four or five songs he was working on. So, I've always got things I can work on.

I sometimes wonder if I'll be able to write another hit and, since songwriting is what I do for a living, I really need to do that. But that's not why I write. I write because I can't help but write.

The first time I ever met Harlan Howard, he asked me, "Kid, what gives you the right?" I said, "The right, what are you talking about?" "What gives you the right?" I said, "Harlan, I'm sorry, I don't understand."

"Well, you're hanging around all these highfalutin songwriters. What gives you the right?" I laughed, I said, "Man, what do you mean?" He goes, "What have you written?" I went, "Oh, Harlan, I don't like to talk about that. There's a lot of other stuff we can talk about."

He said, "I'm asking you. You ain't wrote as many hits as me, I know you ain't wrote as many songs. You might have wrote as many hits, I don't know, but you ain't wrote as many songs." I said, "Well, I ain't written as many hits, Harlan." He said, "Well, I'm asking you, what did you write?"

I said, "Well, you know, the one that brought me to the dance, was a song called, 'I Love The Way You Love Me.'" He goes, "John Michael Montgomery, 1992." He said, "That was real cute. Started a whole rash of that shit, didn't you?"

I said, "I guess." He said, "What else did you write?" I said, "Man, really, I don't like talking about that." He said, "Hell, what's the last thing you wrote? What was your last hit?" I said, "'How Do You Like Me Now,' Toby Keith."

Harlan reached across the table—his hand was kind of shaking—and he said: "Now I want to shake your hand, but be real gentle, I bruise easy." I grabbed his hand and said, "Harlan, thank you, but that song ain't all that. I've written a lot better than that." He said,

"You said something that millions and millions of people want to say, wanted to say, and you said it for them, and that's what our job is."

"I have too, but ain't neither one of us written anything that more people wanted to say."

Him saying that to me just pointed out that I'm taking myself too damn serious. There's the second-biggest copyright of my career, and I'm disparaging it. And Harlan, in his graceful and gentle way, let me know, "Don't take yourself so seriously. You said something that millions and millions of people want to say, wanted to say, and you said it for them, and that's what our job is."

What kind of notebooks do you keep? Do you have an idea book?

I've got a book of blank pages that my wife gave to me. Usually, on the left-hand side, I write the whole song. I never erase. I scratch through things, so that it'll have the history of how I arrived. Then, once I get the lyric absolutely right, I put it on the right-hand side of the page, in as neat handwriting as I can. In this book, there are a few pages where I'll jot down some ideas. I don't have that many ideas. When I do, I usually go ahead and write it.

A lot of people are really good at journaling and I wish I were better at it. I think it can't help but be good, because I know the best cure for writer's block is to write. The best thing the writer can do to keep his tools sharp is to write.

What are your thoughts on hard rhyme versus near-rhymes?

I try, as best I can, to hold myself to the standard of hard rhyme. That's not to say that I always do it. I'm not going to sacrifice what the song needs to say on the altar of hard rhyme.

What I've come to learn, from holding myself to that standard, is that it is not limiting. It actually will force me to be more creative than I might have been, in settling for the easy or soft rhyme. I mean, let's face it, it's easier to approximate rhymes. It gives you more words to choose from. But, with the more words to choose from, it can kind of dilute the creativity.

What does the phrase, "Write from the heart," mean to you?

I'll tell you a story. When I first started writing in earnest, shortly after I was divorced, I went down to audition for the Sunday night writers' show at the Bluebird. The judge was Janis Ian, and she was really complimentary of the song that I played.

I ended up over at the table where she was sitting, and another young writer made the comment, "Janis, I always heard that if you want to write good songs, you write what you know about." And Janis said, "If you want to write great songs, then write about what you don't want people to know about you." And me, ever being the one that wants to get the last word in, I said, "Yeah, and if you want to write awesome songs, write what you don't want to even know about yourself."

Honesty is an exceedingly difficulty thing. If you stop and really reflect on how honest you are, it's pretty daunting. I would not even venture to guess how to tell someone how to be. Every human on the planet, to a greater or lesser extent, will attempt to be what he thinks people want him to be.

I'm still trying to figure out how to do that myself, and sometimes I get close. I think that prayer for me, meditation for some, is so important, because true prayer, first of all, is making a passive admission that there is something out there bigger than you, and it knows it all. Which would imply it knows what you're thinking. A motivation for your prayers is that, if you start stripping away the extraneous, and if you get right down to the bone, you get as close as you can to the part that makes you, you.

I think the whole thing about our pretentious ways starts in adolescence. We're trying to impress our parents. Then, there's the whole peer pressure thing. All of those things just contribute to us not going against the grain, just making sure you fit in. And a lot of people carry that on into their adulthood. Most people never really do much more examination. But most real writers do, and so, whatever trick it is that you do to get there is valid. For me, it's silence.

A lot of times, a device that I like to use in writing love songs is to make it work as a love song to God, or a love song to your lover. I think it makes love songs more interesting. That's not a perspective that I necessarily advertise all that much, because some people are so touchy about religion. It's a creative device that I use, but I'm deadly serious about it.

Some of the best writers that I'm around can be so real that it scares the shit out of me. We really are here to tell it like it is and, somehow, be as personally honest about it as we can. Try not to make up something that we think a lot of people want to hear, and that we think will get us on the radio.

Heck, Toby Keith's record label, at the time that we wrote "How Do You Like Me Now," didn't think that was appropriate, or could get on the radio. Toby and I weren't writing for anything. We were laughing, and talking about old girlfriends, and high school situations; just laughing and having fun writing a song, but telling true stories.

That's not to say that that song wasn't made up but, you know, there's more truth in fiction than you can ever find in nonfiction. Facts and truth: There is a huge gulf between those two things. That's not to say that facts are not important, but truth is the ultimate thing we're all looking for. Facts may not necessarily support the truth.

How important is the opening line?

It's the most important line of the song. It's the message I preach. I believe it too.

I was in a production class at Belmont. One of our assignments was to produce something, and get appointments from three people that were established in the music business, and bring back their responses.

"If you don't get them with that first line, you might not ever get them."

It was a great exercise, because it taught you a whole lot of things. I remember a song of mine that I was playing for Blake Melvis. He actually kind of liked it. He looked at me and said, "What do you think the most important line of the song is?" I said, "The hook." He goes, "Wrong. The most important line of a song is the opening line." I asked why and he said, "Because if you don't get them with that first line, you might not ever get them."

I asked him to give me an example, and he goes, "It's the third-hardest thing I'll ever do, leaving here without you," from "Holding Her and Loving You," Earl Thomas Conley. And that was a breakthrough moment for me. A huge light bulb went on over my head, because I realized that what everybody wants to know is, "If that's the third-hardest thing, what's the second, and what's the first?"

I've always been fairly quick on the uptake, and I realized the ramifications of that real quick. I owe Blake Melvis an eternal debt for calling that to my attention. I walk around all the time trying to come up with a first line. I mean, it's even kind of a joke. When people call and ask, "What are you doing?" I'll say, "I'm just trying to think of a first line." When I write, I generally start with the first line.

A lot of times I've written a first verse and chorus, and realize that what I've written is the second verse. "We Were In Love" was that way. I had written that melody on the way home from the Bluebird one night, and couldn't get any lyrics to it. When I got home, I recorded it because I knew I had a good melody. I sang the melody first, and then I started working out the chords around it. About three o'clock in the morning, I still hadn't come up with any real lyrics. I had some dummy lyrics, but I knew they were just non-sensical stuff. My wife was out of town. I went upstairs to go to sleep. When I got to the top of the stairs I sang, "We were a rock ready to roll. There was a fire down in my soul." I turned around, started walking back down the stairs, and I wrote the chorus, "We were a rock ready to roll. There was a fire down in our souls. And all the whole world had to stand still and turn around us, 'cause that was the deal. And, oh, how those nights where flowing like wine, when I was all yours and you were all mine, and we were in love. Yeah, we were in love."

The way I figure out what's next is, I'll sing it with as much passion as I can and then, wherever it flows, I'll try to go with that. That's when I wrote, "I can still see you when I sleep. There is a picture I still keep, you with your hair in the wind, and me with that crazy grin, under summer skies when dreams were too young to die."

"I can still see you when I sleep" is not an opening line. I knew at the time that it's a great opening line for a second verse, because I've got the story that comes after the story has already been set up.

I wrote all of that, and I took it in the next morning to Allen Shamblin. I played him what I had and said, "Now, I don't have the first verse but I'll play you the second verse, and then I'll sing the chorus, and then I'll sing the second verse again. I played it for him and I asked, "You want in?" He's like sitting on his hands, and he goes, "Man, you know you're already so close." I said, "Allen, I'm bringing it to you because I want you to write it with me." Allen goes, "God almighty, shoot, yeah!" I said, "We just need an opening line."

We talked about it a little bit, and I sang it to him again, and we wrote the lyrics down, so he could look at it and kind of get his brain around the moment and the mood. Then, he goes, "If I could invent a time machine, baby, we'd both be seventeen." And we're off to the races and then, you just paint the story. "Cruising in my first car, necking like movie stars on a Friday night. Do you remember those Friday nights?" And of course everybody does.

So, there was our first line, and what a first line. "If I could invent a time machine." That's such an evocative line.

Talk about using imagery in your songs.

I think imagery is important, but it's not as important to me as emotion. But your question was about imagery. Imagery is important because it lends familiarity; it's furniture. I think Craig Wiseman uses that term when he's teaching classes on song writing. Paint me a picture, and let me see it. It's not a full moon; it's a pale silvery tear dropping across the face of the sky.

I tend to not be so specific, imagery-wise. The stick I swing, if you will, is emotion, the imagery of emotion.

But, for instance, in "We Were In Love" I didn't want to just say, "cruising in my first car." If I said, "cruising in my first Mustang car," well, in my opinion, there's lots of people out there that didn't have a Mustang car as their first car. I'm trying to get more people. In my process of writing, I think that through.

Now, when I got to that second verse, "I can still see you in my sleep. There is a picture I still keep, of you with your hair in the wind, and me with that crazy grin." Okay, now we can see the picture. You can see it through your eyes. I had a picture in my mind of my first girlfriend. She's sitting on the fender and I'm leaning against the fender. She had long hair, and the wind was blowing her hair, and I was laughing. I had that picture in mind, but just me saying that, you've got *your* picture in mind. I don't have to describe your picture for you. I have to paint the colors and the emotion. Everybody's got a picture close to that.

So, I paint with a broad emotional brush. That still paints the picture, and there are ways to make that kind of imagery work, as a lyric, and be extremely effective. There are times that I will employ that, but the most important thing to me is painting the emotion. Or painting the backdrop, so that someone can put himself in the picture and feel the emotion.

What about that "editor voice" that we all have in our head?

I try not to pay as much attention to him. Knowing what that is, when to not pay attention, is rather elusive. I don't know if anyone ever really masters it, but you get better at it.

Experience lets you know that sometimes the editor doesn't know what he wants either. You're both trying to come up with something that will make your soul go, "Yeah!" And that's all the editor's trying to do too, he just goes about it a little differently.

I think the editor is in the craft side of the equation. The editor is the analytical side of the brain. It's frustrating to sit down with someone who just sits there, and just endlessly streams great stuff, creative, interesting, but there's no connection. The act of writing is analytical as well as creative, and you have to balance those two to get a good song.

Songwriting can be a real roller coaster ride. Do you have any tips on how to survive?

We all started writing songs for free, and we're all going to end up writing songs for free. The very fact that I write songs, and people send money, and people want to sing them, never ceases to amaze me, or thrill me. That someone would want to sing one of my songs thrills me beyond measure.

If you write great, commercial songs, the business end of it will take care of itself. Now, there will be people that might screw you out of your money, but there will be enough money there for you to live on. The way I have dealt with the ups and downs aspect of it is, early on, I gained a lot of knowledge about how the business works. You ask so many people who are just getting started, "Well you write a song, and it gets cut, now how do you get your money?" They can't tell you that.

I understand that creative types tend to not be business-oriented, but it's yours, you made it up. If I made it up, then I want to know what they are going to do with it, how they are going to pay me. It's your business to know your business.

I trust that the ups and downs in productivity are a function of my cycle; as a writer, it's the way I work. The obvious thing to guard against is just becoming lazy. You have to guard against not writing, but I don't think you need to worry too much about not finishing, unless you have forty or fifty songs unfinished. Now, you might ought to think about finishing one or two of those. The ups and downs are an issue of faith, an issue of trust, and it will all be all right. Just show up. Show up and write. And, when you show up, really be there.

4
BOB DiPIERO

Bob's first writing deal was with Combine Music, where his first cut, "I Can See Forever In Your Eyes," by Reba McEntire, climbed into the Top 20. The Oakridge Boys' "American Made" put DiPiero's name on the map in country music. This hit song achieved numerous awards and was used in a major ad campaign for Miller Beer, and even today has found its way back around for the Baby Ruth candy bar ad.

Through the years, DiPiero has masterfully crafted more than thirteen number one hits, recorded by country music legends including Vince Gill ("Worlds Apart"), Reba McEntire ("Little Rock" and "Till You Love Me"), Shenandoah ("The Church on Cumberland Road"), and George Strait ("Blue Clear Sky"). Some of DiPiero's hit singles include "Anywhere But Here" (Sammy Kershaw), "Mirror, Mirror" (Diamond Rio), "Bad Day To Let You Go" (Bryan White), and "Do You Want To Make Something Of It" (JoDee Messina). Also included in the list is "Kiss Me, I'm Gone" (Marty Stuart), "Give My Heart To You (Billy Ray Cyrus), "Poor Me" (Joe Diffie), "Walking Away A Winner" (Kathy Mattea), "We're So Good Together" (Reba McEntire), "I Got My Baby" (Faith Hill), and "Good Times" (Anita Cochran).

Bob has received several awards for his contributions to country music, including CMA's Triple Play Award in 1995 for "Wink" (Neal McCoy), "Take Me As I Am" (Faith Hill), and "Till You Love Me" (Reba McEntire). In 1995, he also received BMI's Robert J. Burton Award for Neal McCoy's "Wink" for most-performed country song of the year. In 1996, DiPiero's hits "Blue Clear Sky" (George Strait), "Daddy's Money" (Ricochet), and "Worlds Apart" (Vince Gill) garnered him a second CMA Triple Play award. DiPiero was awarded Song of the Year for "Worlds Apart" at the Country Radio Music Awards in 1997. In 1998, he was named Songwriter of the Year at the Nashville Music Awards and in 2000, he was named Songwriter of the Year by Sony/ATV, Nashville.

www.bobdipiero.com

Would you start off by giving us some insight into how you got into songwriting?

My songwriting grew out of my being in a rock and roll band. I'm a child of the Beatles. I saw them on Ed Sullivan, and from that point on I just wanted to play in a band.

I never wanted to be Elvis; the Beatles were always the model. One thing that I picked up on early was the fact that John Lennon and Paul McCartney wrote the songs for the band. They didn't go somewhere else to get the songs; they were the guys who were writing the songs.

I would get the album and read every piece of type on it. Early on, they were recording a lot of Chuck Berry songs, and as their careers progressed they went from writing three songs on their album to writing ten songs on the album. I was just following their lead. You're in a band, you get a guitar, you buy an amp, you buy a van, and you write songs.

It came natural to me. It wasn't hard, because I was so obsessed with music that anything that had to do with music was fun to me. So writing songs was never work, it was always play.

Are there specific places or things that inspire you?

Actually, I would prefer writing in a windowless room somewhere in North Dakota; the less distraction the better. When I'm writing, I'm so in that moment that it doesn't matter if I'm on the beach with a bunch of naked people running out in front of me. If I'm in the moment of writing a song that I'm really passionate about, then the place is inconsequential to me.

> "When I'm writing, I'm so in that moment that it doesn't matter if I'm on the beach with a bunch of naked people running out in front of me."

There are no magic-touch spots or inspiration zones. My office is inspirational to me only because I know the history of this office. I know the people who have had this office before me. I've heard songs that have been written here. So, it's an inspirational place, but I don't need to be here to write.

Places really aren't a big deal to me; it's the people that are in the places. I'm a co-writing animal. I enjoy co-writing. I enjoy another mind to work with. That's inspiring to me. They [co-writers] don't even have to be as good as I am, just as passionate or as inspired to write as I am. The place becomes a non-issue. I've gone to Europe, to songwriting getaways, to different wonderful places all over the world, literally, to write songs. But sometimes, it almost gets in the way of writing songs.

Songwriting is so personal. You might ask someone else, and they might say, I have to be in this room at two o'clock on Thursday, because that's when I know I'm at my creative peak. They believe that and, because they believe it, it's the truth. I find there is no one way. The way is what works for you.

What I did early on is try to figure myself out, as a writer; figure out what it takes for me to write. I am not saying, "What does it take to write a hit song?" but "What does it take to write a song? What do I need, and what's going to get in my way?" If I need to be in a small room in Nashville, Tennessee, at midnight, every time I write a song, that's going to get in my way. I am not always going to be in Nashville at midnight, because my brain travels with me where ever I go.

How much of your encouragement comes from within?

I think that the encouragement that comes from within is the absolute keystone to a writer. In the early days of a writer's career, nobody is going to bet on that person, nobody.

You're embarking on a career where 1 percent of the people who say, "I'm going to be a songwriter," will be a songwriter. And, of that 1 percent, maybe 1 percent of those will actually have a full-blown, long-living career as a songwriter.

The odds are astronomically stacked against you. I've seen so many writers along the way, from beginning writers to writers with a lot of success, talk themselves out of a career. Because "It's too hard," because "I can't do it anymore," because "I've dried up, I have writer's block," because whatever reason you tell yourself.

I believe your mind is the ultimate writing instrument. It doesn't matter what kind of guitar you play, doesn't matter what room you're in. It is your mind that creates it all. A young writer, a new writer—you just have to be slightly crazy.

You have to be unreasonable because you are doing something that is unreasonable. You're making stuff up out of the air. It's not like you're taking wood or nails and building a house. You're taking nothing and turning it into words and music that someone, around the world, might be singing for the next twenty years. That's a hard concept to get your head around.

As a young writer, failure was never an option for me. It just wasn't in my brain. For as long as I'm alive, I'm going to write songs. I may not have a million-seller in a year or two, or ten years, or twenty years, or maybe ever, but I'm going to write. As long as I was able to write songs, and create stuff, that meant I was successful.

For a young writer, that's a good yardstick. If you're creating songs, you are on the right track. Are they good songs? Well, probably not if you are a brand-new writer, because you are still learning the craft. Even if you are one of the most gifted, genetically-engineered songwriters to be born on the planet, you are still learning how to use that gift. So the early songs that you write are not going to be anything compared to the songs you write a week from that point, two weeks, a year from that point.

Are there specific activities that act as catalysts for creativity?

Yeah, actually what has become part of my creative process is traveling. It doesn't matter where, just the physical act of leaving point *a*, and traveling to point *b*, and leaving behind that static thing that is your life. Leaving it, and going to this place that has nothing to do with your routine, that's random and moving, and you're in it. You're on a plane with a hundred people. You're overhearing bits and pieces of conversations. You're in a cab; you're eating in a restaurant you've never been in. And all around you, there are people living their lives.

I think a big part of being a writer is being a voyeur, just watching and observing. To me, the best way to do that is to get out there and travel. You don't have to go to Maui, go to Cleveland. Just the physical act of leaving your routine and going somewhere else shakes all the cobwebs out.

Sometimes I'll go on a trip to write, like New York or L.A. I'll write there, and I always manage to write something worthwhile. But what I have always found is, it's not what I would write while I am there that is so interesting to me, but what I write three or four days, or a week, or two weeks after that trip. I've now had all this new input. I don't know what that input might be because it's so random.

But you see things happen, you place yourself in different scenes. You run into a man you've never met, a woman you never met. You have these conversations you'd never have if you were just in this place you call home. So, for me, just the act of traveling is really a part of being a writer. If I ever feel myself getting stale, I just go somewhere. You don't have to spend a million dollars. You get in a car, go somewhere, spend a night in a motel, turn around and come back. Shake it up!

Are you aware of the cycles of creativity?

I think a cycle is involved in creativity. I think it's like athletes have moments in time when they are just perfect, when all the training, all the exercising, all the work they've done just comes together and they're just perfect. There come those times, where it's just pouring out, at least for me.

I look at someone like Bob Dylan, who has just put out a CD, and some people say it's the best work of his life. He's not over, he's not even close to being over. Bruce Springsteen has just put out a CD. He's on the cover of *Time* magazine, thirty years after he was first on the cover. He's still just as creative, just as vital, as he was then. He's just reporting on the human condition thirty years later. Does it come in cycles? I think a level of excellence might come in cycles, but truly creative people, I think, are creative all the time.

What I wrote Tuesday may not be the best thing I ever wrote in my life, but I'm still writing. I'm still in the physical act of writing. So part of me doesn't care if I wrote "Take Me As I Am" or "Take the Trash Out." I'm just doing what I feel I am meant to do, which is just to be a creative person.

What's the role of the subconscious mind in songwriting?

The subconscious is just like that classic, underground river that's flowing, and you're standing on top of it. I've talked to other writers about this, how they'll write songs one day, just trying to matter, and two months later, or a year later, that song actually has a whole different meaning than they intended it to. And it fits a part of their life.

What is a hit song? I don't know. If I knew, I'd write one every day! A song gets written that plugs into so many people's lives. Did you do that consciously? Well, consciously you're trying to write a song, but your subconscious is the guy who is yelling out, "Hey, write about this! Hey, why don't you say that?"

I just read this article on Richard Rodgers and *Oklahoma*. Huge songs. The poor guy had a very barren life. He was very depressed. It was the alcohol. Yet he wrote these incredibly beautiful love songs. Makes you wonder where they came from. I think the only way he could get that work was subconsciously.

Have you ever had the experience of a song just pouring out of you in its entirety?

Yeah, that happens. I wish it happened all the time. When it does, that song has value, a lot of value on a lot of different levels. It's emotionally valuable, and it's financially valuable. Songs like that are pure emotion. They are not edited. I think that's how songs get ruined, just thinking about it too much. Editing yourself out of a good song, or talking yourself out of something good.

It's just intuitive writing, it just kind of falls out. A song I wrote with Vince Gill called "Worlds Apart" was like that. In less than an hour, that song was written. We had our guitars and were just playing around and, all of a sudden, this song appeared.

The song I wrote with Karen Staley, "Take Me As I Am," was like that. We spent the whole morning trying to write something, and came up with absolutely zero, two or three hours just staring at each other. We ended up going to lunch, talking about random stuff in our lives. When we came back I said, "I've got this idea, about 'I don't need a bed of roses 'cause roses whither away.'" That's one of those songs that I think was speaking to me subconsciously.

Do you meditate?

I've always worked at a form of meditation. Lately, what works for me is, first thing in the morning, when there are no interruptions, when everything around me is very silent and I can just be alone with my thoughts, I can just empty out my head and listen to what's floating around in there. Think, or not think, just having that moment of silence.

For me, the most important thing, as a writer, is silence. I need

"For me, the most important thing, as a writer, is silence."

big chunks of it. Not that I need to be alone, or be a recluse, or hide from the world, but I do need periods of time when I do not listen to music or watch television, I don't have a guitar in my hand, and I'm not carrying on any conversation. It's almost like opening a window and breathing fresh air. You're not outputting. You're just being.

Is there a certain time of day that you feel you write better?

I think that's the morning. I've been doing this as a career. I treat it not just as a creative whirlwind, but also as a business. So I do it on a regular basis and a regular time. Usually, I'm my best when I'm clearest, and that's in the morning when I haven't had a bunch of interruptions or the day hasn't come crashing in on me.

I think a young writer needs to realize you can write anywhere, anytime. That doesn't mean you have to sit down and complete a whole song. Sometimes, the most important thing about writing is getting that concept, or that title, or that one little chunk of melody that everything grows out from. I find myself doing that driving a car. Your mind isn't engaged in actually trying to do your driving, but there's that part of your brain that is working on it.

I remember reading an article on Mozart, how he would compose at a billiard table. He would just roll the ball and let it bounce back into his hand. His brain was involved in this mechanical thing of rolling the ball, but his creative mind was doing something else. It's almost like you don't scare it away. I think young writers can become too self-conscious of the exact physical act of writing.

You have an idea for something you want to say in a song. What process do you go through to develop the story?

If I have an idea for a song, I try to put myself in as the character of that song, like I'm the guy in the song. Say it's a female central figure, obviously I'm not a woman, but I try. I guess that's what actors do, try to role-play. What would this character really say, not what would show up on a Hallmark holiday card. What emotions would *really* be involved in this title? Whoever's saying this, would they really say that? Role-play is the big thing.

How many songs do you generally have in progress at one time?

I don't have a lot of things in progress. I'm a pretty immediate writer. I might have ideas I have scrawled away in little bits and pieces, but I don't consider that a song in progress. I consider that collecting and storing ideas.

It's pretty typical to finish a song in one session. But when I say "typical," a red light goes off. I think being typical is the death of creativity. If things start becoming typical, that's not a good thing. It's time to get on a plane, time to get in the car, and open the windows, and turn up the radio.

It's just my style as a writer. It's such an immediate thing. If I find an idea that really boggles my imagination, I'll probably finish it. I don't say that as a braggart. It doesn't mean it is going to be a better song than one by someone who spends three or four days on a song, it's just the way that I write. I'm kind of like a chef, you know, "What's fresh today? Loneliness? Hope? Let's use whatever's out there, the catch of the day. Let's write it."

We've all heard the phrase "from the heart." What does it mean to you?

Authentic. Authentic to you, to what life you've experienced. "I Hope You Dance" is so from the heart. It's such a great song on so many levels. It's great because this person isn't preaching to you. She's just wishing you well. That's from the heart. If it rings true, if it sounds real, it's from the heart.

The song "The Night They Drove Old Dixie Down" takes place in the Civil War. These guys didn't live through the Civil War, but it was so from the heart. It was so real. It was so genuine, that it meant something.

People are talking about the song Steve Earle wrote, the Taliban Song. He wasn't in Afghanistan. And I don't think he's talking about if they're right or wrong. I think he was role-playing. I think he was being this John Walker Lindh guy, and trying to get into his brain. It was heartfelt enough. Everybody in the country is talking about it.

I'm of the belief that those first bursts of ideas and inspiration are usually the best ideas, because they are immediate. I've witnessed a lot of writers over-analyzing their work, even as they are doing it, to the point that it freezes them, that it becomes painful. It becomes painful for me, as a co-writer, to write with that person because they're so turning every word over and over.

"Over-analyzing something, especially in the initial stages of writing, can be the death of a song."

I'm not saying that you don't rewrite. I think rewriting is the cog that makes the wheel turn around. Once you get something out there, you really focus on it. But not as I'm originally trying to put something out. Over-analyzing something, especially in the initial stages of writing, can be the death of a song. Let it go by, you can always come back and change it.

I call it "keeping the forward motion." Let's just keep the ball in play, rather than sitting here analyzing one or two words until the whole writing process just grinds to a halt. That can be a detriment to the creative process.

I had this one class in college where this guy said, "Try not to judge your art. Let others judge your art for you." That really made an impact on me. I've written songs that, if I were an artist, I wouldn't have recorded. But that's what I wrote that day and it meant something to somebody, and I'm glad it did.

You really start liking a song when it hits the Top 10, you know. You don't like it too much until it becomes a hit, and then you love it. But, if I were to judge everything I did, I would do maybe 20, maybe 10 percent of it, because I am a musical Nazi.

I eat it, sleep it, drink it, and drive it. That's all I do. So my bar of excellence is ridiculous. It's very important to me to realize that I'm just trying to speak the language of everybody who's out there. I'm not trying to placate anybody, or write down to anybody. I'm just trying to speak that language of the people, of every man. I just let it go.

Do you ever feel like everything has already been said?

I've heard other writers say that. But I think the flip side to that is, everything's been said before, but *I've* never said it. This is *my* take on what everybody's already said.

There's only one me and, as a writer, that's a powerful statement. That gives you the unique opportunity to say something that's never been said before because you're saying it in your way.

Yeah, everything's been said before, and there are the four basic colors. Why paint a picture because they've used all the same colors? It's your version of those mixtures of colors that matters.

Do you think of yourself as disciplined?

I think of myself as a disciplined writer, not a disciplined person. I wish I had as much discipline in certain areas of my life as I have in my writing.

I show up every day. I show up when I'm supposed to show up, and where I'm supposed to show up (give or take ten or twenty minutes). That sounds like a very flippant answer, but it's not. You've got to suit up, and show up, in order to be in the game.

I'll show up when I just don't feel like the world needs another song. Just like, "I don't know about this person I'm writing with. I don't really feel like I'm into it." It would be so easy for me to pick up the phone and make an excuse. I'm sick. I have to iron my socks, whatever.

But I think that is part of my upbringing, my Midwest, blue-collar upbringing. You get up in the morning, and you put your pants on, and you go to work. So many times I've shown up when I didn't want to, and something great has come out of it. If I don't show up, I might miss something.

Is your writing style altered by writing on a different instrument?

Well, I do have favorite guitars. I think Dennis Linde, who is just a genius songwriter, said that a good guitar has a bunch of songs in it, and you just have to pull them out. Unfortunately, I bought into that, and I have too many guitars. Certain guitars are just kind of inspiring to play as a musician.

Craig Wiseman is an incredible songwriter and he's probably one of the worst guitar players I've ever been around. But, as a non-guitar player, he is absolutely brilliant because he has no boundaries. They didn't tell him he couldn't do that. I've studied guitar so much that it's almost like I know too much. I want to write more like somebody who's a sixteen-year-old kid who has just picked up an instrument and doesn't know that you can't do that. It's a great perspective.

How important is imagery in songwriting?

I love imagery in a song. You're writing a movie. You're putting people in a place with furniture, and trees, and rain, and windows, and doors, and red cars, and black guns. Imagery is great.

I think each song will dictate what you need, and what you don't need. There isn't any one hard and fast rule.

Imagery is really useful. But I don't think that if you don't have imagery, you don't have a good song. It's all about placement, and sometimes it's what you don't say that's almost as important was what you do say.

What is the hardest part about writing a song?

It's that verse they want you to rewrite. To me, that is the hardest verse to write, when someone says, "Love this song, love it, fantastic, except we want you to rewrite it." I'm not against rewrites, unless it doesn't seem that there needs to be a rewrite.

You're in the moment, when you're writing the song. You've already spent a lot of time and energy on a song to complete it, and as a songwriter you've given at least 110 percent. Then, for someone to say, "We need you to rewrite this song," to me, that's the single most painful exercise in songwriting. Unless there is something we glaringly missed the first time through.

I just had something like that happen, where it's like, "Oh, we've already recorded the song. It's fantastic, we love it, it's tremendous. Can you rewrite the first verse? All of it, just rewrite all of it." Wait a minute. "You want us to reinvent the wheel?" We did, and it sucked because it wasn't genuine, it wasn't heartfelt.

That happened with the song "Blue Clear Sky." Tony Brown called and he said, "Love the song, but we want to call it 'Clear Blue Sky,' not 'Blue Clear Sky.'" But, to me, the whole song was the turn of the phrase. It's "out of the blue," not "out of the clear." It's "out of the blue it happened." People do say, "out of the clear blue sky." But to me the cool thing was turning it around. And "out of the blue clear sky, out of nowhere" was so totally different and unique. So I said, "Tony, you know what? I can be the biggest song whore in Nashville, and I want a George Strait cut, but I think you'll screw it up if you do that." They left it "Blue Clear

Sky," but I think they actually tried to sing it, "clear blue sky," and it didn't work.

I'm never afraid to work. But to rewrite something, when you've already said the words you wanted to say, it's hard.

What are the basic songwriting skills a young writer should develop?

I think a good songwriter has to be a good storyteller. Not so much telling story songs, but just telling the story. A good songwriter has to be a great communicator. You must be able to communicate what it is you're trying to say, whether it's melodically or lyrically.

That means you have to be a good listener. I think listening is the first step, because you need something to draw from. The best place to draw from is either a very active imagination, or real life.

> **"I think listening is the first step, because you need something to draw from."**

In real life, it's easy just to run your yap and not even be able to hear what is going on around you. I think the tools of a good songwriter are listening, communicating, and a sense of discovery.

The hardest part is saying it the right way. Saying it exactly the right way, in exactly the right amount of words, with exactly the right melody. That's the hardest part, because you don't know what that is. You don't know that you've done it, or not done it, until you've put it in front of another human being and they respond to it.

Knowing how much is enough, how many words are too many words, how much song is too much song. Do you really need a bridge? Do you not need a bridge? Does it need to be three minutes long? Does it need to be four minutes long?

Do you read a lot?

Yeah, I read a lot. Reading is a great place to get ideas. It's kind of like traveling with the mind. You get your mind out of your little room, and go traveling. You go to the eighteenth century, and you go to summer, and to somebody's life, and some love affair.

I'm pretty widely read. I read fiction, biographies, autobiographies, how-to books. I read personal betterment books. I read a lot of trash too. Reading trash is important. It sounds funny, but it's real.

I read a lot of magazines. How are people speaking today? It's real important to write in the language that people speak.

Do you solo write at all?

Some, but not a lot. It becomes a pretty lonely process to me. Lately, I've been doing more solo writing than I have in quite some time. Don't know why. I've always wanted to. I guess it's just the time of the season to do that.

I like the actual mechanics of writing with somebody. That synergy. It's "one and one equals three." It's that energy that's contained between.

What are the advantages and disadvantages to co-writing?

To me, the advantage of co-writing is that two heads are better than one. You have immediate feedback, as you are in the process of writing. But, then again, it becomes very important to pick the right co-writer. Pick someone that you respect and trust.

How does that happen?

Trial and error. They'll bring a whole way of looking at things that you would not consider, because you haven't lived their life. They're looking at the same song idea, but they're looking at it through their eyes, and it turns into something bigger than the both of you. It's a combination of two people's vision. That makes for a great song.

Have you ever had any bad co-writing experiences?

Oh yeah, sure. It's terrible. It's worse than going to the dentist. It's just painful and your stomach gets tied up in knots. Usually if it's bad, it's not a matter of, "We didn't come up with anything." It's a matter of somebody's ego running rampant. Or, I've been in a position where somebody wants to change a line, just to change it. Because they think they need to, they haven't mattered enough.

It's usually a question of ego. I've spent days coming up with nothing but, to me, that's okay because I've been trying and they've been trying. Some days you eat the bear, and some days the bear eats you. It just is what it is.

But I've had some experiences where it just isn't fun. It's got to be fun, because that's the best part of the writing experience, not winning a Grammy. It's having fun that day because, chances are, you're *not* going to win a Grammy. Might as well be in the moment and enjoy it. I just don't suffer fools gladly. Everybody who is a creative person has an ego. An ego is part of being creative, but you don't have to be a jerk.

What about that "editor voice" that we all have in our head?

I think the editor is your intuition. As a young writer, you develop your intuition as fast as you develop your technique. You learn to trust yourself, to trust your intuition, to trust your gut feeling. To listen to yourself when you should, and not pay attention to yourself when you're just knocking off crap. That editor inside you is like an instant editor.

I've seen writers who edited themselves into writer's block because they edit too much. Let the idea come out. Even when it's wrong, let it out. You can always go back and change it. Don't get hung up in the minutiae of writing. The editor in you should be working for you, not against you.

Let's say you have just finished writing a song that you feel is really special. Do you ever experience, even for a moment, the fear that it might be your last?

No, but I've had the experience of being wrong. I thought it was earth-shatteringly great, and I'll play it for someone and they say, "Oh, okay, but this other song over here, I love this one." And that's the one where I was thinking, "I don't know if I'll play that one for them or not."

That goes back to letting others judge what you do. That kind of thinking is very unhealthy for a creative person. If you think you'll never write again, then you're right.

What advice can you give on dealing with the fear of failure?

Failure and success are sisters; they're the same thing almost. Fear is, "I'm going to fail and, in my parents' eyes, I'll be nothing. In my friends' eyes, I'll have a life thrown away trying to be a songwriter." Or, "I will be living in poverty when I fail."

But what does the fear of success mean? "I don't deserve this. I don't deserve to be successful. I'm really not this good. I didn't really write this song, it was a mistake. I shouldn't be successful. I don't deserve it." When I hear the fear of success, I think that's what that means, "I don't deserve it."

That's clearly not something in your thought process.

Oh, it has been in the past, especially early in my career. Early eighties, when I had my first success as a songwriter, I felt, "I don't deserve this. These guys have been here five to ten years longer than I have and I just walked into town and, literally two years later, I've got a number one song. This isn't right. Somebody's going to come and take it away from me." It's that fear of success.

Now, I've worked my ass off. Any success that comes my way, I feel very comfortable with it because I know how long I've worked at it, and I know what I've taken to get to this point.

Roosevelt said, "The only thing we have to fear, is fear itself." Fear is one of the most freezing agents to the creative mind. "I'm afraid I'll never write another song that good again. I'll never write another song. I'll never write a good song. I'll never write, period. I'll never write anything that I like. I'll never write anything that my mother likes. I'll never write anything that ever gets recorded by anybody anywhere in the world."

That's all fear-based. That's all negative input that you're telling yourself, "Okay, I got a song recorded, but I don't deserve it. Why did this happen? I feel like some sort of a sham."

Fear is a very dark word. And in the creative world, it's death.

What is "writer's block"?

I've never really had writer's block. My problem's always been musical diarrhea. I can't turn it off. It's not always good. I'm not saying that everything I write is a pearl of wisdom, from the mouth of God, through my brilliant mind, to the masses.

You can write about a mailbox. You can write about a coffee table. It's not going to be great, but it's going to be something. I think most writer's block is self-induced. It's nothing physical. It's *all* mental.

What do you recommend to get around writer's block?

Write! Just write. Write something terrible. Write something shitty. Write as if there is no such thing as writer's block. It's never been something, in my creative career, that has gotten in my way.

The writers I have written with over the years, who have continued success, I've never heard any of them say, "I have writer's block." I've never heard Craig [Wiseman], or Tom Shapiro, or Don Cook, or Bobby Braddock say, "I'm suffering from writer's block." They might say, "I'm not writing anything I like." Or, "You know, it seems I'm just writing shit lately." But I've never heard them say, "I just can't write anymore." They can't help writing, from what I've seen.

You may have talked to people who've struggled through years of writer's block. Well, I think there's something else in play there. There's something psychologically going on, something in their lives that they might want to draw attention away from.

You can look at the body of work of a writer and see there was a moment in time when they were just writing incredible stuff. But if you look at a career, a career is long. You're not having hits every day, every month, every year, but you are creative.

Idea block, I have a hard time responding to that. All you have to do is raise these blinds and there are hundreds of ideas. Just look outside and there are ideas everywhere. Not necessarily good ideas. I'm not saying they're brilliant, but there are ideas.

Do you feel that discipline and creativity are tied together?

Yes. I think you can squander your creativity by not being disciplined. I think Picasso was unbelievably creative, but he was also incredibly disciplined to show up every day at his studio and turn out canvas, after canvas, after canvas, after canvas. Bruce Springsteen didn't turn out his new CD in a vacuum; he went somewhere and sat down with a guitar. There might be twelve songs on that new CD of his, but I bet you he wrote thirty, at least, to get those twelve songs. There was discipline involved.

Obviously, there was a lot of creativity involved in executing the ideas, in executing the thoughts he was trying to convey, but there was also discipline in conveying those thoughts. In getting those ideas on paper, or getting them on tape, and recording them, and performing them. That requires discipline to get them going.

Songwriting can be a real roller coaster ride. Do you have any tips on how to survive?

Yes, enjoy yourself along the way. It'll be over sooner than you think. If you're not having fun, it's your own fault. You are doing something that the majority of people on this planet will never get a chance to do, to be creative, to be in the moment, to be making something that shouldn't have any value, but has incredible value.

You need to celebrate that while you're doing it. You don't need to make it a painful process, just protect yourself from life, because life has a way of beating creativity down if you let it. And, if you really do find your way into a career as a songwriter, protect yourself there, because you know you are entering the world of egos run amuck, politics for politics' sake, dollars over creativity. As a songwriter, it's my job to be unreasonable, and to be a dreamer, to make stuff up. That's my job, and by God I'm going to do my job. Man, I'm going to have a good time doing it.

5
STEWART HARRIS

Formerly an artist with Mercury Records, the writer/artist experience has given Harris an understanding of and ability to communicate with artists, as evidenced by his number one hits written with Travis Tritt, Little Texas, and John Berry. Now, 17 million records later, Stewart and Travis Tritt are still working together, as evidenced on Travis's latest records. As Stewart so loves to do, he is writing with several new artist for projects, including Jamie Lee Thurston, Kelly Lang, and Sony recording artist Tammy Cochran, who co-penned, along with Stewart and Jim McBride, her single, "Angels in Waiting."

Stewart has enjoyed a successful songwriting career, which includes nine number one hits, three film awards and ten prestigious Million Air Awards from BMI for songs receiving over one million airplays. Both Alabama and South Carolina claim Harris as a son. The Alabama Music Hall of Fame bestowed the Creator's Award on him in early 1999, and later that year he was inducted into the South Carolina Entertainment Hall of Fame. He's had songs recorded by Wynonna, Travis Tritt, Neil Diamond, Waylon Jennings, Reba McEntire, Marshall Tucker Band, John Michael Montgomery, and many others.

Cuts include "No One Else On Earth" (#1 Wynonna), "I'm Gonna Be Somebody," "Drift Off To Dream," "Can I Trust You With My Heart" (all #1 Travis Tritt), "Rose In Paradise" (#1 Waylon Jennings), and "Standing On The Edge Of Goodbye" (#1 John Berry).

How did you get started in songwriting?

I left the University of South Carolina in 1970. I had had kind of an epiphany. I was jotting down songs, instead of listening to the sociology teacher. This was all in my senior year. I was raised by educators, so I just thought I was supposed to go to college. I'd floundered around and changed majors about five times, and finally, it dawned on me that day, that I had to leave and go do this.

I thought my father was going to kill me because I just packed up and went home, but he was very good about it. My father's a literary writer. He asked, "What are you going to do?" I said, "The only thing I know to do is to start. I'll play in Augusta, Georgia, to make enough money to get to Atlanta, and see where I go from there." I was really performing more.

Had you been performing while you were still in college?

I'd been performing since I was about twelve. I was really kind of a folkie, playing a lot of political rallies, whatever you can do in South Carolina and Georgia. I had a band when I was sixteen. I had been writing a little bit, and writing ideas, but I was really doing a lot of James Taylor, Paul Simon, all of the current folk-rock stuff.

I got to Atlanta and, from there, got a gig in New York. Six months out of the University of South Carolina, I was in the middle of Manhattan, green as I could be. I lived at the YMCA and had no money, just really living week to week. Finally, I couldn't afford to live there anymore, so I went to the Jersey shore, where everything was going on.

Bruce Springsteen was at Asbury Park at that time. I was playing just south of there. After that, I went to Prince Edward Island, Canada, where I began writing a little bit more. I actually recorded some of my material and they were playing it on the radio in Canada. That's when I got the disease.

Where were you when heard yourself on the radio?

I was standing on this big cliff, on Prince Edward Island. I heard my song on the radio and I thought, "Okay, that's it. That's what I'm going to do." I got a manager, and moved to Washington, D.C.

All of this happened, really, pretty fast, within about a year and a half. When I got to D.C., it was a really wonderful period. John Denver had just left there to go on the road. Starland Vocal Band was coming up. That's where I met Harry Warner, and that's when everything began.

Harry was managing Jerry Reed at the time. He had been asked to book all the inauguration functions for Nixon, so he was staying at the Twin Bridges Marriott, where I was performing. He came up to me one night after my show and asked me if I'd written this particular song that I sang. I think it was an old Woody Guthrie song. I said, "No, but I have written a couple of things." At that time I'd still only written maybe six or seven songs, because I was still doing cover stuff and still learning all the new stuff that was coming out.

Harry said, "Send me some songs," and gave me his address. I was still performing, and that was still my main focus. All of a sudden, one day I got a package in the mail. I had to pick it up at the post office. It's this huge, heavy box, and I thought, "What in the world is this?" I take it home, open it up, and it is full of Jerry Reed, Chet Atkins, and Ray Stevens albums, and a handwritten note on the top that says, "Looking forward to hearing your songs, Harry."

I thought, "Stewart, you'd better get on the ball." So, I instantly started writing some more. I polished off a couple of things that I had done before. I sent songs to Harry, and he called up and said, "Move down here. You can play around here, and we'll give you a $125-a-week publishing deal." I arrived in Nashville during CMA week, in 1975, and they had me a record deal with United Artists within four months of being here.

Then, that deal went south because of publishing. They wanted all the publishing. So, Harry went to Jerry Kennedy, over at Mercury, and Jerry said, "I don't care about publishing. I like it. Let me do this record." That was six months into it. So, I had my deal.

Jerry did the absolute best he could. Mercury Records actually released my singles pop and country because they couldn't figure out what I was. It was a real progressive move on their part, during that period of time. He stuck with me for three singles.

Ten CC had just released a huge record, so I was kind of under the shadow of that in the pop world, and I was really still too pop for the country market. Harry and I asked off the label until we could figure out what was going on.

During that period of time, Jerry Reed cut a couple of my songs, and Donna Fargo cut "Ragamuffin Man." That was my first Top 20, and that's when things began to turn, because I thought, "This is interesting. I can write for this person, or this person, and I can write like I want to, and I don't have to find it all right here." I was having trouble finding what I did, because I had R&B influences. I had folk-rock influences. I was having trouble putting it all in one artist.

When I started getting things cut, then, of course, the checks starting to come. At that time, BMI was doing advances so, all of a sudden, I was kind of in high cotton and thinking, "Maybe this is good."

Right about that time, Jerry got into the movies. Harry came to me and said, "Burt Reynolds wants this particular song for the movie *Hooper*, and he'll be here this afternoon, so come on by and you can talk to him, and you can write the song." Dick Feller, who also wrote for Jerry Reed's company, had always written with Jerry before, like, *East Bound and Down*, and things for *Smokey and the Bandit* films. This was my turn to have something to do in that. It really worked well for me, because what he needed wasn't necessarily a country song.

Jerry was getting further into the movies. I got the distinct feeling, and Harry had hinted, that Jerry Reed Enterprises, as a musical entity, might be closing down. Charlie Monk offered me a deal with April Blackwood. I was writing a lot with Keith Stegall, who wrote for them, so I went with April Blackwood, which later became CBS songs. I stayed with them for six and a half years. That's when the number ones started coming. "Hurricane," "Lonely Nights," "Rose In Paradise," those were all number ones. April Blackwood and CBS songs got me a lot of cuts. We had cuts in TV and films, and outside of this market. The whole world opened up for me in the early eighties.

I still wanted to do an album, but I think that was more ego than anything else. One day I said to myself, "Why don't you write down how much of being an artist you enjoy, and how much you enjoy writing?" And then, at the bottom of the page I put how much I'd made as an artist, and how much money I'd made writing. I said, "You know what? If you put all of the *artist* energy over in the *writer* column, you can have a long, long career." That's when I became a songwriter, period. That was the defining moment.

Shortly after that, is when SBK bought CBS, and I asked out of my deal. I didn't know what I was going to do, but Waylon Jennings's cut of "Rose In Paradise" came out that year, so I think I went to the bank and got a line of credit. My wife was doing really well at the time, so financially I was okay, but that was kind of a turning point. I think that was 1986. I went for a year without publishing and formed my own company.

Were you still getting cuts?

Not really, but "Rose In Paradise" was carrying me all the way. It was screaming up the charts. It was a really big record.

Then one day, a year later, I was getting a little worried. It was a really bad time in the music industry. It was kind of like it is now, big buyouts, things closing down, people not getting deals. Artists were not at the best that they had been. Older ones were getting older. There were no young ones coming along that were sticking.

A friend of mine asked if I'd noticed that Harvey Shapiro had reopened CBS Music Publishing out of New York. He had been the number two man at CBS, and Harvey and I just got along wonderfully. There was a real camaraderie between us.

I had fourteen R&B songs, and four country songs, and I got in the car and went up to see Harvey. It was one of the funniest things. I look back on that, and you couldn't have written this in a movie.

He said, "Come on in. Show me what you got." I said, "Harvey, I want you to forget about all those country hits, and listen to this." We went to lunch and he said, "We're going to do this deal. I'm going to give you 50–50 publishing, because there have been two major writers who have always resented me because I had 100 percent of their publishing. I'm starting you off with 50–50 because I don't want you to ever resent me."

I was so excited I was halfway down the Jersey turnpike before I remembered to call my wife. That really started, probably, the biggest part of my publishing life. The agreement with Harvey was that whatever pop songs I wrote, they would do up there in New York. The country stuff I would pitch myself down here.

Sony bought CBS Music Publishing the next year. We just transferred all my stuff then, down here. Then, they bought Tree, and I was just kind of absorbed into the whole Sony network. I've been through all the corporate buyouts. It was like a minefield for a while.

That's a lot of change.

It was a lot of change. There are some songwriters who have been with one place. My friend Harlan Howard was with Tree forever, until he started his own company.

Then, one day, Warner Brothers called me and said that there was a young guy from Atlanta who was performing "Rose In Paradise" and the two people he wanted to write with were me and Jim McBride. That was Travis Tritt, and that started the whole string of stuff with Travis.

I was also working with Jill Colucci during that time and, because Jill was scheduled to sing the theme for *America's Funniest Home Videos*, we got the opportunity to write the lyrics. We had to write them in forty-five minutes because they were going into a meeting. We just took a shot and got it. The early nineties was just a flurry of wonderful stuff, BMI Awards, Film Awards, L.A., London, New York.

Then my wife and I decided that we would start an independent publishing company. It was a wonderful experience, though I don't know that I'd ever do it again, unless I was funded to the max. We were actually doing pretty well until my wife and I fell apart. We closed the company when we got divorced, and I signed with peermusic in 2000.

You've come a long way, but it sounds like it's been a good road.

I love what I do. I don't know of any writers who don't get insecurity. My good friend Harlan would sometimes fall into that, "Boy, I need this one more song." I go through those kinds of things, but it just seems normal to me now. And there is life over fifty for a writer.

There is good life over fifty, because I am having a wonderful time right now. I'm working with a couple of great country artists that I really believe will be big country acts. And then, of course, Jim McBride and I have the song "Angels In Waiting" with Tammy Cochran.

I'm having a great time with country music, and I'm writing pop music again. There's a circle of people in town that are successfully farming music out to L.A. and New York, and I'm getting in that circle again, and it's fun. I've come too long, and bit too many nails off, not to enjoy it right now.

I was talking to my friend Don Pfrimmer one day. He said, "Look, you're never going to retire, you're just like me. What can you do that you can get up in the morning and have your day exactly the way you want it? You can go to the mailbox later on and see if there's a royalty check there or not. What are you thinking, man?"

I get up every day and I thank God that this is what I do. You get tired of it sometimes and, if you do, then you take a week off and go do something. Go fishing and come back.

Are there any places or things that are inspirational for you, or spark the creativity?

I have a great sense of place. I go back to South Carolina, to the Barrier Islands, south of Charleston, rent a house, and listen to the ocean.

I always take a tape recorder with me when I drive. There's something about having your hands occupied, and that part of your brain that has to drive occupied, that frees the other side of the brain to get ideas. I used to drive out to L.A. I would always arrive there with a big bag of ideas. I didn't usually write songs while I was on the road, I wrote down ideas, hooks, and the concepts for the songs. Then, that gave me something to do when I got out there.

And I really love working out of the house. I've been meditating for twenty-seven years so, a lot of times, I will try to just be as quiet as I can for a period of time. Not long, usually a day and a half, up to three days, and just write down ideas. Give myself a chance to rest and listen to what's going on. I come up here to my office, for instance, and be quiet for extended periods of time, until stuff starts to come again.

I went to my father years ago, the first time I thought I had writer's block, and he said, "Look at it this way; if you go to a well and you take buckets of water out of the well, and you are constantly taking buckets out of the well, pretty soon that well's going to be empty. You've got to give it a chance to fill back up, and then you can go to the well again."

I think sometimes, in the Nashville writing process, it gets to where you feel like you're taking final exams. There's a lot of pressure. If you really need a cut and you work harder, and harder, and harder, to get that, I think that's where a lot of us writers get kind of irritated, and don't like what we're doing, or complain about what we do.

There is a natural rhythm each one of us has. Some of us work harder than others. I couldn't work as hard as Kim Williams. But he has his natural rhythm, and once I find my rhythm, I know when I'm in it. Part of it is the number of years I've been writing, but part of it is the appreciation of the gift, and the care of that gift.

It changes, and so I constantly try to ask myself where am I right now, and what is the most comfortable, because when I am the most comfortable, it's like a light that's always coming through you, and all you really have to do is keep your window clean. If you keep your window clean, you can always see the light coming through. I think it was Guy Clark who called it the banks of the river. You're just the banks of the river. You just barely direct the flow. That's all you do.

"Inspiration demands a certain amount of discipline."

If the window's getting cloudy and you can't see, then there's probably something in your personality that is bothering you, or you're going too fast, or you're just not stopping to look around to find the ideas, because they are here.

All of that said, inspiration, I think, also demands a certain amount of discipline. You've got to care for this gift. We hear music in our heads and we hear lyrics in our heads. And we are charged to tend this gift.

My mother gave me a wonderful saying—I don't know where it came from—"I go to my studio each day. Often nothing happens, but woe be to he who is not there when the angel comes bearing gifts." There are some days that I can come in here and pick up this guitar and everything falls out. There are other days when I come in here and it goes, "Not today, baby." I just know you have to listen to that.

On the days that I'm uninspired, I'll take a walk. A lot of times just getting outside, taking a walk, I come back and everything opens up. There's a whole new perspective. As I've grown older, I find that if I exercise, that kind of gets the body satisfied. Then you can sit for the period of time that you need, to have that flow again.

What is creativity?

Creativity is trying to understand God. I really believe that's pretty much the root of it. We're all seeking to paint him, or play him, or sing to him. I view music as a prayer. It has been for me. It has been my religion.

Music connects us to people that we'll never meet in our whole lives. Wynonna's song, "No One Else On Earth," was done during the halftime of one of the Super Bowls, back in 1994, I guess. I was having a few beers with a friend of mine here and, right in the middle of our conversation, he says, "What was it like to have a billion people hearing your song at the same time?" I said, "Well, you know what? I've never really thought of it in that way." He said, "You need to think about that." I did, and boy, it got pretty overwhelming. You think about how you can influence individuals.

This is why I say it's all about our wanting to reach out, and I think when we reach out to one another we reach out to God. I remember one of those late-night conversations with Guy Clark. I was just kind of rattling on and I said, "Well, you know, what we do is not exactly brain surgery." Guy said, "Oh, really?"

That's all he said. And then I started thinking about that and I realized, "You're right. It is." You can change people's perspective. You can change people's minds. You can do surgery on people. People that are sad, you can make them happy. People that are in need of something to identify with, you can do it. It's huge what you can do.

I know that I've been personally affected that way many times, even by some of my contemporaries. When Allen Shamblin and Mike Reid wrote "I Can't Make You Love Me," man, I dropped to my knees. It was a form of awe, and jealousy, and love for them all at the same time.

What about the role of the subconscious mind?

Huge. That's where you go every day and you tap in. When I come up here and I put a guitar in my lap, that's where it is. That's one of the reasons I meditate, because I want that membrane, between consciousness and subconsciousness, as thin as I can get it.

That creates its problems for us too, because in a very competitive, not so nice business, writers constantly try to keep their shells soft, so you can be sensitive to the world, so you can be sensitive to your subconscious, so you can be sensitive to what you're really even supposed to write, or want to write. Then, you get the slings and arrows that come from the disappointments, and the hardships that come from the creative life.

What about dreams? Have you ever dreamed songs?

I've dreamed ideas for songs. There was one time that I was in Richmond, Virginia, playing a gig. I was asleep one night in my hotel, and I dreamed a song. I bolted up. I knew I had to write it down, because I knew that it would go away. I could not find a pen, so I picked up the phone and called the front desk and said, "Don't ask me any questions, and just write this down." So, this girl started writing it down and she said, "Are you all right, Mr. Harris?" I said, "I'm a songwriter."

I think one time I dreamed a whole song and just lost the whole thing. And you know, of course, in your dreams they're going to be hits, so you don't want to lose them. But usually, where dreams are concerned, I'm either learning something or I'm letting something go. That's why I say that dreams are more of the preparation to the meditations. There's something more channeled about the meditations.

If you have an idea for a song, what is your process to take this little gem and develop it?

When you get the inspiration, the inspiration usually takes you there. A lot of times you'll get an idea for something that you think would be a very good idea, and when I do that, if I'm co-writing I usually like to do a lot of brainstorming.

Once I lay a bed of music, that helps me know where to go with it, and where to put the emotional emphasis. There are emotional highs and lows in songs, or *highs* and *highers* in songs, and the music dictates that more to me.

Then, sometimes, you really have to dig into the intellectual process, if you're doing a story song. For instance, when Jim McBride and I were writing "Rose In Paradise," we didn't start with the hook and write backwards. We started with the concept, "Is this lady going to disappear?"

For those that don't know "Rose In Paradise," it is a song about a young girl who marries a banker, and the banker turns out to be a jealous man. The chorus is, "Every time he'd talk about her, you could see the fire in his eyes. He'd say 'I would walk through hell on Sunday to keep my rose in paradise.'" Well, that's some pretty, almost evil stuff. He's going to control her in some way, although in his mind, he's not controlling her because he loves her so much, but he really is, and he may not even know that himself.

We developed it further when we introduced the gardener. While the banker's out of town, he wants the gardener to keep an eye on her. She disappears and, in the end, you don't know whether she went away with the gardener, or whether she is truly buried out in the garden.

That just developed out of our seeing just how bizarre we could get and still keep a mystery going. We had DJs calling us going "Well, did he do it or not?" We'd say, "We don't know. We're not really sure."

"If you can give yourself goose bumps, nine times out of ten you can give your audience goose bumps."

Each time is a little different, but I think, basically, if you're co-writing, it's brainstorming for a little while until that one that gives you goose bumps says, "Go on." I've always called goose bumps *hidden indicators*, because if you can give yourself goose bumps, nine times out of ten you can give your audience goose bumps.

If you're writing by yourself, you should walk away, and come back to it, and see what you've got. You be your own co-writer. The process takes a little longer, but usually you'll find that evolution.

Do you keep notebooks and idea books?

I used to do it all the time. Now, I don't do it as much, and I can't really tell you why. I still seem to find more ideas out of the music. Those seem to be the better songs that I write. If I get too studious about what I do, I think my work sucks.

A blank sheet of paper—now what?

It kind of it depends on how secure I am at the time. I can look at it as just a wonderful thing. I love paper and pen. I never have been able to write on computer. I'll type it up later, when it's time to turn it in to the publisher.

When Hemingway was asked that question, "What is it like to stare at a blank sheet of paper?" He said, "I never do." They said, "What do you mean?" He said, "As soon as I turn the page, I write 'the,' so I no longer have a blank page."

God didn't give you this gift to take it away from you, so there's not really any writer's block. A blank sheet of paper doesn't bother me.

How important, to you, is the opening line?

Very important. Harlan was the one that said to me, "If you can write in the first line of the song, what the whole song is about, then by the time they get to the chorus they think they've heard it before."

I began to think about that, and then I went back and looked at some of my hits, and it was true. It told you so much, if not in the first line, then in the first, second, and third lines. As much information as you can give them. You can create mystery, if that's what your purpose is, but I think, in general, opening lines either have to give you a lot of information about what you're getting ready to hear, the ride that you're getting ready to take, or it has to be so beautiful musically and evoke such emotion in you.

I think songs today are really what poetry was to other generations. So much is said in poetry in a very, very short time. That's one of the things that has always helped me, is reading poetry. After you do that for a while, you kind of naturally go for the most information in the shortest period.

My father, years ago, told me something that stuck with me. He said, "Just cut out the dead wood. When it's not needed, simplify. Take it out."

That took you to a good place for songwriting, didn't it?

It did. I used to start out far more complicated than I do now. It takes a while, sometimes, to get around to that simplicity, but simplicity has to do with a certain amount of knowledge of what you're doing. Otherwise, it can be just too simple.

A lot of times, for instance, writing a positive love ballad, there's a fine line between hip and drip, and that can be just the smallest little thing, whether it's in your opening line, or any of the other lines. But if you're really going to come up with another powerful way of saying, "I love you," it's often just the turn of the word.

What advice do you have to share with us on rewrites?

I'm a bad one to ask. I don't like rewrites. I will do it if I have a respected co-writer. I will do it if it really makes that much difference to my publisher, but in general, I believe in getting it right the first time. Kind of like refried beans, you know. I mean, why do you re-fry them? Why don't you fry them right the first time?

Jim McBride and I were talking about it one day. We've done about four rewrites that I can think of, where the artist or the producer asked for it, and we never got the cut. We wouldn't rewrite "Rose In Paradise" and three artists walked right up to the door on that, and would not cut it. They wanted us to change the line "I would walk through hell on Sunday to keep my rose in paradise." But we weren't changing that line. That's such a powerful line. I understand why some people are afraid of it.

We stuck by our guns. Judy Harris was pitching it for Loretta Lynn one day. Loretta listened to it and said, "Boy, that's a great song, but I can't do it. That's not for me at all, but Waylon would kill that. You've got to get that to Waylon."

So, we played it for Waylon and he said, "Put it under a rock. I'll be back in six months." It took Waylon Jennings for someone to sing that line effectively.

Another time, Wynonna wanted "No One Else on Earth." Jill and I and Sam originally wrote, "No one can touch me like, no one can love me like you," and they called back and said, "Wy doesn't really want to sing 'touch me.'" We spent a little time thinking about other lines and, finally, they were ready to cut the song and they said, "Wy thinks, 'No one can love me like, no one can love me like you.'" And we said, "Yeah, great!" We wanted the cut and it didn't mean that much to us, but we felt like the right way was, "No one can touch me, no one can love me." It gives you more information. But we figured, if she's emotional about the other way then, by God, do it that way.

What about imagery in songwriting? How important is that?

Tremendous! Paint pictures, especially in country music. But, imagery, along with alliteration in the lyric, you take those two and put them together and you've got a poem. When you have a poem on top of music, you've got a really wonderful song.

"The Gambler" takes you on a train ride. Puts you at the table. You're there. Those are wonderful things. "I'm Gonna Be Somebody," that's the story about everybody, depending on what you want to do.

It just happens to tell the story of Jill [Colucci's] and my lives. The other unique thing about that one is that it doesn't rhyme, anywhere. We didn't try to do that, we just wrote it. Not one word rhymes with another. That was an interesting thing, and we didn't even think about it.

That's why I think there are different kinds of writers. Some writers like hard rhymes. Harlan liked a hard rhyme. I'll go with half-rhymes. I'll go with combined words too. I'll break all kinds of rules. Probably, I benefited by not knowing all the rules when I started off. I just kind of learned on the road. I think it makes for some interesting things to happen.

What are good basic skills that we need to develop as writers?

Discipline. I don't know whether that's a skill. I think it is.

I love alliteration and consonants, which are two of the oldest techniques of the craft. In love songs, I like soft alliteration. If I'm writing an attitude song, I use more aggressive consonants, to make it a little harder.

Musical movement. I just finished a song where I waited an extra bar for the hook, at the end of the second chorus, just to create some anticipation for the listener. If you just wrote a line and it's clever, does it emote emotion? Does it hit you just between the eyes, or does it hit you in the sternum also?

Don't underestimate your audience. Go ahead and write from the heart. I remember the first time I heard "Bluer than Blue," and I heard the line, "I can run through the house screaming." I thought, "Man, that just jumped out." It wakes you up for the rest of the song. It says, "Listen to this, I'm telling you exactly what's happening when I'm bluer than blue." It shakes you. It was a bold, bold move in a song like that. Be bold, but don't be bold for the sake of being bold.

I also, sometimes, will write a line in a song that's a little less than the other lines. If I've written three, kind of, rapid-fire lines in a row, I'll write something that gives the mind a rest, just for them to comprehend what was just said, because if you keep rapid-firing, sometimes you can lose your listener.

Talk to us about writer's block.

Doesn't exist. It's nonexistent, a figment of the imagination. There are times, certainly, that you feel stupid, and you feel like, "Okay, I've written the last song that I'm ever going to write in my life." No, but you may need to go do something else for a little while. You might just need some time away, to step away and look at what you've been writing.

I have certain times of the year that I'll run out of things. I'm affected by the dying of the year, and the blooming of the year, spring and fall. Winter, I could be a bear and go into hibernation. My songs will probably be a little darker in the winter. I try to write as little as I can in the summer. A lot of times, as a result of that I write some really good songs.

But, my most creative times are when you get the first whiff of honeysuckle. I usually get in a really good rhythm. And then, I get real reflective in the fall. Feel the dying.

I really don't believe God gives you this talent and then goes, "You can't do it! I'm taking it away."

What do you think is the most intimidating thing about songwriting?

Occasionally, it will hit me, the odds of what I do. The odds of getting a song recorded, of that song becoming a single, climbing up the charts. That's pretty intimidating. But I think the most intimidating is your responsibility to your listener, and to your art, and your craft. It's a pretty noble endeavor. If we treat it that way, I think it honors what we do.

Give us some tips on surviving the roller coaster ride.

Believe in yourself. That's the most important, because on the days that nobody cuts your songs, and nobody will give you a writer's deal, nobody's listening to your songs, you have to have the belief in yourself to get out of bed, and to go walk out there, and take a deep breath, and go after it.

Try to get in touch with yourself as much as you can and ask yourself, when you're really miserable, what it is that's making you miserable. Is it something in your life, or is it the fact that you think you should be a millionaire by now and at the top of the food chain, and you're not? Then, maybe, you're putting too much pressure on yourself.

I think that's what I've seen more than any thing else with marvelously talented writers who have not had that first one. There are some majorly talented people that it never happens to, and that's really, really unfortunate, because then there are some less talented, that know how to manipulate the game. It's like any other business.

If somebody, some producer that you respect, really doesn't like one of your songs, take a look at it and see if maybe you're not stacking up, or maybe this one wasn't right, or maybe you didn't know enough about the artist to pitch the right song. Little things like that.

It's really kind of practical stuff that you would apply to another business. If you were a salesperson, for instance, you'd deal with a guy that says "no" all the time. A really good salesman thrives on that person that says "no". Creative people don't do that.

Emotionally, keep yourself strong and positive. It's a good life. I don't care where you are on the food chain of this thing, it's a good life. It's wonderful.

6

CAROLYN DAWN JOHNSON

Carolyn's incredible work ethic, coupled with natural talent, has carried her in a few short years to places she only dared to dream about as a young girl. The release of her first album to the United States capped a year in which her success as a songwriter merited a number one hit ("Single White Female" for Chely Wright), a single for Jo Dee Messina ("Down Time"), and the highly-coveted Music Row *magazine's Breakthrough Songwriter of the Year award for 2000. Just six months after the Canadian release of* Room With A View, *she celebrated two number one singles and videos in Canada for "Georgia" and "Complicated." The Academy of Country Music honored her with a nomination for Top New Female Vocalist 2000.*

Comprised entirely of Carolyn Dawn Johnson's writings, Room With A View *is obviously the work of someone able to bring the highly personal into play while making art. "Georgia," "Complicated," "Room With A View," "Masterpiece," and "One Day Closer"—in fact, all of her songs—are clearly proof that Carolyn is a master at transforming simple stories into richly detailed pictorials.*

Room With A View *is also a vivid display of Carolyn's impressive reputation within the Nashville music community. Notable guests on the album include Martina McBride, Marty Stuart, Kim Carnes, Matraca Berg, Al Anderson, Mary Ann Kennedy, and other artists whose respect for Carolyn's music led them to lend their singing and playing talents. All of these elements were assembled in a first-time collaboration between Carolyn and producer Paul Worley (Dixie Chicks, Martina McBride).*

www.carolyndawnjohnson.com

How did you get into songwriting?

When I was a teenager, I wrote songs really for my own enjoyment. Looking back now, I see that it was pretty therapeutic for me, because I wrote a lot of poetry and I put music to that. I didn't think that that was going to be my life, I really didn't. That's not what I thought my career might be. But, after I graduated from high school, I was still writing, and I started playing some of these songs for my friends. I was always a music lover. I would read the credits of records and see who the writers were. Something just kept stirring inside me, and I kept doing it.

When I decided to actually chase my music career was when I really felt that the songwriting was part of it. It wasn't just about being the singer, for me. I wanted to do both. I was about nineteen when I just realized that maybe I had a gift, a little bit more than just normal. But I was also learning about the business, and learning about the world of the music business.

I was in Edmonton and then I moved to Vancouver, to pursue my music career in Canada. Seemed like the bigger music scenes were in Vancouver and Toronto.

I didn't really know where to start. I just knew that people always wanted me to sing for every event, and I was writing these songs that meant a lot to me. I was nervous about exposing them, but as I started doing that, and found out that people were really liking them, I started believing in myself. It wasn't just my little secret anymore.

As I grew as a writer, I still wrote from a pretty personal place, usually things I had experienced. I felt like there was a lot of growth that needed to happen. I tried to be realistic about it, but I believed that I could nurture my talent and, if I did, my creativity would grow and get better.

I don't know how your creativity gets better, but you can expand it, and you can use it, and exercise it just like anything else. The more you do that, I think, the better you become, and the better flow there is of the ideas, and the lyrics, and the inspiration.

When I was about twenty was the first time I started asking myself, "Are you doing this? Do you have a strong feeling within?" I decided that I really didn't know, but time was going to go on, whether I did anything about it or not. So, I went for it.

That's the advice I try and give to anybody who's trying to make it in anything. You can sit and not do anything about it. Five years are going to go by anyway. Or you can take those five years, keep going on with your life, but do something about it.

Did you have a deal of any sort while you were still in Canada?

No, I didn't. I didn't get a deal until I came down here to Nashville. I started making trips here in early 1994. I, officially, was planted here in 1997. That's when I was able to just be, kind of, a real part of the community.

But I made myself very present when I was here anyway. When I came for a visit, I was out everywhere. I was listening to music. I got up and played everywhere that they would let me. Coming to a town like Nashville, where there's such a wealth of talent, is very scary. But, the greatest thing is to get up there and do it, because you place yourself in the middle of what's going on. You can sit and listen to music all night and go, "'Man, that song just wasn't very good." And then you can go, "That song was great! Do my songs stack up? I need to get better. I need to go and sit up on stage, and have people coming up to me, and tell me how great a song is, just how I do to the other writers when I listen to their music." I strive for that.

It also made me a much better guitar player, because I couldn't rely on anybody else to play the music for me. I had to go up and do it myself.

I think we really need to be able to support ourselves, internally, if we hope to succeed as songwriters. Do you agree?

Supporting yourself internally is very important. It's strange, because it's like you have to convince yourself that you're worth it, and that you're good enough. You probably are! But, if you don't believe it, then you've already shot yourself in the foot, and you probably won't make it. So, you have to keep encouraging yourself.

I read a lot of positive books. Some of them you've probably heard of: *If You Think You Can, You Can*, and *How to Win Friends and Influence People*. There's another one, that this Australian writer did, which is one of my favorite books, very easy reading. It's called *Being Happy*. I still pull that book out because there are so many different subjects that it covers.

That's, actually, where I got that line in "Single White Female," "to put it in a nutshell." I had gone to this songwriting seminar, and some of the songwriters said, "Tell yourself every morning, 'I'm a great songwriter. I am worth this. I am very talented.'"

Then, in some of the books you read, they say, "Don't say anything negative, because what comes out of your mouth goes back in your ears. It goes in your brain." I try to do that, I just keep believing.

Another thing I learned from those books is to liken yourself to people you admire. If there's someone you want to be like, ask yourself what they're like. What do you know about them?

What I learned about Nashville, and some of the great writers, is that, first of all, they work very hard. They don't do it just on a whim. Most of them are treating it like a job, Monday through Friday. That doesn't necessarily mean that they might be writing Monday to Friday every week; but maybe Tuesday they're doing a demo session. Maybe Wednesday they're reading magazines in the morning, and they write in the afternoon. They're always doing something to further their career.

One thing that's a goal of mine is to do something every day that gets me closer to the big picture. Every day, whether it's singing for fifteen minutes, or doing something like practicing guitar, or just doing some creative exercises to get some more titles, or just do something every day.

> **"One thing that's a goal of mine is to do something every day that gets me closer to the big picture."**

I still tell myself positive things, because I think you have to have that encouragement from yourself. But I also believe it would be nice if you had one or two other people that really believed in you, whether it's your parents, one of your best friends, somebody that can be a good support system for you. Not everybody has that.

Was your family supportive?

My family was supportive. Whether or not they thought I was a great songwriter or not is another issue, but they believed in me, and they believed that whatever I put my mind to I could do. But they did see talent, as far as music goes. They nurtured it. I took piano lessons since I was five, and sang in every concert there was. My mom and dad really supported me.

What do you think creativity is?

I think it's like this mystery that we have inside of us. We all have our own variations of it, and you have to find a way to allow whatever you were given inside to come out. Whether you're a painter with amazing hands, or whatever, there's got to be something more, inside that person, to come up with whatever they paint.

For me, I just think my creativity is definitely a gift. Everybody has it. I really believe it. We all use it in our own different ways. Mine specializes in musical things, and ideas, and stories. I guess that's it. No two people are the same. It's like a snowflake.

Do you have a special writing room that you prefer?

My favorite place to write is at my first publishing company, Patrick Joseph Music. It's in a little house over off of Wedgwood, in Nashville. That was where I got my first publishing deal. I was so thrilled, so excited, to be considered a staff writer. I was very inspired. I just was on such a high to be doing what I loved for a living. I couldn't get enough of that place. There's one room in there, I've written a lot of my songs in there, a lot of things that have been cuts. When I go in there, I'm there to write. I think my mind knows that. My body knows that, and the rest of the world sort of goes away. It allows it to just be in the place where I'm going to create some songs.

I do write at home. Early morning, late at night, those are special times for me. I think in the morning I'm fresh, as long as it's not a rush in the morning. I remember reading, in your other book, some of the other writers talking about at nighttime, when you get tired, how your editor goes to sleep. Why is it that, when you lay in bed, and you're almost asleep, you come up with these cool ideas? Because there's nobody talking, telling you, you can't, or thinking about the other things.

There's always so much going on in your life that you have to find a way to get rid of that, so that stuff that's underlying comes out.

The writer's room at Patrick Joseph, does it have lots of windows, or is it four stone walls such that you can't see out?

It's got a glass door and a window. Sometimes we open the door, and just listen to birds, and have fresh air. There's a fireplace in this one particular room too, so if it's rainy and cold, just flip a switch and it's on. There's a piano in there, a couch, and a couple chairs.

That ended up being my favorite room. It just really conditioned itself to being my favorite place.

Do you think that creativity comes in cycles?

I think you can have spurts of it, absolutely. It depends on how much you exercise it. I've been out on the road a lot lately, so I don't spend as much time writing. I have to almost force creativity.

Some people say, "How can you force creativity?" People who don't write like we do don't understand it. If I didn't sit down and set apart some time to get my juices flowing, then they just wouldn't flow. I have to start playing some music or going through my little book of ideas, and just start thinking about life, get myself to thinking in that mode. Once I do, it could be a couple hours down the road, but something comes out.

I've gone weeks where I didn't even sit down and have guitar, and pen, and paper, or anything. Or, I've actually gotten an idea and was lazy about it, and didn't write it down, and lost it. I've learned, from doing that, that you should always write it down.

But, on the road I can get lazy that way. I can only say laziness, because I just get out of the mode of capturing it when it comes around. Whereas, when I'm really on fire, I write everything down, and I'm not wasting a letter, a word. I'm always thinking, "That could be something."

Are there any activities that are really conducive to stimulating your creativity?

Walking. If I'm on the treadmill, or something like that, I'll get to thinking about things. It can be one of two things on the treadmill, business or creativity. I mean, sometimes I'm on there, and thinking about everything I have to do. I have a piece of paper there to jot down my list.

But then, the main thing that always gets me really creative, is sitting down with an instrument. The music will always give me ideas. I can come up with melodies for days. If I'm stuck writing lyrics, the melodies will take me to one. If I feel like I don't have anything worth talking about, then I just play.

The sound coming out from the body of the guitar always is inspiring to me. Piano is not my main instrument to write on, but it used to be my main instrument to play. Sometimes I'll get on it, and the sound of it will put me in some sort of mood. I'll start playing something and, next thing I know, I'm like, "What is this about? What could this be about?" You start singing words over it, and it turns into something. It takes you in another direction.

Do you ever find yourself in a rut with your writing?

I don't ever feel like I've been in a rut up to this point. But I will say, once again, that since my artist career has taken off, being on the road puts me in ruts. I get on my management company and say, "The writing's what got me here. I have to have some time."

Then, when I get that time to write, my manager asks me, "How'd it go?" I'll tell him, "When I have days like this, it makes my life bearable."

The writing's a true release for me. I love it. I think it's helped me, as a person, be more confident in myself.

Is there a time of day that you feel like you're more creative?

Getting started off in the morning. Sit down, coffee sitting there, sun coming in wherever you're at. Not early morning. I've gotten used to certain habits, like ten o'clock in the morning. Even writing by myself, I kind of set myself patterns. Once again, that was from viewing other people that were successful. They treated it like that, and I thought, "Well, I'm going to do that."

Then, in the evenings, I love just being sort of tired and hanging out in my living room. I can get real creative that way. But I do, also, find it's harder for me to stick to something late at night. I have to record something and work on it later.

Do you like to have several songs in progress, or do you prefer to take one and finish it?

I'd rather take one and finish it, but there are times when I have many different songs on the go. I don't like that. I get frustrated, and I lose track of them. I lose the initial moment of what the song was.

Do you write on the bus, now that you're touring so much?

Not very much, I'm getting better at learning how to do that. And I say "learning," because it's learning how to set aside time. I travel with my band, so we're all on there, and there's not a lot of space and, even if I'm in the back by myself, I just don't feel like I'm in my own private place. I need to feel like nobody's listening to me. I don't like people listening to me write.

Do you keep notebooks and idea books?

Absolutely. I have them with me in my backpack. I have a notepad and a couple different journals that I keep up with. I've looked at this thing so many times. I've looked at these ideas, and none of them are doing anything for me. And then, the next time you pull it out, one of them pops out, so it's worth it to keep around. Sometimes, I just write ideas down, even though they don't seem like anything. They're just a bunch of words I'd better put in here.

Does reading books and seeing movies help you as a writer?

Movies, I think, are awesome to go and watch. A movie comes out and there's a great line in it and then, you know, there's fifty songs pitched to Faith Hill with the same title because we all saw the movie. But we've all got our own interpretations. It's like, who can get it to her first. Besides that, movies are moving for me, anyway. I love watching them, so it's kind of like an escape for me. When you do have that escape, it's like in that place where your creativity is flourishing, it's sort of an escape as well. And so, it's a creative place for me, to just go there and go to a different place, and feel those emotions. I get ideas from movies, definitely.

Reading is a thing that comes and goes for me. I'll go through a period of reading, and then I won't pick up a book for a long time. I read for my enjoyment, but most of the time it's about things I'm interested in, it's not fictitious things. So, my reading isn't necessarily an inspiration for me, as far as ideas or anything go. I think movies definitely have more of that. I know a lot of writers that use books for ideas, and that's awesome, but I'm not that disciplined. I'm always wanting to learn something from my reading. I have a hard time reading just for fun.

Do you think it's possible to overanalyze a song idea?

Absolutely, I definitely do. I have done that. I've tried to re-write, and re-write, and re-write, and just gotten so tired of it, and the song never goes anywhere.

Also, you can overanalyze the rules. None of us knows exactly what any rules are, we just think we know what they are.

I think our subconscious is a big factor in writing a great song because, if we've grown up with music, and we've listened to music all these years, there's something inside of us that knows what's good and what's not, as far as music goes. And when you're not realistic about that, you only hurt yourself.

Do you think of yourself as a disciplined writer?

Yes, I didn't used to be, but I am now. All my friends that have had success are disciplined people. They don't take it as something that just happens, they take it very seriously. They work at it. And when I did, that's when I started reaping the rewards of my hard work. And it is work. As much as you enjoy it, the discipline part of it is hard to maintain. I'm so thankful that I was taught discipline growing up. You set your mind to something, and you just do it. Next thing you know, all these things happen because of it.

How important is it to have a strong opening line?

I think a strong opening line is very important, but sometimes it depends on the song. I mean, you want to have the best opening line ever, but sometimes the simplest thing can be the best opening line. You might not have a great opening line, but the chorus kills.

I think it's important to try for the great opening line, but you want every line to have a reason for being there.

Talk to us about using imagery in your writing.

I learned how important it was. I didn't use to specifically think about it. I just, kind of, wrote my emotions and feelings. I realized, after somebody pointed it out, "Here's why that song's so great, because it has such imagery. I can totally picture what's coming up."

I need to remember that, when I write my songs. Not every song needs that, but usually there is something where you can sit back, close your eyes, and feel like that story's unraveling to you. Whether it's a story song or not, you know, like a picture of what's going on.

What do you think are the basic skills a person should work on developing, as a songwriter?

Well, there are lots of songwriters that don't play instruments, and they do fine, but I think the more musical you can be, the more you can expand on your songwriting. So, I think it's important to try and be some sort of a musician. As I got better on the guitar, I'd learn a new groove and then I'd write ten more songs, because it would inspire something different.

I think that, to be a professional songwriter, discipline is something that you have to have. You need to constantly find ways to expand your horizons, expand your mind.

Nobody can teach you exactly how to write a song. I'm pretty sure of that. You have to teach yourself, and bring your own individuality to it. For me, as a songwriter, wanting to be a professional songwriter, I learned that it had nothing to do with the creative part. It has everything to do with getting your songs heard. And, learning how to be tactful in this business, such that people aren't going to want to shut the door every time I turn the corner because I'm annoying.

Coming to Nashville was a huge thing, to spend some time here and see what you're up against. One thing that I heard a long time ago, that I thought was amazing, Woody Bomar said, "You don't have to move to Nashville. It could be a lot easier for you if you did. Just remember that if you're not here, you're up against people like me, who are here every day, and working my butt off to get my song heard."

I said, "Why can't I stay on my farm and, when I write songs, send them in?"

He was like, "You can do that, but know that if you are working at this at a hobby level, you can expect hobby-level results."

What do you think is the hardest part about writing a song?
Finishing it. I come up with great ideas, and melodies, for days, but actually doing the idea and the melody justice, and finishing it, seems like that's always the biggest challenge.

What do you feel are the advantages and the disadvantages of co-writing?
The advantage, for me, is that when I feel like, "Gosh, I don't feel like doing anything today," but I have an obligation to somebody, I'm going to be there. And I'll not let them down, and I'm going to pull my weight, because I'm not going to walk away with them thinking that I've got nothing to give. It always makes you reach a little bit further inside yourself. I never want to walk away from a situation where someone goes, "Man, why is she in this town?" That's an exaggeration, but I take a lot of pride in what I do, actually making it happen, and the joy of having that positive feedback.

"I come up with great ideas, and melodies, for days, but actually doing the idea and the melody justice, and finishing it, seems like that's always the biggest challenge."

There are lines that I may never have written. I wasn't sure if I believed in them or not, but someone else did. Having that vibe, and the bouncing back and forth thing, which I'm amazed at.

I definitely have my handful of writers that I stick with now, and it's hard for me to venture outside of my circle right now, because I'm comfortable that if we don't get something that day, we'll get it another day. And if I walk in there, I'm not afraid to say anything, even if it's the dumbest thing in the world. That may make them say something, and then I might say something else, and the next thing you know, we've come up with something great.

And, there's a lot of joy in celebrating a song with somebody. I've made a lot of great friendships because of my co-writing situations.

Do you feel like there are any disadvantages to co-writing?
Yes, if you're not with the right person. You can waste a good idea and it ends up being watered down because you usually end up settling for certain things. Because you're not as comfortable with that person, both of you are, kind of, just saying "yes" to things you might not normally say "yes" to because it's easier that way, and more comfortable.

We were talking once about doing a three-way write. If one person doesn't like the line, just keep searching, because when you find something that all three of you like, then you're all happy.

I took that to heart, and there've been times when I have not spoken up because I was in a situation where I was just nervous, and didn't feel right about it, and it wasn't their fault.

You find your own places, where you flourish, and that's where you need to go. It takes going through a lot of people to find that situation. We all go through it, so everybody understands it.

Are you very active in writing melodies for your songs?

Absolutely, melody is my strongest thing. I've definitely gotten a lot stronger in that department in the last few years, and gotten a lot more confident. So I'm more creative that way, and I work at it. It's gotten to be more important.

But, I don't want to be a melody hog.

Have you ever written with somebody whose is equally as strong a melody writer as you?

Absolutely, I have. But the fun thing about it is, if you find those people, and you have a good relationship with them, then you come up with cool things that are a combination. It's very inspiring.

Let's talk about that "editor voice" we touched on earlier and, if you would, offer some advice on dealing with that.

I think that the editor is important, but I think that you need to allow all those first things to come out. The original lyrics, the original ideas, put them on paper. And, when you get to a place you feel like you're almost done, then allow yourself to, kind of, go back.

I think there's some danger in editing along the way, because you might be able to use some of those lines or words later on in the song, or maybe in another song. The editor can do too much sometimes. That's part of that overanalyzing thing.

What do you think "writer's block" is?

Fear.

Have you ever had writer's block?

I've been burnt out before, where I wrote, and wrote, and wrote, and the next thing I know, it's like, "I can't do a thing right."

I don't know that it's necessarily that I couldn't do it. I think I just felt I was uninteresting. I felt like I didn't anything left to talk about.

I've never sat down and thought, "I can't do this." It's never been like that. But I have had days where you toss ideas around, and nothing locks. You just have to walk away from that and go, "That's just today. I'll be fine." You have to realize, it's a passing moment. You've got more songs in you.

> **"Never hang on to your last song. Never believe it's the last song you're going to write. There's always a better one coming."**

I think some of the best advice I was ever given was, "Never hang on to your last song. Never believe it's the last song you're going to write. There's always a better one coming."

Give us some advice on getting past the fear of failure.

You've got to find a way. It's easy for me to say that, while things are going good right now, but there were times that were miserable. And you falter a little bit. You just have to believe that you love what you're doing. Whether or not you're ever super-successful, if you still enjoy doing this, then it's okay.

I live with it, now that I'm on the charts. I live with, "What if nobody plays my song?" I have to tell myself, "If they don't play it, I can still sing. I can still sing around town. I will be fine."

Fear is a terrible thing. You've just got to not let it consume you. I always try and believe that I jump into my fear and just go, "I'm not going to let you do this to me. I am going to still show up tomorrow."

Sometimes, I'll go into a writing appointment and I'll be saying, "I haven't written in like a month and a half." I'm putting all these disclaimers on it because I'm so worried, "What if nothing happens?" The next thing you know, an hour later, you get onto something, and you're kind of excited, and you're having a good time, and you go home that night and you say, "What was I thinking?"

Don't even allow yourself to say those words, because you're setting yourself up for failure by talking about it, and thinking about it, and consuming yourself with thoughts that you might fail.

Songwriting is like a roller coaster ride, a lot of highs and a lot of lows. It's rare that you have a nice straight path. Would you give us some advice on how to survive that ride?

Don't quit, whatever you do. Keep doing it. When you experience the lows, you've got to know that everybody has those. Nobody has a consistent, run for the money, kind of thing.

When you look at the hot writers every year, everybody thinks they are gods, and then, the next year, it's someone else and it's not them. They're still writing though, and they're still getting cuts, just not these huge ones. So, when you have those great moments, revel in them, and be happy, and be excited because you may never have it again, but you have had it.

When you are at a low, just remember that you are still doing what you love. Music is one of the greatest things ever. I think we're all really lucky. So, take the highs, have a great time, and just know that you're coming down.

I'm a huge fan of Marty Stewart. He said something to me one time like, "Just remember, we'll all end up in the bargain bin one day. If you understand that, just go have a great time."

I thought that was neat because there is no one person that can sustain something, for his or her entire life. People like Dolly Parton, she's had her ups and downs. She's still around. She's a huge icon, really, and she probably will be till the day she dies. And that's great, but you can't tell me her life is perfect every moment.

Cherish it. Have fun with it. I have so many great people around me, and songwriting is really, truly the heart of what I do. I'm not sure which I'd rather have. I really wouldn't want to have one more than the other, but I will say that starting with a blank piece of paper, and ending with a song, is probably one of the best feelings I'll ever have.

The lows do make you appreciate the highs, and that's a sweet thing. I love the journey. I look at some of the things I did to get here, just playing in those little coffee shops, what a great time it was. You make so many great friends. We're all struggling trying to do it, but it's a very nurturing town if you're working hard.

And, once you get to that certain place, you really can't go back. I mean, once I'm not a recording artist anymore and I'm just songwriting, I'll have more of that life again, but I'll never go back to the beginning. Those were really precious moments.

7

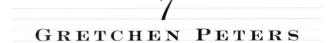

Known as a writer of intelligent and introspective songs in the
country/folk/pop vein, Gretchen Peters achieved notoriety through country stars
covering her material. Among the artists to have had hits with her songs are
Trisha Yearwood, Pam Tillis, George Strait, Martina McBride, Patty Loveless,
and Faith Hill. Peters was born in Westchester County, New York, and lived
there until her parents divorced when she was eight. She moved with her mother
to Boulder, Colorado, where as a teenager she was writing songs and performing
in the town's thriving live music scene. She moved to Nashville in 1988 and
signed several writing deals before moving to Sony/ATV in 1992. Having written
a string of critically acclaimed hits, Peters received her first Grammy nomination
for Song of the Year in 1995 for "Independence Day" (recorded by Martina
McBride), her powerful anthem about a woman who fights back against an
abusive husband. In the Country Music Awards that year, the song took home
the same award, as well as a CMA Video of the Year in 1994. She was nominated again for a Song of the Year Grammy in 1996 with the Patty Loveless
chart-topper, "You Don't Even Know Who I Am." But Peters's scope isn't limited
to the country music arena, as she has demonstrated with several songs written
with rock artist Bryan Adams, including songs from the DreamWorks animated
feature, Spirit—Stallion of The Cimarron. The current hit single from that
film is "Here I Am," recorded by Adams.

Gretchen is working on her own recording project for Europe and is in the
early stages of composing an operetta commissioned by the Nashville Chamber
Orchestra to debut in 2004.

Other cuts include "Chill of an Early Fall" (#1 George Strait), "Let That Pony
Run" (Top 5 Pam Tillis) and "The Secret of Life" (Top 5 Faith Hill).

www.gretchenpeters.com

How did you get into songwriting?

I really started out as a musician. All I wanted to do was just play songs, and I didn't even really think about where songs came from, at that point.

As a teenager, I started getting into certain kinds of music, mostly folk, and rock, and that sort of hybrid of country/rock that was going on in the seventies. I had friends who were playing in bands and were slipping in the occasional original song and, on a whim, I thought, "I bet I could do that." I tried, and seemed to have some kind of a knack for it. But it wasn't like, "Oh, this is what I want to do. I want to be a songwriter!" I wanted to be a musician, and I was. It was all just part of what you did: playing live, writing songs, and if you were really lucky, going into a studio, which was like a big apple on the tree.

Even when I got to Nashville, I still looked at it that way, like it was all part of one big thing. Not that songwriting, in particular, was what I really wanted to do, it was just music. I look at it as parts of a whole.

When I got here I realized that I had to do something. Credibility was really important to me, and it seemed that the road to credibility was through writing.

People posed the question a lot, like they do to people who are new here, "What do you want to be, an artist or a writer?" I really had never thought of it in terms of an either/or situation, but I got a writing deal within three months of being here. So I wrote, because that's what they were paying me to do. But I still didn't have in my mind, "I came to Nashville to be a songwriter."

Are there specific places or things that inspire you?

Traveling is really inspirational to me. Not in the sense that I write while I travel, but I feel like I fill my well when I travel.

I've always been a big reader. It's hard for me to say whether that's inspiration, because I've never *not* been a reader. I have a feeling that it keeps my head full of characters, ideas, situations, and certainly allows me the freedom to make things up. It's true you should write what you know, but you'd have to lead a pretty insane life to write all the things there are to write about, if you weren't a reader, and didn't have somewhat of an imagination.

I've always found that I have to be alone. I've never been able to understand the writer that says, "Well, I was sitting around in the kitchen with my wife the other day, and I was writing," and I'm thinking, "How, in God's name, could you do that?" I have to be alone.

I talked with Jamie O'Hara about this one time and we were laughing, because neither one of us really thought there was anyone else on earth like us. We were so paranoid about someone overhearing us when we were writing, that we really couldn't relax, and settle down, and do it, till everyone else was out of the house. That's why I built myself an office out in the woods, that's not attached to the house, because I don't want anyone hearing me.

I don't know how else to describe it. It feels like a very private activity to me. And lately, I've been finding that I write the best when I go away. I just came back a few days ago from Florida. I went down there for five days, and I wrote, and wrote, and wrote. It's almost like a binge. I can go from seven or eight in the morning, till eight or nine at night, and I can't do that at home. So, it's really wherever, whatever it takes for me, but solitude is always in the mix.

How much of your encouragement to do this comes from within?

At the beginning stages, you pretty much feel like everyone is saying, "You're out of your mind, what makes you think you can do this?" We all, to a greater or lesser extent, have felt that. I am lucky to have a husband who was an absolute believer in me. And, my father was a freelance writer most of his life, so it wasn't as if he could say, "You can't do that."

We all feel that, even from ourselves. Even internally, we feel like, "Who am I fooling?" And then you go through the litany in your head, of the statistical improbability of making it. It helps if you have a champion.

I had some sort of a blind spot. I thought, "I'm sorry, but the rules and statistics do not apply to me," and I believed that. It's not something that I psyched myself into believing. That's just how I felt, and it got me through.

Now that I look back, I think it sounds like I had a very easy route. I moved to Nashville in 1987 and in three months, I had a publishing deal, and a year later I had a cut. That sounds great, but I spent ten years before that playing in clubs in Colorado.

I remember plenty of nights when I should have looked at the room and gone, "What am I doing this for?" I starved for ten years and we had no money. Through all that, you have to naturally come to some moments of doubt, but I just had this blind spot about it, and it got me through all that.

New songwriters think there's going to be a point when you get over that internal feeling of not being good enough, "I might not be able to do this." I don't really think you get over that. Every time I sit down to write, I think, "I don't know how to do this, and this is the time that the world is going to find out that I don't know how to do this."

I don't think new writers really realize that, and I think it would be a comfort to realize it. We all start with a blank piece of paper, every time. It's not like it gets any easier. In fact, I think it gets a lot harder, as your standards go up. It's taking a big leap into the unknown. You get a little more comfortable with that, but it's not like I know some big secret that beginning songwriters don't know.

What is creativity?

For me, it feels like a tension; sometimes even anger, or a hurt, or a negative feeling. But underlying, there's a need. The best analogy, for me, is the sand that gets inside of the oyster. It's the irritant that makes the oyster create the pearl. You can't make those pearls unless you have that thing that is urging you on. Creativity is like a need, a hunger. It's a need because it causes action. It causes you to make something, to do something, to say something.

> **"Creativity is like a need, a hunger.... It causes you to make something, to do something, to say something."**

Are specific activities, such as driving, showering, or mowing the lawn, conducive to creativity?

I think walking is underrated for that. It has something to do with the rhythm of the walking. There's something about physical rhythm that brings things out musically.

There's another activity, that doesn't seem like much of an activity, and that's napping. I totally believe in that.

Do you have a place in your writer's room where you can nap?

When I built my office, I put a really comfortable couch in there for that very reason. Number one, I really love napping. And, number two, it can't hurt if you're stuck to try it out.

I just had this happen a few days ago when I was down in Florida. I was stuck on something, and I thought, "Well, okay, I'll just quit for a while and go take a walk." And within five minutes, as soon as I started walking, the right line came to me.

I think, a lot of times the thing that helps shake you loose when you don't know what the answer is, is something physical. Sleeping, which is physical, or walking, can be really helpful.

Are you aware of the cycles of creativity?

Definitely. When I first moved to Nashville I did what everybody did, which was write every day. I wrote in the morning, four or five hours. Life got more complicated when I had my first record deal, and that went out the window. I became more of a binge writer.

I would plan to have three uninterrupted weeks with nothing to do but write. I wasn't actually writing the whole song in those three weeks. I had been collecting little bits and pieces along the way. I would actually be finishing things up, which is really some of the hard work.

After you took those three weeks off to write, were you able to write immediately, or did it take you a while to get going again?

There is definitely a period of getting the machinery up and running again. In fact, that's something I fight a lot. If it's been three four weeks since I've written anything, I really start to dread getting that machinery cranked up again.

It feels like you're going into a factory that's been dark for a long time, and you have to crank, and get the wheels going again. It's not a pleasant thing. I guess, after a while, from experience, I know that I'm going to sit in there, and nothing's going to happen for several days, even weeks.

I don't know why I don't write every day, except I just don't want to anymore. I get more pleasure now, really waiting until I need to write. I'm not really making a value judgment about either, I don't know that either one's really better; it's just what's right for me right now.

Talk about the role of your subconscious mind in songwriting.

I am a huge believer in that. In fact I think, in a lot of ways, your whole job as a writer is to get out of the way of your subconscious mind, as much as possible. Your conscious mind, your editor, so to speak, is always in the room with you, saying, "Well, this won't work, and this doesn't make sense."

You need that voice, but you don't need it till later. You generally need to kick that person out of the room and let the subconscious happen. That's where you get the genius lines, and the stuff that later you look back on and go, "God, did I write that?"

The conscious mind, the editor, is just cobbling it all together and helping it all make sense. I think your song is the most perfect right before you start writing it, because you have this beautiful vision of it in your mind, and you haven't screwed it up yet.

The longer you can stay in that frame of mind, and get as much of that out, before you have to start going in and making sense of it, the better.

It's kind of like a sculptor with a piece of rock. You just want to take away what needs to be taken away. It's not that you're making something, it's that you're revealing something. Your subconscious knows, somehow, on some level, what's the truest message, what's the best thing, what's right musically and lyrically.

"I think your song is the most perfect right before you start writing it, because you have this beautiful vision of it in your mind, and you haven't screwed it up yet."

Have you ever experienced a period when the flow of your creativity seemed endless?

I have, and usually it's right before I go mental, and crash. Usually, I've gone through the whole horrible process of getting the machinery started up. Then things start cruising along fine. I hit a few snags, but I'm okay, still moving. Then, I get into the manic, "Everything I do is great," phase. And right after that, I hit the wall.

It's great, because you can get into that thing where all the synapses are firing right, and everything's looking up, and lining up, and you feel like you could write two songs per day forever. You can't, of course. In my case, I'll burn out fairly shortly after getting that feeling.

I think you really have to fill the well up. You need to let it fill up again and go through that cycle. The fallow periods are really important to me. If I try to write when I don't have anything to say, I come out with superficial stuff, that's pretty disposable. I'm just not happy with that, and it hasn't really been very successful for me. The things that have been successful have been the things that really meant a lot when I wrote them.

It's a talent, to be able to craft a song that's just a pure piece of confection. People have a lot of success with that and, more power to them. I don't think that's my forte.

When you have an idea for something you want to say in a song, what process do you go through to develop the story?

It sort of works a little bit differently for me. With "Independence Day," for example, I have this chorus and I don't really know what it means, but I know there's a story. I have a general idea what the story is, but I don't know the specifics. I don't know who the characters are and I don't know how it's supposed to end.

The whole process of writing that song was letting the story, the characters, tell me where it wanted to go. It was a feeling of, "It's out there, and I have to find it." It wasn't me deciding how it was going to go. Although, I tried changing the ending a thousand different ways and, ultimately, I realized, "I can't. I'm not in control of it. It's what it is and I have to find it." It's like a riddle. It was a matter more of uncovering a story, than determining the story.

I've had that experience with more than just that song. When there's a story involved, it's more about listening to what the song wants. It's just an instinct thing. You play the song back to yourself and you go, "That's not real." You get to this certain point in the song and you think, "That's not what happens, that's not right." It strikes a false note. "Okay, I'm not there yet. I haven't found the arc of the story yet."

That's what happened with "Independence Day." First, I had the chorus. Then, I got the first verse and then, the second verse, and I thought, "Okay, we know what's happened, we know that this little child's father is abusing her mother, and she gets out of the way." Then there was the problem of the third verse, and I wrote it several different ways.

I tried to make it nonviolent at the end. I don't know how I thought I was going to do that, given that it was a violent situation. But I'd try something, and I'd listen to it. And there was just something in me that said, "That's not right. That's not what happens." It's just a feeling of, "I don't buy that." It's an instinct.

How many songs are you generally writing on at one time?

Probably on an average, eight or nine. I have a big pile of paper, and then there's the master paper, which is all of the ideas that I've never thrown away. On the top of that pile, is a hot pile, of about eight or nine things, that I keep going.

You just have all of this sitting on the desk, and you see which one strikes you for the day?

Yeah, I just flip from one thing to the other a lot. I don't generally sit down and say, "Okay, I'm going to hammer this one out." I think it's because I feel songs are like soufflés. They'll fall if you work on them too hard, or if you handle them too much.

You just glance at it, and maybe you'll get a little bit of an idea, and you'll add that, and then go on to another thing. I just feel like heavy handling will bruise them, or something.

Do you keep any notebooks?

No, I can't do the notebook thing, because it's too linear, by virtue of the way the notebook is put together. If you have a big stack of papers, you can just shuffle them, put things on top, and rearrange. It's piles of paper for me.

Then, the computer thing added a whole new dimension.

Good or bad?

Well, both, actually. There are times when I feel like I really want to write with a pen and paper. And when I feel that way, I do that. Then there are times when I really want to see it on a computer screen, and I want to manipulate the words, the way you can with a computer.

That's usually later in the process, when I feel like I'm really getting there. I want to see it up on the screen, and put in my extra little ideas that didn't work, down at the bottom so I can hang on to them. Then, sometimes, I'll print that out and scribble on it. So, it's like a mixture of writing and computer typing.

Give us an idea what a handwritten lyric sheet might look like for you.

It's got crap all over page. One of the big questions when you're writing is, "What am I trying to say?" You always have to keep that in mind.

If it's really early on, and I have this little ephemeral couple of lines, I'll do a little summary at the top of the page that says, "This is about whatever," whatever the real actual theme might be, and that gives me a compass when I go back to it.

It sounds more like a note to yourself, than a line of lyric.

It's just a note to myself to remind me to get back into that head-space. Then, there will be couplets, and extra rhyming words, out to the side, and stuff everywhere.

I finished a song last week that I've had lying around for a really long time and, when I took all the papers that related to that song and put them away, the pile of papers for that song was an inch thick. I looked at it and I thought, "Boy, I really needed to write that song apparently!"

So, sometimes, there's not just one lyric sheet. Sometimes there are twenty, or thirty, in different phases of doneness.

And it all goes in a folder at the end?

When the song is done, I put it in the file cabinet, because I'm terrified to throw anything away. You know, they ended up using my lyric sheet for "Independence Day" in the Country Music Hall of Fame, which was incredible. It was also frightening for me to give that to them, because there were lines on it that didn't get used, and there was some bad stuff.

Like I said, I look at it like a very private activity, and to show somebody a lyric sheet with things you didn't use, things that you tried, dead-end roads that you went down, it's just a little bit daunting. But I also thought, "God, how cool would it be!"

Do you feel different about the songs that just seem to pour out, as opposed to those that you struggle over?

"You Don't Even Know Who I Am" is the only song I can remember pretty much writing in one sitting. I sat down right here on the floor. I found that spot of sun on the floor, and I sat on there. I was all alone in the house, and I just *wrote* that song.

It never works that way for me. I never write something in one sitting. I went back several times looking for that spot. It was like the dome of creativity, but I never found it again.

How did that feel?

Oh, it was amazing! I never know, after I write something, if it's any good or not. I didn't have the feeling of, "Oh, my God, I just sat here, and it took me two hours, and I wrote a number one song!" I didn't have that feeling, because who knows? I didn't even know if it might really suck. But I knew it was done. I sensed, and I felt, "Whatever this is, I finished it." I had an inkling that it was pretty good.

I'm really bad about judging my songs. I don't know what I would do without my husband, because he tells me if it's any good or not. Then I believe it. I have an inkling usually, but I need that first reassurance.

A blank sheet of paper—now what?

No, that's awful—blank sheets of paper. I realized something, not too long ago. When I'm talking to somebody, like now, about the process of writing, what I remember is finishing songs. I can tell you the whole process of "Independence Day," how I finished it, and how I struggled with this and with that, and how long it took. But I can't remember writing the first part, the initial part, of anything. I don't know when that happened, and I don't know what I was thinking about.

It's like there are two distinct stages. There's the stage we were just talking about, getting the idea and letting the unconscious kind of work on it. Obviously, at some point, I wrote something down and then left it alone. That's the part I don't remember doing. The part I do remember doing is the cobbling together, the work, the finishing, and the flushing it out.

I think what happens is, while I'm in the process of finishing something else, I get another idea, and I'll write it down and not even think about it. It's so offhand, I'm not even aware I'm doing it.

Is there such a thing as overanalyzing an idea?

There's overanalyzing, from the standpoint of making it make sense. Sometimes things make emotional sense, and they don't necessarily make grammatical sense.

And then there's my least favorite kind, which is overanalyzing in terms of the market. We all run into this trap at one time or another. You come up with an idea. There's a line in there that you know will make the song un-cutable. Then, you start playing that "devil's game," "Well, if I just maybe softened this a little bit." Sometimes that's okay, but sometimes you're totally compromising what the song is all about.

That would have happened for "Independence Day," if you had overanalyzed the market.

Absolutely, and I thought a lot about doing it. But the classic "overanalyzation" is just when you can't see the forest for the trees. You're inside this song and you're trying to claw your way out, and saying, "Well, if he did that, why would she do that?" That becomes sort of plot analysis.

That's when you have to extricate yourself, and go back to that thing that should be at the top of your page that says, "What am I trying to say?"

We've all heard the phrase "from the heart." What does it mean to you?

I have mixed feelings about that phrase. I think what it really means, is "from the instinct."

When I hear the phrase "from the heart," I get a little bit nervous, because I don't like unbridled sentimentality. Some of the authors I like—Fitzgerald, Hemingway—that's not sentimental writing, that's cerebral writing. There's absolute gut instinct behind it.

I'm not saying it's a bad thing to write what you feel. I think that's a very important thing. You can touch people emotionally, but you have to be disciplined about it. There has to be discipline and instinct, as well as heart.

If it were just about writing from the heart, anything anybody wrote would be fine. But you're not the audience; you're *of* the audience. Your job is to put into words what they can't, or to put them in such a way that it blindsides them and takes them by surprise.

You're not going to move anybody by saying, "I loved him so much, I thought I would die when he left." You have to be disciplined enough, instinctive enough, and feel the emotion enough, to say it in a way that they wouldn't think of saying it, so it cuts them.

That's my problem with the whole "from the heart" thing. I think sometimes people take that to mean, "All I have to do is say how I feel." Well, that's not all you have to do at all. You have to say it in a devastatingly new way, and that takes a lot of discipline and restraint.

Songs benefit greatly from restraint. A lot of people believe it's not what you say; it's what you don't say. That kind of restraint takes discipline. You have to trust that, by glancing on the subject, you're going to affect somebody, emotionally, more than putting your finger on the subject. Describing the pictures around what happened when he left is far more devastating emotionally than just saying, "He left and now I'm sad." That takes intellectual discipline.

I'm not saying you shouldn't feel the emotions. You have to be emotionally in the place, but I think it's just the combination of all those things. There is a discipline. There's an instinct, and there's a heart, and they all have to work together.

How does that happen for you? Do you get an overall sense of what is happening and then back up and supply the images?

Sometimes. But sometimes, the images come first. Sometimes the scenery, the visual stuff, comes first and you ask, "What is this picture describing, what has happened to you?" That happens to me a lot because I tend to think visually. A lot of times, I'll see a character doing something, or in some situation, and I won't even know what's happening, and I have to let that story tell itself to me in a way.

But, on the other hand, let's say you have a chorus, and it moves you, and you're really happy with it. It's around this theme of being left, of loss. Then you have to write the verses. That's when you have to say, "Okay, it wouldn't be effective to say, 'He left me, da, da, da,' and then the chorus." Like in "You Don't Even Know Who I Am," it was far more effective to say, "She left the keys. She left the car in the driveway." Just paint the picture. Then, when the chorus comes, you get the meat. You understand what happened. That's an example of painting the scenery, rather than just sharing the information.

Do you ever feel like everything has already been said?

Oh, yes, that's the corollary to "I'll never write another song again." Yeah, I do all the time, and I halfway believe it. That's the fight of a writer. That's the sort of spiritual quest of a writer, to constantly be carrying that torch in the night. There is another idea out there and I will find it.

It helps if you think of it in terms of *finding* ideas instead of *having* ideas. You take too much of the credit on yourself if you think "I created this song, I wrote this song," rather than "I found this song." It takes some of the heat off, when you realize it's a process of feeling around out there in the subconscious world for ideas.

Everybody feels like all the song ideas are taken. Look around you. There are a hundred song ideas in this room. They're out there; you just have to find them. I think it's a little easier to think of it that way, because you don't feel so responsible.

Do you think of yourself as disciplined?

I guess my friends would say that I am, but I don't.

Why would they say that?

They've seen me doggedly pursuing this for so many years. What they don't see is me thinking, "How lucky can I get?"

Despite how hard it is sometimes, when I'm down there writing by myself, or I'm in a studio, I'm thinking, "This is the stuff I've always wanted to do, and somebody's paying me to do it."

You don't need discipline to do that. Most of the time it's really, really fun, but sometimes it's a real pain. Sometimes the realities of the business suck. But I've had straight jobs, and I know what that's like. Getting up at seven o'clock in the morning and going to a job that you hate, that's discipline. I don't really look at this as discipline. I do screw around and not work, all the time, so it's hard for me to think of myself as disciplined. Let's say I have good follow-through.

How important is the opening line?

I thing it's really, really important. I think you're 50 percent of the way there. It's important for the writer, and the listener too.

First of all, for the writer, if you come up with a great title and a great opening line, you are so on your way. That opening line is going to be the propulsion that gets you to the end of the song. The opening is where they decide, "Wow, I'm intrigued by this," or "God, not another one of these songs."

It's like a path, a garden path. Does the entry into this little garden path look inviting? Do you want to go down that path? That's what the opening line is.

Generally speaking, I'm the type that would get the opening line first. I don't often get a hit chorus, or a hook first. That's probably a little backwards, or weird, maybe. A lot of times, I'll end up with three verses I just love, and no chorus or hook, and a "what the hell am I going to do now" kind of thing.

I get it that way because verses are very second nature for me to write. I'm all about developing the narrative of the story. The chorus is sometimes a nasty necessity. That probably comes from my folk background. I'm perfectly happy with songs that don't have choruses at all.

But, on the other hand, I like songs that are hooky, and I like songs that make me want to hear them again and again. I'm not immune to that at all. I like to write them. But I'd say, maybe 70 percent of the time, I'm more the type that would develop an opening line, or an opening couplet, and then say, "Oh, what have I gotten myself into?"

How important is imagery in songwriting?

It's very important to me. I'm always looking more for the visual way of telling the story than to just say what happened. I've written songs with both, but I love songs that feel like movies to me.

That's one of my big problems with videos. I just can't stand the idea that somebody is giving me the image to have in my head. I would much rather listen to a song and, if it's a great song, I'll have my own images.

I think images are incredibly powerful, because they'll hit you in the subconscious more than a straight narrative, telling of the facts will. The way all nonverbal things do. The way music does, the way painting does. Anything visual is going to hit you on more levels than just an intellectual level.

I encourage young writers to try and find ways to use visual images in their songs to tell the story. I think that's a common trap that you can fall into when you're starting out, is to tell what happened. But we've all heard that story before, and we've all heard it in those words before. If you can put the setting out in the desert, and tell me about the barrenness of the desert, give me some kind of image to hang onto that will invoke that image that you're trying to convey, then you're going to be farther along to affecting me emotionally.

What is the hardest part about writing a song?

It's all hard, and the more I do it, the harder it gets. The little target that you're aiming at gets smaller and smaller, the better you get.

I guess the hardest part about writing though, if I had to really isolate it, is all the mental noise about doing it. There's nothing tangible there. If you sew a potholder, you can look at it and say, "I sewed that potholder correctly."

It's very difficult to know where you stand with songs. It's all completely subjective. You might get some feedback down the road, if your song is a big hit, and then you can say, "Yeah, I wrote a good song." But that's probably going to happen at least a year from the time you're sitting there writing it.

All the mental noise around writing, "Is this good? Is this bad? Does this suck? Does this not suck? Am I crazy for thinking I can do this?" All of that, with nothing tangible to balance that out, is the hardest part about writing.

That's why I think songwriters, myself included, like to do things with their hands as an antidote to this, because it's all in your head so much. For me, one of the most satisfying things I can do is sew. I love to sew because you make it, and it's there. You can hold it, you can use it, and you can wear it, or whatever. It's so reassuringly tangible.

What are the basic skills a person should develop to become a good songwriter?

I remember doing this in the beginning, and I have seen evidence of it in a lot of beginning writers. They get so involved in the rhymes and what sounds good, that they really lose track of the fact that every single line has to serve the purpose of "What are you trying to say?" Every line has to, at least, not throw you off the path and, hopefully, further you down the path of what you are trying to say.

I think another key is developing a good sense of respect for your own instincts. The way that you can get derailed with that is listening to the radio so much that you figure, "I have to write what's on the radio," or you listen to people tell you, "I think you ought to do this."

I always tell new writers the best way to deal with feedback or critiques is, if it strikes a chord in you and you think, "Oh, I was worried about that line, and I didn't want to admit it," then you need to listen to it. If it makes you feel like, "No, that's the point of this song," if you want to fight about it, then fight about it. Stand up for your line, but respect that instinct that's inside of you.

I think new writers are so anxious to get some success going and get something happening that they're willing to subjugate all their own opinions and feelings about their writing, and try whatever anybody tells them. Some of that is okay, but you have to respect your own abilities.

For instance, when I was first starting out, I was encouraged to co-write like everybody who moves here. Thank God I had a really wise and understanding publisher, who saw me floundering around trying to co-write, failing miserably at it, and said, "Why are you torturing yourself like this? You're writing beautifully on your own. You write better on your own than you do with anybody else." He let me off the hook.

What are the advantages and disadvantages to co-writing?

That's different for every writer. The reason people like me don't co-write is we only see the disadvantages. It's hard for me to say what the advantages are, because if I say what they are I'd probably be taking advantage of them, and I'm not.

I do co-write with Bryan Adams. That's my one co-writing thing, and it's taken so many years for us to get comfortable, to feed ideas to each other without thinking about it. It's a very intimate process, and that's probably why I don't co-write more. The advantage, obviously, is that you share the burden, and you get a different perspective.

My major problem with co-writing is that, if I have an idea for a song, the other person is just in the way. It's that whole thing about the song being just a concept, and it's most wonderful before you've screwed it up, and written it. At that point of the song, I can't even verbalize to another person what it is. It wouldn't sound like anything. It's so preverbal.

That's why I find it difficult, because that's the point at which I'm getting the most inspiration, and I can't even tell you what it's about.

I'm not the kind of person that generally has the big hook chorus idea. So, if I have a couple of lines, and they're not really that much, I'm sure my co-writer would be asking, "What?"

When I wrote "Let That Pony Run," all I had for the longest time was the word "pony" written in my notebook. If you walk into a co-writing session and you say, "How about the word, *pony?*" they're going to go, "And, what else?" But for me, just the word made all kinds of things happen inside of me.

That's one of those songs that I had no idea what it was about. It ended up being a story that I really kind of found my way to, slowly and instinctively. I don't think you can do that with another person. Maybe you can, if you've worked together for a very long time, and you just sort of are mind-locked.

So, I think co-writing is a different process. By nature, it has to be more cerebral, more linear, because you have to already be able to express your ideas and words to your co-writer as in, "I want to say this." Sometimes, for me, ideas come and they're just not that verbal. I just have sort of a feeling, and that's just not possible to do with another writer.

Talk about that "editor voice" that we all have in our head?

I think the difference is, is it a critic or an editor? An editor is full of helpful suggestions, and a critic is telling you, "You stink." I think you have to make sort of a bargain with yourself which is, "All right, I'll let you in, but not until I get to a certain point with this song. For the first three hours, I sit down with this song, you have to stay out of the room and you have to let me play." For me, anyway, that makes it a little bit easier, knowing I'm not going to suppress that voice forever, but I have permission to suppress while I play.

It's really about playing, in the beginning of anything creative. Watch children, that's how they are creative, they play. And that's how writers do it. We just play with things.

The longer you can stay with the act of playing, the better. You have to make a bargain with yourself that you won't let that person in for that period of time, so you feel safe doing dumb stuff, and writing dumb stuff, and saying dumb stuff, and it's all okay.

What advice can you give on dealing with the fear of failure?

Heroes aren't fearless. It's not that they don't have fear, it's that they have fear but go ahead anyway. That's how I feel about fear of failure.

"There's not any level of fame, or fortune, or accomplishment that you're going to reach, where you're going to cease to feel that you've just written a terrible song."

There's not any level of fame, or fortune, or accomplishment that you're going to reach, where you're going to cease to feel that you've just written a terrible song. Fear of failure is always going to be there. It's not going to kill you, is really the bottom line.

My worst moments are playing my new songs for my husband. It is excruciating. I hate it. I want to disappear in a hole. It's so vulnerable. You've just written these songs, you don't know how you feel about them. You don't know how the world will feel about them. You don't know if they're any good or not. And you're laying them out there to be crucified. It's awful. As long as I do this, I will go through this. I guess you just have to learn that it won't kill you. And it's not going to change. It kind of ceases to be a part of the picture because, if I want to do this songwriting thing, I'm going to have to face it.

Is there competition among songwriters in Nashville?

Yeah, there's competitiveness. And some of it is good, I think. I remember one of the first things I did, when I first moved to Nashville, was go to a Harlan Howard Birthday Bash. I heard Kennedy Rose and I thought, "I could do that. I could be that good," and at the very same moment I thought, "I will never be that good, and I need to just go home and forget about it." That was a great thing for me.

A little bit of overconfidence and belief in your self, and a little bit of humility, is a good cocktail. It's a thing that will spur you on to try. It's a motivator. I would call that competitive, in a sense. Not competitive in the sense that I hated them because they were so good. I loved them, but I also had that kind of feeling of, "Yeah, I want to try. I'm game for this," tempered with feelings of complete humility because they were so great, and are so great. So, that's a wonderful thing.

The other thing I experienced when I first moved to Nashville, which was good for me, was that I really *heard* songs for the first time. I heard Don Schlitz at the Bluebird Cafe play "The Gambler." I'd heard that song a thousand times on the radio, but I never really heard it, till I heard him do it. I never really heard the story. I never heard the words. I guess because of the medium. When it comes out of the radio its one thing, when you're there and you're watching the person, suddenly something clicked in me about how every word is important. How you tell the story is vitally important.

I was, up to that point, trying to write things that sounded like what's on the radio. When I heard him, I realized it's not about writing what sounds like what's on the radio, it's about telling a story with a perfect economy of words. Then I got it.

8

HUGH PRESTWOOD

Hugh Prestwood has been writing hits for two decades. He was discovered in 1978 by Judy Collins, who gave him his first hit ("Hard Times For Lovers") and subsequently recorded five more of his songs.

A staff songwriter for BMG music, Prestwood has penned #1 hits for Randy Travis ("Hard Rock Bottom Of Your Heart"), Trisha Yearwood ("The Song Remembers When"), Michael Johnson ("The Moon Is Still Over Her Shoulder"), Shenandoah ("Ghost In This House"), Crystal Gayle ("The Sound Of Goodbye"), and Collin Raye ("On The Verge"). He has also composed hits for Highway 101 ("Bing Bang Boom"), Anne Murray ("Feed This Fire"), Michael Johnson ("That's That"), Ty England ("Smoke In Her Eyes"), and Kathy Mattea ("Asking Us To Dance"). Other artists who have recorded his songs include Conway Twitty, Lee Greenwood, Don Williams, Jackie De Shannon, Verne Gosdin, Maura O'Connell, Tanya Tucker, and The Judds.

In 1991, Prestwood was honored at the annual BMI Awards with the twenty-third Robert J. Burton Song Of The Year award for "Hard Rock Bottom Of Your Heart." He was also picked by Billboard *magazine as the #2 country songwriter of that year.* Billboard *currently lists "Hard Rock Bottom Of Your Heart" as the fifth-biggest country hit of this decade.*

Prestwood made his recording debut on RCA records in 1993 with the album Signatures 3, *featuring five of Nashville's top writers doing their own songs. In 1994 Prestwood won a Prime Time Emmy Award for Outstanding Individual Achievement In Music And Lyrics for his composition "The Song Remembers When," featured in the Disney special,* "Trisha Yearwood—The Song Remembers When." *The song was also nominated for a CableACE Award for Best Original Song, and was voted Song Of The Year by members of the Nashville Songwriters Association (NSAI).*

In 1997 his song, "On The Verge," was listed by Billboard *magazine as the fourth-biggest country hit of the year.*

Three of Prestwood's songs have been nominated for Grammys in the "best performance" category: "Sound Of Goodbye," performed by Crystal Gayle; "Hard Rock Bottom Of Your Heart," performed by Randy Travis; and "Ghost In This House," performed by Shenandoah.

www.hughprestwood.com

How did you become a songwriter?

I was raised in a middle-class family. My mother was a teacher, and later became a college professor. My grandparents, on my father's side, had both been musicians, but I didn't even know that until later, when I myself was a musician.

I was a pretty introverted kid, and pretty shy. I started playing the guitar when I was about ten. They used to leave the radio on a country station for me to go to sleep, and maybe that's why I just had to have a guitar. Over the next few years, I became a pretty decent guitar player. Didn't write any songs, but I played in bands and did things like that.

As a freshman in college, I had my first serious romance, but it didn't work out. I was crushed, so I decided to go visit my father in Alabama, and while I was there I wrote my first couple of songs.

Then I went back to El Paso, where I'm from, and proceeded to be a guitar player for another ten years, without writing another song. So, I didn't start writing songs till I was, maybe, twenty-seven.

I read a lot of poetry, and I always thought that I should write songs, but I just never did. What really sort of triggered it was that I got in a band that was doing top 40 hits. And the whole, "do your own music," thing was starting to kick in. This was in the late sixties, and the idea of doing original material suddenly seemed like a reasonable thing, so I started writing a few songs for the band. They were well received. I mean the band thought they were good.

It kept you encouraged.

I was so impressionable really, had I gotten some negative thing at that point, I probably wouldn't have written anymore.

How did you get into writing for the commercial market?

I've had a couple of what I call major accidents in my career. In the course of playing around in El Paso, I used to accompany a girl who was a great singer. She went off to pursue a singing career and, in a couple years, ended up on Broadway, in a big musical. She was an ingénue in a Richard Rogers musical called *Two By Two*. In the meantime, I had started to write these songs. We were good friends, so I had sent her a tape that I made, with me playing my guitar. She called me and said she loved the song.

CBS got interested in her as an artist, and they told her, "We'll do a whole session on you and, if it works out, we'll sign you, but you pick out your material." So, here comes the great accident. She phones me up and says, "Let's do your songs in this session." And I can honestly say, even though I may have had many a fantasy about being in the music business, it just never seemed at all a possibility.

I was teaching school when I got out of college, and playing in this group at night. Then, here I was in New York, doing this session. The producer got interested in me as a singer/songwriter, and he signed me and was trying to get me a record deal. That came and went, but that was a sort of professional validation that maybe I had talent.

I went back to Texas and continued teaching for another year or so. Karen Taylor-Good was also in El Paso, and we formed a duo and I quit teaching. We did that for about a year, and then I decided to go back to New York and give it a shot. I decided I could live with myself if I failed, but I couldn't live with myself if I didn't try.

Although country was the first music I was really into, I had drifted into folk music. So when I went to New York, I was trying to be James Taylor, The Second. I was not interested in country, at that point.

My big break came when I was discovered by Judy Collins and Tom Paxton, after I knocked around for several years. I played a showcase and Tom Paxton was there, and he came up to me and was very complimentary. I had, by that point, a lot of that folky stuff, that I thought would be really great for Judy Collins, and so I asked him if he would get them to her. He said he would, and he did.

About a year went by, between that happening and the day Judy Collins called up. And that was my big, huge break. She recorded "Hard Times For Lovers," which was my first, sort-of hit, back in 1978. It got me my first staff writing job.

After a year or so, I got into another staff writing job for Tommy West, who did all of Jim Croce's stuff. He had started producing acts out of Nashville, and he was going to record me.

In the meantime, I told Judy Collins one day that I was going to go down to Nashville and see what was going on down there. She told me to look up Jimmy Bowen. I didn't even know who he was but she had been talking to him about doing her next album. So I went down to Nashville, and I gave Jimmy Bowen a tape that had three songs on it, one of which was a song called "Sound of Goodbye."

All of a sudden one day, after I got back to New York, I got this phone call that said, "Guess what the first single off Crystal Gayle's album is?" It was "Sound of Goodbye."

The interesting thing about this is that they had her single picked out, but they didn't know who wrote the song. At some point, my name fell off this thing. I understand it was quite a frantic period. Tommy had taken me down to Nashville to do some recording in the same studio where Jimmy Bowen was at. Finally, one engineer talked to another engineer, and they figured out whose song it was.

So, Tommy West started MTM records, and that's really when I became connected with Nashville on a full-time level, although I didn't move down here. That was in 1985. I was a staff writer and would-be artist for MTM for four years.

After about two years with nothing happening, Michael Johnson came into my life and he's the one who really got me off the ground. Even though I had this number one record with Crystal Gayle, I was still some guy from New York. Michael recorded "The Moon is Still Over Her Shoulder," and that was another big hit. Then he recorded "That's That," which was a pretty good hit. That's when I think I was sort of welcomed into the club.

Do you write every day, and how many songs do you write in a year?

On any day that I don't have to go anywhere or be out of town, I try to write. I try to write about a dozen songs a year, so I write about a song a month.

I only write one song at a time. I get very involved in it. I always say I could write a song a week if it were just the melodies, but there's always a few lines of lyric I can't get happy with for another two weeks.

I've found out I'm freshest in the morning, so I try to write then. I usually stop in the afternoon and do business, or try to exercise. And then a lot of times, at night, I'll go back up and sort of go over what I've done that morning.

Do you think that helps, to listen in the evening?

Yeah, I might be watching television or something, and about nine o'clock, I'll tell my wife, "I think I'll go up and listen." I always say *listen* to my song, because I usually like to put something that I'm working on down on tape, then go up and listen to it. In the morning, I'm just working it. In the evening, I'm just really grooving on it. I get a lot of ideas that way. I should do this, or I should change that.

You prefer listening to it on tape, rather than playing it live?

There's something about the grooving end of it. I usually do it on earphones too, because I don't want my wife to hear me playing this thing over and over again. I will put in earphones, and I'll have a drink, and really try to relax, and just groove and dig. Just get off on the song, as much as I can.

Have you ever been a person to set goals for yourself?

I'm not much of a goal-setter. I mean, I have goals, but I don't have time set for my goals.

> **"I have the world's biggest stove, with two million back burners. The front burner's my song, and in the back are all these things I should do, or want to do."**

The main thing for me is writing songs. I always say I have the world's biggest stove, with two million back burners. The front burner's my song, and in the back are all these things I should do, or want to do. I like to work on my songs, but I'm not really a self-disciplined kind of person. I always just write until I'm tired of writing.

I always say, I don't write one minute more than I want to write. If it's an hour and I get tired, then I stop. One of my great goals is to enjoy the process. I can get into it and be up there, hour after hour, on a song, but other times not. It's suddenly becoming work. The whole point of songwriting is not to have to work; it's never going to become like labor to me.

What is your definition of good luck?

I don't care how much talent you have, you've got to have some luck, and I've certainly had some amazing luck. A perfect example is the one I already gave you. I suddenly get up in New York, and get signed to a producer, totally without trying to do anything.

A great stroke of luck is just having Michael Johnson exist. He really did open the doors for me. I'm a great believer in luck, but I'm not sure if I could give you a good definition of "good luck" except that, to my mind, you have to be prepared for the good luck. When good luck comes, you have to be ready.

I always think that one of the worst things that can happen to somebody is to get lucky too soon, and they can't follow it up, there's too much pressure on them to follow it up. I was very lucky with my success.

I think I have a very good attitude about the success that I've had, in terms of taking it for what it is, and not getting into the bullshit aspect of it too much. Trying to really appreciate how lucky you are to have any success. I'm sure that most writers do understand that you never know what's going to happen next year. This may be it. You've just got to keep doing it and hoping that something happens once in a while.

Do you ever co-write?

Once in a blue moon I do. I really don't like it. Every time I decide to give it another try (I do this about once every three years), it's usually because somebody really great has asked me to. Say you're getting together at 10:00, and you're going to write till 1:00 or something, as soon as I get in that room at 10:15, I'm trapped. This whole idea that I have to sit here, now becomes an incredible burden to me.

One of my great revelations was when Judy Collins got me my first staff writing job. I suddenly didn't have to go to work anymore, and I thought, "Boy, this is great. I can write all day." That first week, I was going to write till five o'clock. After about two hours, I thought, "Geez, I'm tired of writing. I'm going to have to think of something else to do." The first thing I do is I feel trapped.

I want this to be a labor of love. This is not going to be something I have to do. When I co-write, then I suddenly have to do it.

Then, the other thing is (which I'm sure you've heard), I have a terrible time telling another writer I really respect that I don't like what he just did. You know what I mean? So I tend to say, "Oh, okay."

Then, ultimately, it's really that I want to do it all myself. In some funny way, it's like I'm like a painter. I don't want anyone else to have this brush. I want to do it all. I want to, even though, I think, so many great songs have been co-written.

Is time for "quiet" important to your songwriting?

Yeah. My ideal way to write is to feel very secure in a relationship, but be very alone at the time I'm writing. Like when my wife's at work. It's something where I really want to feel like no one can hear me.

That's another reason I have problems with co-writing. I'm overly sensitive about being heard. Even when I was a kid, learning to play the guitar, if I heard my mother in the next room, I would stop playing. I just didn't want to be judged.

I wrote my first few songs when I went down to Alabama to visit my father, when I was eighteen. He was a lawyer, and he would go into work. I didn't have any friends around there, so I was alone in this house out in Alabama. There's something about that that gets me going.

Do you find that, every so often, you just have to tell people "No," in order to prioritize time for your writing?

Yeah. What's funny is, my writing style is very slow, and it's based on probably going so long without having any success. I just feel like I've got all the time in the world. I just take my time.

When I finally started having some success, along with it comes, "Would you do this?" Or, "Would you do that? Would you play this or play that?" It really threw a wrench in my writing. I have to say, I'm not very good at saying "No," but I say it a lot more than I used to.

Another thing that seems to be crucial to my writing is to feel like I have a large block of time in front of me. If I feel like I have nothing to do for like a month, then I really like to write.

I often think that I'd love for my wife and I to rent some place in the middle of nowhere, once in a while. I almost did that a couple years ago. There's always so damn many things you've got to deal with, you know?

As a matter of fact, I always tell my songwriting students, "You need to establish that space. If you live in an apartment with somebody, you just have to work that out somehow."

I used to live with a girl, and I asked her if she would watch television at night while I wrote, because I didn't want to be heard. Having the television on in the other room masked what I was doing. I always tell [my students], "You've got to get your family to leave you alone," same kind of thing.

I always like to use that scene from *The Shining*, where Jack Nicholson's wife comes in and he's writing, and he says, "When you hear this, or when you don't hear it, if I'm in here . . . " He bites her head off for coming in. But I always say, in a way, there's some truth to that scene, because I have to really relax when I write.

Like when I first get up in the morning, and go up to my room. I may goof off for a little bit. I may read the paper and I get into this relaxed state. Then I start to write, and then, if something comes up, like if my wife comes up and says, "I can't find the pliers," or something like that, then it breaks that sort of mood. I train her not to do that unless it can't wait.

Are there specific places that you go, to renew that creative spirit?

You know, it's funny, there are two places that I think of. One of them is sort of real, and one of them is not. The real place is Nashville, meaning when I come down here. I really love my situation because I write away from the music business, and I don't worry about it. I come down; I get a jolt of it. I'm down here for a week, and I get revved up, and I get some people telling me, "Oh, we think you're a great writer." Then I go back home and I write.

The other place where I get revved up is hearing a great song. Every now and then, about once or twice a year, I hear a song and I say, "Whoa, what is this?" That's why I do this. I want to write one of those kinds of songs.

Do you meditate?

No, I don't. Meditation is one of those things that I feel like, from everything I've heard, would be good for me. I'm sort of anxiety-prone. But I've never really gone to somebody to show me how to do it, and I've tried it on my own, and I can't ever seem to do it. I relax, believe it or not, by watching old movies.

So you're meditating, just not in the traditional way?

Right. I always have this feeling, when I'm really writing and enjoying it, that it's almost like I'm doing something I shouldn't be doing. It's like I should be doing my homework, but I'm doing this instead. I should be seeing about that problem with the electric stuff, but I get into this shell and I don't want to get out of it. I won't return phone calls; I won't pay bills when I should, just because I just get in this place and I just don't want to deal with anything else.

Do you read a lot?

Yeah, I do. As a matter of fact, I've had many an idea from reading. "Ghost In This House" came out of *Grapes Of Wrath*, although it came from the movie. "The Song Remembers When" came from a poem by Ann Sexton.

So you read a lot of poetry?

I read poetry. I used to read a lot of fiction. Now I read more nonfiction stuff. I mainly get my fiction from movies. I always tell my students that they should read poetry. I was an English major in college, and I read a lot of poetry. I really think it makes a difference, especially when you read poets that have meter and rhyme. You pick up an ear for that, after a while.

I was reading this biography of Ann Sexton, and they started talking about this poem that really helped make her first big dent as a poet. It was this poem called *Music Swims Back to You*. There's an old lady in a nursing home, and the radio's playing. The music's taking her back and she says, "This song remembers more that I do." I thought, "Wow, that is a great way to put it, like it's the song that has memories."

I'm looking for those ideas where something in me goes off. If I can get a musical idea going, that really emotionally gets me going, then I feel emotionally inspired to try to write a lyric to it.

Do you get melodic ideas in your head, or do melodies come from playing your guitar?

I never have a melodic idea in my head until I begin to play. I hear other people say they were driving in their car and they got this melodic idea. To me, melodies are not interesting until they are laid upon a chord progression. I always begin to play chords and just noodle around, and then I begin to improvise a melody.

I always say that the stronger the melody I can come up with, the more gasoline I have in my tank to work on the words. If the melody really works for me, I can work on the words a long time. If the melody isn't that good, then I run out of gas.

"I always say that the stronger the melody I can come up with, the more gasoline I have in my tank to work on the words."

The normal process for me is to begin to noodle around and plug in a phrase and then, usually what happens is, I'll just do some musical thing combined with some little lyric thing, and then there's that spark.

When I was in Boy Scouts, one of the things we would do is build fires. We would take flint and steel and make a little spark, and this charred cloth, then you'd nurse it up into a fire. That, to me, is how writing a song is in many ways. I get a little spark, and I'm very careful with the spark. I never let anybody hear this thing until I know the fire's going. I never play my wife (who's the first person I ever play anything for) something in that stage. At that stage, it could just be blown out too easily if I get any kind of reaction that isn't positive.

I'll tell you one of the things which I think is good for me, is that I'll get this little thing going, maybe no more than thirty seconds long, with a line in it, and I'll put it on tape. Then I will purposely not think about it, or listen to it again, till the next day. It'll be like the only time in the process where it's like it isn't my song. I'll hear it neutrally, and a lot of times I'll say, "Oh, right there, change that." Once you get into it, then you start to lose your perspective a little bit, so I like to step away.

What about the connection between your subconscious mind and your creativity?

I think there is a very strong connection. I don't know how aware I am of it, but having taught songwriting for a long time, I really have come to believe that the real thing you have to have as a songwriter, you can't be taught. It's some kind of connection between your gut feeling and your brain, some kind of instinct you have that says, "Go here." I think one of the lessons you have to learn as a songwriter is to go there. Let your instincts and your brain tell you where to go.

Usually when I'm working it's all instinctual. Lyrically, there's definitely some kind of subconscious thing going on. I'll be struggling over some damn line for two hours, and then I'm in the shower, and suddenly there it is. I wasn't even thinking about it. There's some kind of connection there.

I try to write songs these days where I do have a strong emotional investment in an idea, and I've been there, and I know what I'm talking about. I look back over my past and I try to really bring it up. I love, in my songs, to have some pieces of things that really happened to me.

Do you think being open-minded is a key ingredient to being a good songwriter?

Being open-minded is a key ingredient to being a human being. I believe that a songwriter ought to really write to the common man. That's who you're speaking to. You've got to love humanity and be open-minded to everybody.

My wife comes from a farming background, in Nebraska. I love to be around these sorts of people, and get a sense of them. You almost forget people like that exist. Television makes you think that the whole world is completely different than it is.

I think the songwriter is some kind of preacher, in a way. We're lucky that we have this sort of microphone where we can share our views. You should just be open to all kinds of input, but you've got to try to distill it and give it back.

Have you ever had a song come to you in its entirety?

I used to have this theory that God had a quota. You get *x* amount of freebies, then you start having to dig for them. God cut me off a long time ago. I use to have songs that were like, "Where'd that come from?" I haven't had one of those in fifteen years.

I'm a real fussy thing about getting perfect rhymes, and getting the lyric to where I'm happy with every line. To do that, invariably, there are a couple lines, or more, that I just can't get happy with. It's not like I'm trying to write incredible lines, I just want a line that I'm happy with. That's where I grind to a halt.

It depends on the type of song you're trying to write too. You hear these guys say, "I wrote this song really quick." A lot of times, it's just a song that didn't require a great deal of imagery. I don't think Joni Mitchell ever had one just come right through. Those words are too crafted. I would find that most depressing if she could just write that incredible lyric at a rapid rate.

Do you ever make it a point to vary the location, when you write?

No, I don't seem to have any problem going up to my studio. I feel pretty comfortable up there. The main thing is, I want to feel alone up there. It's very important for me to feel that I have no demands on me during this period, and to just get in a relaxed state. I can do it in my studio. But, I think I could write anywhere as long as I felt alone with it.

Do you have things in yours studio that you would miss if you tried to write somewhere else?

Mainly, my equipment. Because the melody seems to come together so much sooner than the lyric does and, to maintain my interest during those two weeks it's going to take me to get the lyric right, I essentially begin to do the demo of the song. I do the guitar tracks. I do the drums. I paint myself into a corner. I have to finish this thing because I've done all this work on this demo, and all I need is two lines. That does keep me going.

Talk to us about the inner critic.

With every song I write, I go through this period where I think, "This is the greatest song I've ever written." Then, "This is a piece of crap." Then, "This is great; no, it's a piece of crap. Now it's great."

My wife is my great secret weapon, though, because she really is a great fan of what I do. One of the reasons I think she has been so good for me is that she gives me back such positive feedback on what I do. So many times, I'll be in one of these states where I think a song is terrible. I'll play it for her and she says, "Oh, that's fantastic!" I think that's such a great thing to have in your household, someone that thinks what you do is great.

Do you ever have "writer's block"?

I always say to my students, "There are two things that cause writer's block. One is, you're trying to write a hit. You're trying to do what you think they want." And then, "The other thing is that your palette is too limited. Go learn some new progressions, go get some more musical information."

I'm a guitar player. My keyboard-playing palette has got like two colors on it. If I had to write on that for long, I'd get blocked and I'd have to go and learn piano better. But that's what I'd have to do.

If I can get some music going, I start thinking of ideas. So, I don't think I have a problem. Lyrically, I can always get ideas, and then the hard part is to make them work.

What is your motivation?

Definitely, to communicate. What else is the point of it? I have things I want to say.

I always tell my songwriting students, "One of the biggest decisions you have to make as songwriters is, do you want to have hits?" That may seem like a funny thing to say, but what that means is, "Are you willing to do what it takes to have a hit?"

A lot of people around here can write these artsy little esoteric things, and have a hip cult following. If you want to do that, that's totally valid. If you want to have a hit, you've got to do these certain things.

To me, the ultimate trick is to be totally put into this box. You can't do this, and can't do that. The song's too long, and it's got to be about love, and it's got to be this, and got to be that— somehow, to pull off this thing, in spite of all these boundaries. It's fresh. It hasn't been done exactly that way.

Someone once said without that box, it's like playing tennis without the line. Just hit the ball anywhere you want. To me, there's no satisfaction to that. So, in a way, having to write a song less than four minutes long, and to do this and do that is the great challenge, and that's where the great satisfaction comes in, for me.

Although, the one thing I regret is that there are certain things I just can't say, because no one's going to cut them. I don't mean offensive things. I can't write a song about political things. It's just not going to get cut.

The rules are what make the game really neat. Being original is not a thing I'm very impressed by. To be original is very easy. Let me write a song about this television set and what it looks like from the back. No one's done that before.

Write a song that says, "I love you," and try and be original with that! That is hard as hell, because it's been done so many times, and done well so many times.

Talk to us about the role your intuition plays in songwriting.

I think it's the most important thing. Your brain is right up there, but you've got to let your gut feelings lead you around. I always say that writing a song is coming to lots of little forks in the road, "Do I do this chord or that chord? Should I say this or say that?"

To me, anytime I have a choice where my brain and my gut feeling disagree, I always go with my gut feeling. A lot of times they agree, but ultimately I think the last word has to be your instinct. And that's the thing you can't teach. I do think you get more tuned into it the more you write. You listen to that voice more.

> "Anytime I have a choice where my brain and my gut feeling disagree, I always go with my gut feeling."

Just like your ears get more tuned to listening for song titles when someone talks, your ears get tuned to hearing your inner voice. A lot of time the things that make a song really exceptional are dangerous things. You have to stick your neck out once in a while.

The song that really got me started with Judy Collins was a song called "Dorothy." It was a very unusual song about what happened to Dorothy when she got back from Oz. I had this idea one day. I bet when she got back from Oz, in about two weeks, she wished she'd gone back, because it was such an amazing place.

It's really a sad song. It's about regret. Jim Ed Norman ended up cutting it on Jackie DeShannon, even before Judy Collins came along. He said he'd been listening to all these songs about *Baby*, and *I love you*, and suddenly, this song came out about *Dorothy*. I think that's how, sometimes, you get noticed. You've got to do some unusual things once in a while.

They may not cut the song, but they'll think, "Wow, that's an unusual song," and ask what else you've got.

What do you think has made you a successful songwriter?

I think it's several things. I've paid my dues. I've hung in there. Hanging in there is one of the important things. Sticking it out for years before something happens. I have a good musical instinct in me, and I think I'm a good lyricist because I've read a lot of poetry.

I really, truly think that having someone around, like my wife, is the other great thing. If you can surround yourself with people who believe in what you do, then you're way ahead. I also think the opposite is true, that if you're around someone who does not believe in what you do, then it's very destructive to your success.

Believing in yourself is one of hardest things you have to accomplish. I'm a great believer in thinking positive, and I'm not a naturally positive person.

My mother was an educational psychology professor. She was always trying to tell me things that would help me be more positive. I'd think, "Well, okay, what the hell does that mean?" I could never make any sense of what it meant. Then one day, many years later, she said "With positive thinking, you have to practice it like piano. You have to practice it every day." Something about that statement really started to affect me, and I made up my mind to do it.

One time I had some interest and it fell through. I said to myself, "You know, I'm doing something here. I keep getting interest, and nothing happens from it." I realized, at that point in my life, that I really expected this stuff to fall through. If I got involved with somebody, I expected them to eventually dump me. If I got involved with anyone in business, I expected them to eventually see what a fraud I was. That was what was happening.

I also heard about this therapist named Albert Ellis. He said "Nobody badmouths you like you do." The first thing he would have you do is to go around carrying a notebook and make a note about how many times a day you would say something bad about yourself, to yourself. You don't realize how many times a day you do it.

Ultimately, I ended up with a system, which is, "Don't fill in any blank with anything negative." What that means is that until I know differently, I'm not going to put any negative in there.

My mother also gave me a thing about spontaneity. It said, "Spontaneity is, at worst, a neutral thing. It can be a good thing a lot of times. So if you feel like doing something, you shouldn't second-guess it so much."

How do you balance business and writing?

I try to write 75 percent of the time, and take care of business 25 percent of the time. I am not natural at that sort of thing. I can go to a party and stand around the whole time, and leave.

My mother always told me that a lot of studies of successful people have shown that their friends have had a lot to do with their success. So I need to try to be friends with people who are in a position to help my career, and I try to make phone calls. I dread that kind of stuff.

I used to know this guy who said he had his spring offensive and fall offensive. Like, twice a year, he would go out and suffer the rejection, and all that crap you've got to go through. I try to come down here and call on a few people, but, in general, I put it off as long as I can. But I do what I've got to do.

I think one of the things a lot of writers don't see, is how many talented people are down here. For you to be heard down here, you have to do some yelling, leaping up and down.

If you were advising someone that hasn't achieved his commercial success yet, what two or three elements would you tell them that they really need to work on?

That's easy. First of all, I tell them you've got to think long-term. Don't think you'll be doing this for a year, and something's going to happen. Think about doing this the next ten years, and if you're lucky, something will happen.

And, in order for you to do this the next ten years, you're going to have to find a way to love the process. You have to get off on writing songs, not get off on having them cut.

Another thing I tell them is, be the best musician you can be. Go to the Bluebird. Most of these guys are damn good players. And they're damn good singers.

Be as good a singer as you can be. Even if you don't sing your own demos, you'll be able to communicate them better to the singer, and you're going to have different ideas for melodies. You're not going to write things that singers want to do, if you can't sing a little.

I always tell them to think long-term. Go take some lessons, both instrumentally and vocally, so you can be the best you can be at that. You don't have to make a living at it, but it will help.

9
MIKE REID

Mike retired from the Cincinnati Bengals football team in 1980 and moved to Nashville to pursue songwriting. Since 1983, when Reid scored his first number one country hit song, "Inside," by Ronnie Milsap, he has composed more than thirty Top 10 country and pop hits. Twenty-one of those records have gone all the way to number one on the charts.

He was the recipient of ASCAP's Songwriter of the Year award in 1985, and one of the many songs that Milsap recorded—"Stranger In My House"—earned a Grammy award. In addition to Milsap, Reid has had his songs recorded by Bonnie Raitt, Anita Baker, Bette Midler, Prince, George Michael, Nancy Wilson, Etta James, Kenny Rogers, Anne Murray, Wynonna Judd, Alabama, Joe Cocker, Tanya Tucker, Willie Nelson, Collin Raye, and Tim McGraw. Among the songs that Mike has composed are "I Can't Make You Love Me" (Raitt, Michael, and Prince), "My Strongest Weakness" and "To Be Loved By You" (Judd), "In This Life" (Raye and Midler), "Sometimes I Wonder Why" (Baker), "Forever's As Far As I'll Go" (Alabama), and "Everywhere" (McGraw).

In 1992, Reid composed the score for Quilts, *a modern dance piece created by Andrew Krichels and Donna Rizzo of The Tennessee Dance Theatre. Following the premiere, Reid, Krichels, and Rizzo received The Governor's Award for the Arts in Tennessee for their work on* Quilts. *In addition, Reid was commissioned by the Kandinsky Trio of Roanoke, Virginia, to write a piece for piano trio and storyteller. The piece, entitled "The Cantankerous Blacksmith," premiered in the fall of 1995.*

Reid has collaborated with librettist Sarah Schlesinger on a one-act opera commissioned by the Metropolitan Opera Guild and Opera Memphis that explores the myth of celebrity in contemporary American sports. The opera, entitled Different Fields, *received its premiere in New York City at the New Victory Theatre on Broadway.* Different Fields *has since been produced in Memphis and Nashville and by The Cincinnati Opera.*

Reid and Schlesinger's musical, entitled The Ballad of Little Jo, *received a 1998 Richard Rodgers Foundation Award.*

How did you get started in songwriting?

I took piano lessons as a very young kid. I did all right but I wasn't gifted. There was a designated amount of time that my dad said I had to practice, and I had a difficult time focusing all my energies on the lesson for the whole time, and not wandering off into some improvisational who knows what, making up little pieces of music on my own. They weren't songs, but I think any kind of creative impulse is an attempt to bring form to chaos. So maybe, as a kid, there was lots of energy inside that had to have somewhere to go. But they weren't formed into anything like a song.

I came into writing songs very late in life. I was playing professional football for the Bengals back in the seventies, and I think that's the first time I started dabbling, and putting a few words together, and picking a melody that might be appropriate for those words. I never really decided that I wanted to be a songwriter, anymore than I really decided I wanted to be a football player.

Writing for success was never really a motivation. Well, it probably was when I first moved to town. To try to learn what this commercial form was, because it's pretty substantially different. It requires that you pay attention to it, if your desire is to get people to record your songs.

Going from being an athlete, into music, thus far I've managed to avoid a real job. Who knows what we are? I think we, maybe, wander through life and are drawn to activities that might help reveal those sorts of things.

But you took music in college, so you had an idea you wanted to be in music.

I was a terrible student. I was there with a football scholarship at the beginning of Joe Paterno's football program at Penn State. I was never fired up by anything other than music, and I realized, if I was going to utilize these four years that were being paid for by this football scholarship, I'd better study something that made sense. I was not a good compositional or theory student, but music just sort of made sense.

How did you end up in Nashville?

I stopped football in the mid-seventies, and, against all common sense, I started playing music. But I've always thought one must overcome common sense if you're going to achieve anything that might be fun, or halfway interesting. I had a little band and we played some on the road. I was young, and had a little bit of money saved and no family, and it was great fun.

We lived in condemned hotels and that sort of thing. All those stories that you look back on, and they were hardly a hardship, they were just an enormous amount of fun. I'm talking about being on the road where you wake up and you think, "For God's sake, I spent the night here?"

The band broke up, and the owner of this club that I played in The Village called and said, "I want you to come back." I told him, "I'm sorry, but I've fired my band." He said, "Great! The whole time you were here, all I wanted was to hear what you were like by yourself." So I went and played by myself, opened up for three other acts.

While I was playing there, a booking agent saw me and booked me to play a circuit up and down the Southeast coast. So I started playing and earned my living, traveled around maybe thirty-five weeks a year. These were the kinds of joints where you played a couple weeks at a time. They weren't "one-nighters."

This friend of mine had written a song that everyone thought Kenny Rogers should record, and he asked me to sing the demo. When he sent it down to Nashville, they didn't like the song, but they wanted to know who the guy singing was, and they got in touch with me.

I had come off the road pretty bummed. I really felt a wider audience was necessary for people to maybe hear what I wrote, without really having me around. That meant getting on a record somehow. This was right at the time when this guy called from Nashville. So I drove down here and talked with ATV about being a singer. In the process I played them a few of my songs and they said, "We'll give you a hundred dollars a week and you can be a staff writer, but you have to come here." That was 1980. I had just been married a little while, and Suzy was a little excited about trying Nashville out.

The first eighteen months that I was with ATV, nothing that I wrote made any sense to anybody there. Not only were songs not put on hold, but people were calling and promising they would *never* record that.

Not really, but that was the way I felt. I was writing by the numbers. I was observing the charts. Listening to the radio, which I hadn't done a lot of. I was trying to construct them. Building verses that seemed to possess some sort of emotion. It never occurred to me to ask myself, "Is it true?"

I think, in all creative art, life must be the protagonist, and what other life do you know about? The experiences don't have to be specific, but you have to understand the emotional terrain. That just wasn't happening, it was going nowhere, they were wasting their hundred dollars on me.

But I met a guy, Rob Galbraith. I think ATV was administering a company he had with Ronnie Milsap. I was flirting with leaving town, thinking I just wasn't a writer. I felt like I wasn't even remotely close to it. I remember feeling the same about those songs as I felt about mowing the grass. Probably even less, because I really get emotional mowing the grass. It takes me back to when I was a kid, and family stuff, and my dad. I was working in what should be an emotional medium, and not feeling anything about some of this stuff.

ATV said, "That's it, we're done with you." So, Rob Galbraith said, "Well, bring me some songs." I brought him the best I had. It wasn't very good, but he heard something in it. I've always said to young writers, "You don't have to get the whole town believing in you. You have to get one person believing in you."

I walked out of that meeting feeling like Jimmy Webb. Sometimes just that little turn in the way you feel about what you're doing, does the trick. I think it's helpful, too, when somebody grants you permission. I think trying to be aware of that in children is to grant them permission to attempt to express what it is that they actually might truly be feeling. I think that is what Rob did for me. He not only granted it, but he insisted.

He would say to me, "Do you think that's believable? Do you think people actually feel that? What's the next thing she would say to him in that song?" One of the things Rob taught me, early on, was to tell the story.

And in all the writing I've done, whether it's in theater or anything else, when I get lost, I generally sit back, stop, and say, "What's the story?" If you have that sense of what story the song is trying to tell, lines begin then to get clearer.

"The commercial song is a pretty standard container. If you think of it in terms of the old Coke bottle, that's the size it is."

Everyone pretty well understands the song form. The commercial song is a pretty standard container. That container has a couple variations but, for the most part, it's the same shape and size. If you think of it in terms of the old Coke bottle, that's the size it is. It's going to be that color and its going to hold that much. That's empirical information. Here's the data I can give you: keep your intros to ten seconds, get to the chorus in thirty-five to forty seconds, put the title of the song as the first line of the chorus, and keep the song to about three minutes and fifteen seconds.

Now, that doesn't mean that what I've given you is a form that is going to increase the chances of someone recognizing it as a popular song. It's just that it's going to have the same kind of shape or form as most other songs.

Rob was trying to help me, but what he couldn't tell me was what to put in that container. I was putting versions of other people's ideas and experiences in that container. Rob was trying to tell me that I had to put myself in there. What relationship do you have with the emotion, or with the material, of your own life? This is what any expression is going to be made of. And that's why in art or in the creative process, life must be the protagonist.

I think it's hard to understand what one should do with things like that. You can admire it the way you can admire any beautiful attractive thing. But the thing that causes you to really go there, and own it, and buy it, and want to be around it, is recognition of your own life experiences. Whether it's a song, a poem, a piece of theater, sculpture, whatever.

I've always asked myself, and I've asked other writers, "Why do you write? You may not know exactly but give me the general feeling about why you write." Inevitably, you hear, "I need to express myself, because I have things to say. To express how I feel."

And my next question, generally, is, "Why is it then, that you write like everyone else?" Why is it then, we all start out writing like other people? I think, generally, at heart, most of us feel like our everydayness is simply not interesting. In fact, I think the power of great songs is in the way they can capture the small intense experience of everyday living, of everyday life. I love that in songs.

So, essentially, the journey is about understanding oneself, to the point that it becomes clearer and clearer what the contents are, that go into the container. I've had the experience too, of feeling that the container was just too limiting. It was going to have to be broken apart, or expanded, or the shape of it changed. And that's how you get yourself into the trouble of writing other music that no one wants to hear, which I've done.

So Rob gave you the sense of needing to put yourself into the songs?

For me, it made sense very quickly. I brought him two things, shortly thereafter, that ended up on Ronnie Milsap's next record. One was called "Inside," which was a single back in 1984, and the other was called "It's Just a Rumor." Those were my first cuts. And of course in those days, when Milsap recorded one of your songs, that really put you on the map.

Then, on the next album I wrote the song "Stranger In My House," which did very well. We were sort of off to the races. We had a nice run together, from about 1983 until maybe 1988. I had a great time writing songs, and Ronnie recorded an awful lot of them.

It so happened that what I was writing made sense to Ronnie. By then, he had made a pile of records, and the more records you make, the harder it is for you to find material that keeps you interested, as a performer, as opposed to rehashing the same old thing. It's a difficult thing to find that fresh material, to keep that sound, and that thing fresh. So we had a wonderful time. Ronnie took a lot of my songs to the public sector that no one else would have done. There were some other records too, but predominately it was Ronnie who recorded them.

There comes time for you to strike out a little more on your own, and Ronnie was headed off in another direction. So I ended up on my own for a while, and then I was with David Conrad, and then with Almo Irving.

What is creativity?

I think it might be a response to some sort of disturbance. I think you feel some sort of slight disturbance inside.

I don't know what that is. I have no idea. Why someone is a painter instead of a composer. Why someone is a sculptor, and another is an actor or, in the writing forms, why someone is a poet versus a novelist. Why some people gravitate to song form, rather than string quartets. All of that is sort of a mystery.

But I've often thought that deciding to bring oneself into the external world was some sort of response to some sort of disturbance that was somewhat mysterious and never satisfied. There's never anytime where you hit that spot and say, "Ah, there it is, I've scratched that itch and I don't have to do that anymore."

Do you have a writing room, or special place, where you feel the creativity flows more easily?

When we were looking for a house, Sue liked this one because it has a little guesthouse. She thought it would be a great place for me to work. It has great advantages, because I tend to be over there at six in the morning. The disadvantage is that it tends to be the same place. Sometimes I think it would have been better to get in the car and actually drive someplace else and do some work.

But that room is just where I do, what I call, the "grunt work," which is finding the right collection of words. Writing, as far as getting ideas, and what the song might be about, and who might be in the song, and what's the emotional place—that happens on my walks.

Are you aware of the cycles of creativity?

Let's not romanticize creativity too much. I think that's a mistake. It is work. I think we play tricks on ourselves. I think writer's block is kind of a thinly veiled excuse for either not wanting to do it at the time, or being tired, or maybe being sort of lazy. Writing is a blue-collar occupation. It is a construction job.

> **"Writing is a blue-collar occupation. It is a construction job."**

I don't know about muses descending. I don't really think in those terms. Why somebody seems to be creative, and another person isn't. I guess I would have a hard time backing up the statement, "All people are creative." But, come on, I'm not an extraordinary person. I'm a very ordinary human being. You would have never looked at me, at any point in my childhood, and said, "This boy is destined to go off and make his life in music."

I've done a few little things at the NYU theater department, and I always gravitate towards some of the lesser-talented kids. Because the tools are not up to speed, doesn't mean the heart isn't. Sometimes it just takes longer to get the tool shed filled with all the right tools. It doesn't mean their heart isn't aching, all the time, to get something said in a good clear way.

Essentially, it's about shortening the distance between two points. One point is what you can imagine, what your imagination can conceive of. And this point, way over here, is what you might actually be capable of writing. There's no way around this, it's just writing every day. If you're a writer, I believe you have to write every day. I don't care if it's ten minutes. Because writing every day shortens the distance between those two points.

Young writers might say, "I've got this new song, tell me what you think," and it does nothing for you. Very often, where they are is in what they've imagined. Where you are, is in what they have written. Those points can be very far apart.

My technique is not going to hinder my imagination, because I've learned my tools. They are able to express what it is I'm feeling.

I hear young songwriters' songs that are just awful, and are just absolutely brimming full of emotion. Some of this deep connection people have with their lives, trying to be brought out into the experiential realm, so we can all share it. But there's no technique. There's no sense of how to play an instrument, no sense of how to vocally express something. There's no sense of narrative, how to move from point *a* to *c*. So it's all just emotion and no technique, which tends to bring the chaos of emotion. So, you need technique because the emotions have got to be brought into some form. That's back to the shape of a Coke bottle or container. The realness of the experience they are trying to express is lost, because the technical tools are just simply not up to speed.

I feel like people tend to go through three stages. One, the emotion is real and the chaos is there. Two, they realize they have to fit it into a form, so they study and they learn, but all that "realness" gets left behind. It becomes very dry. And the third stage is where they learn to put it all together.

That's exactly what happened to me. And that's one of the pitfalls of the "marketplace." I think also, generally, we start out writing like other people too. We recognize that there is something in other people's work that we admire, that we would like to be like. I think that's why, in the beginning, when you go around the room and ask people to name their idea of a great song, they will name something that represents an ideal. So you set out to write like that.

It was hard enough for *that* writer to write like that, and it's going to be damn near impossible for you to write like that. So you're nowhere near that ideal and you say, "I'm a miserable failure, and I'm not really getting there." What you're failing at is mimicking someone else's work, which is really not art.

Eventually, you're going to come back and run headlong into that wall, which is you. This is about you. The world is not interested in you being able to write like Billy Joel. Your best chance is when you write like yourself. If you're able to do that, then we'll decide if we like it.

You have a life, you're alive, and you've got the chaos of life. Writers don't have the market cornered on that. When I see this thing about entertainers or writers, that they must feel more deeply than the average guy, I don't believe that for one second. What writers have done is give their lives over to learning the technical aspects, the tools that give voice to the emotion that everybody feels. The sheer arrogance of a writer, believing that he or she feels more than the guy tuning his car, or building the deck on the back of his house, I just don't, for a second, believe it. What it is, is the acquisition of these tools, these techniques, a particular faculty on an instrument, a particular faculty of vocal expression. Writing enough songs that are lyrically confused and muddled, until you begin to understand and have faith in speaking clearly, and directly. Simple, direct language that conveys deep things.

Do you think people need to just write, write, write, and this will eventually happen for them?

That goes beyond writing. I think that's a factor in your relationships with people. Your willingness to stare down the barrel of your own life. To what degree this will happen is always going to be to what degree you are interested in dealing with yourself. That bargain has to be made with yourself.

A writer has to expect one thing. Before any considerations of talent, or gifts, or inspiration, a writer has to make this agreement. First, you have to show up, and you have to show up faithfully. You have this part of yourself, this unseen part of yourself that makes you unlike anything else. I think, within that part of you, that's where your work is. That's what your work will be. That's where you will be.

You make dates with that part of yourself. And you faithfully keep those appointments. It's important to keep them faithfully because that part of you, I believe, desires and wants to show up.

Imagine Romeo and Juliet for a second. One of the great aspects of that relationship is that they made secret appointments, and they showed up. Out of that, came this sweetness of love. What if we go back and consider that one time Romeo doesn't show up. Maybe a couple of nights Juliet shows up an hour late. And maybe one night, Romeo blows it off all together. One night, Juliet really needs him there and he shows up an hour and forty-five minutes late. Everything about the sweetness of that love, everything we know about what that love means to us, is put at risk, if not gone completely.

There is that part in you, it's in Gary Burr, it's in me, and in Allen Shamblin. Because we're not unique, we are human beings. It's in people. You keep appointments with that part of yourself faithfully, because it really wants to show up. It wants to come out. It's not going to show up, if you're not going to show up. It's always there, and it will wait a lifetime if it has to. But it's not going to take part in a faithless relationship.

Is there a certain time of day you prefer to write?

I have the luxury of being able to do nothing but write. I really get this feeling of profound gratitude. And because "this is what I do," I simply have no problem showing up every day.

I have this little ritual. I love that first smell of that first cup of coffee. I love the early morning, I think, because years and years ago, when I played football, I was tired all the time and could never get enough sleep. When I stopped playing football, I discovered the early morning hours.

I love getting up early in the morning, at six o'clock, with that first cup of coffee. I usually start the day out with a piece of music. That just turns something on in me. The things I might listen to are all across the board. Maybe Bach, maybe James Taylor. It might be Allen Shamblin.

Are you a staff writer right now?

No, I'm on my own. I have pursued other kinds of music as well. That's taken me into chamber music, and opera and the theater.

And, speaking of staff writing, I've never been one to take an advance. I've had a lot of friends hound me about that, saying it's really a mistake. I have always believed that if you're having songs recorded, and you're actually making money, you shouldn't take an advance.

It makes no sense to me, in this business, for hugely successful songwriters to be given huge advances. Because the big successful songwriter taking the big advance is, very often, the reason that this extraordinarily young, gifted kid has to cook hamburgers and not get to write all day.

Of course, I don't know. I'm not in the main loop or anything. But it just seems to me that it's profoundly shortsighted for successful songwriters to demand that kind of money, and it's profoundly shortsighted for publishers to give it to them.

From what I hear, publishers seem to be less and less involved in developing young writers. Who will do for them what Rob Galbraith did for me? That is a shame. That is a heartbreak, because there is some wonderfully gifted kid somewhere who just does not have the means to do this. It's a shame that they are not trying to find those people. It's bad for the business. I have a real burr up my butt on this.

Do you like to read?

I read poetry every day. I love to discover new combinations of words. I think reading is probably just continuing to have some sort of relationship with your own tools. I love to be emotionally tossed around by someone's work. I'm rereading *You Can't Go Home Again* by Thomas Wolfe. It's cutting me off at the knees at every page. And that's exactly what his work does for me. It grabs me and tosses me around. I love that.

Wallace Stevens is a favorite poet. His work takes me out of my everyday thing, and my complacency, and it grabs me. Great work grabs you and says, "No, I will compel you to encounter me." I love that I'm at the mercy of that. Whether it's a Beth Neilsen Chapman song, or a beautifully, wonderfully crafted commercial song that turns out to be a hit song that people love, or *Death of a Salesman*—in my view, the great American play of the twentieth century. You can't casually encounter *Death of a Salesman*. Turn on *Will and Grace* or something else if you want a casual encounter. I love the way those things shake you awake.

I've never been one to take a piece of literature and then write a song to that title, as in "Islands in the Stream." "You Can't Go Home Again" is a perfectly good song title, but what would you say? Is there anything that you could possibly bring to that collection of words in song form, that Wolfe hasn't already covered? And better, more intensely, more compellingly, than what you might say? You've got one foot in another guy's garden. Keep your ass in your own garden. Be where God has put you, and dig as deep as you can.

You don't find that intimidating, to see great works and to not be able to express a similar thing in your own way?

It used to. But, you know, if people encountered greatness and then said, "Well, I'll never be as great as that," you could make the argument that nothing after Beethoven would have ever been written. Or nothing after Mozart would have ever been written. Or nothing after Shakespeare would have ever been written. That's the summit. We can all go home, story is over. Think of all we would be living without.

I made my peace with that one night, when I was down in Muscle Shoals. I went by the studio where Mac McAnally was putting the finishing touches on an album. I listened to this record, and walked out of the studio and actually said to myself, "Well, that's it, you're done, quit. You'll never write that well, no matter what."

And, I will give myself this credit: On the three-hour drive home I, at least, had my head out of my butt far enough to realize that people like Mac McAnally do not write to make other people quit writing. People like that set the bar very high. They are doing what they do, that's all. What that kind of work does, if you have any testicular density at all, is cause you to set your bar higher. It causes you to aim higher and not settle.

Generally, we settle by giving in before we say what it is we need to say. As a writer, you can control one thing and one thing only, and that is what is your intent. You can never control what someone thinks of it. God knows you can never control what the business is going to do with it, if it should happen to be picked up by the machinery. It's liable to come out the other end in shreds, for all you know.

> **"As a writer, you can control one thing and one thing only, and that is what is your intent."**

I remember when Allen and I finished "I Can't Make You Love Me " I had a sense of calm. We said what we meant. We came pretty damn close. There are only a handful of songs that come close to what I intended. When you really get what it is you intend, you're fairly immune to criticism because there is this thing that says, "Well, this might not be your cup of tea, but this is what I meant, and I won't turn my back on it. If it's not the flavor of the day, so be it." Life is long. It might be the flavor sometime, you never know.

The odds are against any of us really writing great work. The odds are against any of us doing it, but you know what, you just might. You should never believe anyone who stands in front of you, and says, "You will never create anything wonderful." There's one way I can guarantee you won't: just don't write. Stop, and the verdict is in. One must participate in the sorrows of the world, and if you can bring yourself to say "yes" to it all, put your head down, and say "yes," and keep going, there's just no way to know what will occur.

Is it possible to overanalyze an idea?

Absolutely. Yes. And I'll never be able to save those songs. They don't work. I remember the fire I had for the idea, and the depth of feelings I had for the idea. The songs will, under my hands, never work. Maybe, if I shared the idea with someone, they could help me get on track.

What could you have done to avoid overanalyzing?

Maybe relax a little bit. Not put it under such a writing microscope. Just let things happen. Try to keep the little policeman in your head sedated, or out for coffee, or something. He's a destructive little bastard.

Can you share any words of advice on dealing with that guy?

I seriously believe that you cannot beat your demons by fighting them. You have to bring them to the table and give them their place at the table, whether it's jealousy, envy, or insecurity. When they are brought to the table, they can't lurk in the bushes and ambush your ass, when you least expect it.

It seems to me, in life, we have a choice, and it's one I think a lot of people battle with. The choice is humility or humiliation. Someone who really understands true humility, you really can't humiliate a person like that. Humiliation is around the corner, where we all become ripe for it. When we think we're something we aren't.

I think success can blindside you. Failure, you just take the blow and take the hit, and surround yourself, and hang out with people who love you, get to feel better, and go at it again. Success is a bitch. You can be stepping off the curb and get whacked by it at two hundred miles per hour, and be forever getting yourself back.

That little guy that we're talking about, you can arm-wrestle that little bastard, but he doesn't go away. He's always there and he always wins. So, what's your alternative? You can say, "Okay, come to the table. Here's your spot, let's work a deal." You look at him and say, "Alright, I've fought you, and it hasn't got me anywhere. So I have to ask you one question. What is it that you want?" Always, there's something underneath these emotions, there's something underneath the drive. We all have to get underneath to see what's driving it.

I'll tell you another demon we must recognize, and that is bad, mediocre writing. Bring it to the table. Give it its place in your life. That way it cannot hide and ambush you, when you least expect it. Always be aware of it. We're all capable of writing lousy songs.

How important is the opening line?

An audience is imploring the writer to answer one very important question, "Why are you telling me this?" A listener of your song wants to be interested. You've decided to write this idea because you deem it interesting. And your intent is to marshal your tools, and to put it in a form. To be brought into a relationship with the person because they say, "Yes, I understand this. I have experienced that too."

So your job and responsibility is to not repel them. They want to be interested. Only critics want to dislike something. Human beings don't desire to dislike music. They want to like it. They want to be interested. So you cannot waste their time. Now more than ever, the attention span is shorter, and that opening line has got to say to the listener, "There is a chance you might hear something interesting."

Do you find second verses harder to write than first verses?

Very common problem, when you get that incredible chorus, and you get a first verse that is just honking. I've found two things for writers to look at when they get stuck.

First, you may discover the verse you have is not the first verse, it's the second verse. And the other is, because you're looking for the great line, step back and ask yourself, "What is the story?" Life must be the protagonist.

How important is imagery in songwriting?

Some people refer to it as the furniture in the room. It's showing, rather than just telling, it's painting the picture. Like, with Allen Shamblin's song "He Walked On Water," he just painted that picture. You can see this man. "Starched white shirt, buttoned at the neck."

That kind of writing always compels you to listen. There's an example of the importance of an opening line. It compels you to stay with the song.

What was it like when you first heard your song on the radio?

It stopped me. It didn't excite me, it didn't thrill me; it was like all systems shut off. I guess it was something like a slight sense of shock. Even now, it's a curious thing to hear something you've written on the radio.

It would be nice if you could just thank the great writers. If you could let them know what they did for you. I find it almost impossible to think that something I've written has affected someone that way.

Do you ever get comments from people who have heard your songs, and been touched by them?

My impulse is always to say, "It's not me, it's really you, and what you've brought to the listening of the thing. I used the tools in a good way. It's about your willingness to open up the bags of your life, to know what that feels like. To be so lonesome that all you feel like doing is crying. Or to feel so powerfully about somebody that, 'like a bridge over troubled water,' I will be there for you."

Songwriting can be a real roller coaster ride. Do you have any tips on how to survive?

If you're sufficiently in love with this thing, for the right reasons, you'll figure out a way to survive. The business is a brutal thing, and it tends to separate the wheat from the chaff. It's sufficiently difficult such that, if you're not in love with it, and there's anything else you *can* do, you'll do it. Everybody is in love with having written. Everyone is in love with having been successful.

I have listened to too many great songs in my life that will never see the light of radio. And, whether it was the Bluebird or some other place, I have walked out of there, and not been able to forget the experience of having heard that Don Henry song, or Mac McAnally sing and play, or Michael McDonald, in the midst of his enormous success, play something that no one has ever heard, and just be transported.

You've got to remember that when the business is grinding away in a different direction than where you happen to be. I'm not saying it's not hard. I will pray for you every night, if you are someone who judges the value of your work on where it happens to be on the charts. What a terrible way to live. You're just eating a hole through the center of yourself over things that you literally have no control over. I'm not saying I never went through that.

Hemingway said a writer's integrity was like a woman's virginity, "Once it's gone, it's gone forever." I know, he was Hemingway, but I flat-out disagree with him. You learn by screwing up. You learn by your mistakes, and selling yourself, and selling your integrity down the river. One time causes you to not want to do it again.

I've learned by committing these sins. You're participating, or you're not. You're the Civil War general who says, "You know, men, I'd like to be with you in battle today, but somebody's got to be here, just outside of cannon range. Rest assured that after this battle, I will gather up your remains and see that they are sent home to your families."

Come on, are you down in there participating or not? And if you are, wear boots, because it's messy down there. The creative life is very messy. Almost nothing has ever sprung whole cloth out of anything. It's been a blood-and-guts operation. That's how it's been for me. Wear a cup; you're going take some shots.

That's a good parting comment from a football player.

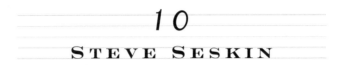

10

STEVE SESKIN

Steve Seskin is one of the most successful writers in Nashville today, with a boatload of songs recorded by Tim McGraw, Neal McCoy, John Michael Montgomery, Kenny Chesney, Collin Raye, Peter Frampton, Waylon Jennings, Alabama, Mark Wills, and Peter, Paul, and Mary. His song "Don't Laugh At Me" was a finalist for CMA Song of the Year in 1999, and has spurred an entire tolerance movement, launched by the Don't Laugh at Me Project. Other Seskin hits include: "I Think About You," "Life's A Dance," "No Doubt About It," "You've Got Love," and "Grown Men Don't Cry."

Steve is also an electrifying performer. "His voice has a natural lilt that can't be learned," writes Joel Selvin in the San Francisco Chronicle. *He's "a really exceptional talent," writes Alan Lewis in the* San Francisco Bay Guardian. *And "the presentation is simple, affective, and effective," writes Jim Carnes in the* Sacramento Union. *Few performers can face an audience with only an acoustic guitar and hotwire its emotions. But that's what happens at Steve's concerts.*

Steve has also distinguished himself as a recording artist. On his records, you can hear the hits as only the writer can present them—as well as other jewels, waiting to be discovered.

In October, 1999, Steve joined forces with noted Music Row song plugger Stephanie Cox to form Larga Vista Music. Steve's song "Grown Men Don't Cry," recorded by Tim McGraw, is the company's first big hit. He also has songs on the current Toby Keith album ("New Orleans") and Aaron Tippin's latest ("Lost").

www.steveseskin.com

How did you become a songwriter?

I started singing and taking piano lessons, at about five or six years old. I went to a place called the High School of Music and Art in New York, but the notion of having a career in music was something that was on the back burner. My parents thought it was a great hobby, but that I should "go get a job." So, I went to college and studied psychology, but I kept playing music.

I went out to California, to look at some grad schools. Maybe it was something about being away from the nest, but the bell went off. Soon, I moved there and started playing in the clubs, and on the streets. I'd kept this all bottled up for a long time, and I'd never performed much in New York.

During that time, I met a lot of incredible singer/songwriters and I used to do their material, but in 1972, I started writing my own songs. From 1972 to 1976, I wrote about twenty songs. In retrospect, they were pretty green around the edges. I always have a lot of emotion, and a lot of heart, in my work, and could pull the heartstrings. You could feel something when you heard the songs, but they weren't that well crafted.

I came close to getting a record deal out of Los Angeles in 1979, but it didn't happen. I was happy, and probably could have done this the rest of my life, but at that time, my songs were only for me. I had absolutely no thoughts of anybody else recording them. I was just writing for what I think should be the real reason you write them today, which is, "I love writing songs, and I love expressing myself, and sharing my joy and my sorrow, and my gift, with other people."

I did a couple of dates in San Francisco with Crystal Gayle, and one night she and her husband came up after they saw my set and said, "You ought to go to Nashville." I said, "Nashville? That's interesting."

At the time, my vision of Nashville was the stereotype that a lot of people get. I'm thinking Loretta Lynn, Conway Twitty, country, country, country. Although I always admired that music, and the way they could put forth a song and make you feel something, it just didn't seem to fit into what my ideal was. But, it was one of those moments where someone looks you in the eye and says, "You should go to Nashville." And you think, "Oh, all right."

So, three months later, I had a meeting at ASCAP with a guy named Merlin Littlefield. I was armed with my little tape of three or four songs, and I walked in there and played my songs. He liked them enough to pick up the phone and call a few publishers.

I got a few appointments, and the first couple of publishers said, "Thanks, we'll call you." Then, at New Clarion Music Group, a woman named Sue Patton was just very taken with what I was doing. She saw my potential and helped me get ensconced in the community. The next day, I was singing a demo for one of their writers.

I never intended to move to Nashville, by the way. That was not in the picture for me, because I loved where I was living, and I don't believe that you should go somewhere that you're not as comfortable as where you are, just for your career. I love it in Nashville, but San Francisco's home.

Of course, I got a lot of flack about that. "Nothing's ever going to happen unless you move here." I said, "I'm not moving here." But, already, I knew on that first trip that I loved it here. I had to figure out how I was going to make it work. I decided, with Sue Patton's help, that the way I could do this was to come here regularly, six or eight times a year.

In 1985, I started coming here every couple months, for a week to ten days at a time. During that time, I signed with New Clarion Music Group. I would come here and I'd write every day, and I started co-writing, which I had never done till I got here.

Was that scary the first time?

Not only scary, I just didn't understand how that could possibly work, because it was such a personal thing for me. There were certain criteria for my writing. One, something had to happen to me for me to write about it. I never wrote about anything but my own life, those early years.

And, two, I never had any discipline in my writing. It was something like, a lightning bolt hits, and you go, "Oh my God, write, write, write." Then it's over, and you're waiting for it to come again.

For the first fifteen years that I wrote songs, I wrote ten songs a year, tops. I didn't think anything was wrong then. One of the beauties of songwriting, to me, is that there are no rules in that sense. There's no right or wrong way to do it. There's the Mike Reid/Hugh Prestwood school of songwriting. Both those guys write six to ten songs a year, and they're all brilliant. Then, there's the Don Schlitz school of songwriting. Don will tell you that he still writes one hundred and fifty songs a year.

I asked him once, "Why do you write so many? That's a lot of songs." He said, "I'm only brilliant 10 percent of the time, so, this way, I get fifteen great songs. If I only wrote fifty songs, I'd only get five."

How many do you write a year?

The big switch I made through co-writing was that I started writing a lot more. Back then, I probably wrote thirty songs a year. Now, it's probably forty or fifty.

I was terrified of co-writing. I didn't understand how it could work. And the fact is, it doesn't work far more often than it does work. I've probably written songs with about one hundred and fifty different co-writers, and there are probably only fifty of them that I've ever written more than one song with.

I look at co-writing like dating. It doesn't always work out. Some people, you have to say, "Let's just be friends. I don't want to go there with you." Co-writing is a very intimate exchange.

I was with New Clarion Music Group for three years, and wrote with a lot of people. A very interesting thing happened to me during that time. Looking back on it now, I wrote some of the worst songs I've ever written. I probably wrote one hundred and fifty songs in those three years, and there are only five of them that I'd play for you.

What I was doing, during that time, was learning. Learning the craft of writing songs. I was learning one of the things that Nashville is so good at, which was how to put together a song. Form, economy, commerciality, are concepts that had never really occurred to me. Before, I was from the school of, "Well, that's how it came out."

Writing had always been a real organic experience for me, and it was the first time that I realized that writing really was, at its best, a combination of those two things. That organic, dreamy, stream of consciousness, unedited, beautiful thing, but then, a period when you reflect on that in an analytical mode, and say, "Okay, all of this came flowing out of me. Now, that's good, but what does this have to do with that, maybe that should be in another song."

I think, in the process of learning that, I wrote some pretty heartless songs. They were very well put together. They rhymed in the right places, but I think I'd lost my voice. I'd lost who I am; that thread that ran through my material was no longer there. It was generic. You couldn't tell that *I* wrote the songs. I was trying too hard. It took three years, but luckily, I got my voice back, along with a whole bunch of newfound knowledge of how to craft a song. I believe that that's when I started writing pretty good stuff.

I left New Clarion Music Group in 1988, and was a free agent for about six months or so. All those years, from 1985 to 1988, I played constantly, at every writer's night I could play. I found it was a great way to meet people, without kind of pushing yourself in their face. You never know what will happen when you put the music out in the universe.

One night, I played my two songs at the Bluebird, and the special guest was Bob DiPiero. He came over to me and said, "I really like those two songs. Are you writing somewhere?" I said, "Well, actually, no. I'm kind of a free agent these days." He said, "We just started this new company called Little Big Town Music, Woody Bomar, and myself, and John Scott Sherrill. We're looking to sign some writers and some songs."

The next day I played him twenty songs and he liked six of them. We decided to do single song contracts on those six songs. When a publisher is willing to do that, I think it's good for the writer, because you get to know each other. Kind of like the courting stage before you get married.

As luck would have it, about two months into that, Alabama cut a song of mine called "She Can." I was in heaven. All year it was supposed to be a single, but it turns out it wasn't. Still, the album sold over a million and a half records.

And, of course, they liked me. They had signed six songs, and had very little invested in this thing, and they got one cut. So, here I was at a company where we had two writers who had all these hits, and really knew their way around the town, and had a reputation. And Woody, as a song plugger, had a lot of success, so this company was happening. It was a good fit for me.

The other thing I realized there is that a good publishing company is built on diversity in the writing staff. I fit into that company very well because you had Bob DiPiero, who's the king of fun, three-minute radio songs, pretty much better than anybody on the planet. Then, you had John Scott Sherrill, who's "Mister Blue-Eyed Soul/R&B." And then, there was me. I was already writing a lot of socially conscious songs, and philosophical message songs, and story songs. So, I fit in there, in that I wasn't in competition with the other two guys.

I kept coming to town and writing songs. In 1990 I had my first single, with Waylon Jennings on a song called "Wrong." Then, another interesting thing happened that was really fortuitous for me.

Bob DiPiero and John Scott Sherrill formed a group called Billy Hill. They were on Warner Brothers Records. They were on the road, they were at meetings all the time, and all of a sudden they weren't writing many songs for Nashville. So, guess who rose to that occasion? I was working harder than ever.

It's not a coincidence that during that time I started getting a lot of cuts. We signed a couple other writers, so the publishing company needed me to be producing some stuff.

The other thing is, at that time, country music was really exploding. New artists like John Michael Montgomery, Kenny Chesney, and Neil McCoy were coming out. That was an amazing time.

I'm very proud to say that Allen Shamblin and I wrote John Michael Montgomery's first single, "Life's A Dance," Kenny Chesney's second single, "All I Need To Know," and Neil McCoy's first hit, "No Doubt About It." New artists, much more than established artists, go back to the well. I had three John Michael Montgomery songs, one on each of his first three records, and three Neil McCoy songs.

Through those years, I just kept writing better and better songs, with better and better co-writers. I always say that you're only as good as your co-writer. I've never been the kind of writer that's gotten a ton of cuts. I know Craig Wiseman's had like three hundred cuts. I don't know how many I've had—something like fifty maybe, is all. But I've always had an incredible single-to-cut ratio. There are writers that have a ton of album cuts, but I've been lucky that a lot of my work has made it to the radio.

If you look at my body of work, "Life's a Dance" and "I Think About You" and "Don't Laugh At Me" are very unusual. But "No Doubt About It" is probably the only love song I've ever had cut. "Daddy's Money" was a song that I still can't believe I wrote. I wrote it with Mark Sanders and Bob DiPiero.

That is a classic case of a co-writing thing. It's not like I didn't participate in it, I did. But I'm not going to be writing too many of those in the future, because it's just not what I do. I think, in an overall view, it's important for a writer to figure out what it is they do. You can broaden that, and you can change it. It can develop, but there ought to be some basic notion of what it is you do.

Bob DiPiero writes fabulous three-minute, forget-about-your-troubles, put-the-top-down-and-drive-to-the-beach songs. He's always said to me, "That's what music's all about, people forgetting their troubles." And I'll say to him, "Hey, music is about people feeling, people laughing, crying." I want to move people. I want to teach people. I want to show people something they might be missing, not from an egotistical, "I know better than you" point of view, but just make them reacquaint themselves with some ideals in their lives that maybe they forgot about.

I think the point of this is that we are both right. Music is about all of that, but you have to figure out what it is that you do best. It took a while for me to figure out what that is, but I certainly know it now. Be comfortable with it. Our unique nature, and our individualities, are our best suit.

I really feel like I have a responsibility to deliver the goods. The world, to me, is hurting. There's a lot going on, and if I can make one life a little easier, or shed some light on something for somebody that makes them rise to the occasion, or deal with some grief in a better manner, what is better than that?

When Sony bought Little Big Town Music, it was a big banner day for the company. I was happy for Woody and the people who were involved in Little Big Town, but on the other hand, a bunch of us were really sad, because life as we knew it had just ended.

It's part of the business. But we had made it twelve years without that happening, and we had this little family there. We never had more than seven or eight writers. We had two song pluggers. The math was very good. At Sony there were a hundred writers and six song pluggers! Do the math.

Long story short, Stephanie Cox, who had been our intern at Little Big Town way back in 1989 to1990, fresh out of college, went to breakfast with me one morning when my contract with Sony was about up. She had lost her job at Universal.

She asked, "What are you going to do?" I said, "I'm looking for a little company like Little Big Town. I want that feeling again. Small suits me." We just looked at each other and said, "Let's start our own darn company. We know what we're doing. We've got the flagship writer and we've got a great song plugger that knows the business. Let's take a shot." That was three years ago. We started Larga Vista Music, and we're sitting here in our offices now doing really well.

We're literally modeling ourselves after Little Big Town, everything we learned from Woody Bomar on how to run a small company, and how to put together a staff of writers. We're utilizing that knowledge to build our company.

I've always said there's nothing wrong with selling your stuff and making money at it. But one of the things I've maintained all these years is that you can mix art and commerce, but don't mix them in the creation. Don't let the commerce poison the art.

I've never been the kind of writer that sits down and goes, "Oh, who's cutting this week?" I say, "Let the song be as pure a creation as it can be." Write what's in your heart and on your mind. When it's done, and you can call it a piece of art, then you can figure out who to sell it to. That's my motto, and it's working for me.

Don't get me wrong. I love when one of my songs ends up on the radio. But, in a way, it's not as important to me as when I go play it at the Bluebird and see if an audience likes it. I think sometimes, in the business, we lose sight of the most important piece of the equation, which is the listener, the people. The entire industry is nothing without them.

> "One of the things I've maintained all these years is that you can mix art and commerce, but don't mix them in the creation. Don't let the commerce poison the art."

I have a lot of songs that I've written that nobody's ever cut, but I know that they're a good piece of work, because they've been validated. Not by some A&R person or some producer, but by an audience who has a tear in their eye, or a chuckle on their mouth. That makes me feel good.

I think every writer needs to get an intrinsic reward out of their writing, for themselves, whether or not anybody else ever validates it on a music business level. I try to keep that perspective. It's hard sometimes, because there's that big carrot dangling, saying, "Write another 'Daddy's Money.' Write another 'Life's A Dance.'" Well, I can't do it that way. I've just got to write what I'm writing today, and hope for the best.

Give me a definition for creativity.

Part of it is an ability to take the thoughts that you might have, and put them down on paper within the context of what we're talking about, writing songs. To put them down in a way that other people can take something from that. We don't write these songs for ourselves. When I finish a song, the first thing I want to do is go play it for somebody.

Open the door for the listener, because the listener doesn't care about you. They only care about you as it relates to them. If you don't cross that line and make somebody think about their own life and say, "Oh, I've been there," or "He understands my pain," or "Wow, that would be great," if you haven't done that, then you haven't accomplished anything. You start with a seed and being creative with it takes it to another place.

I think it's also the notion that you can take something that happens to either yourself or somebody else, and comment on it, and bring it to life. Part of the creative process is being able to fictionalize, because I don't think that we have to write everything exactly like it happened.

We're given a seed to start with and then, sometimes, it's our turn to make things up. I learned from Allen Shamblin, a great writer never lets the facts get in the way of the truth, truth being the *emotional* truth. Why are you writing this song? What's this really about? What are we trying to touch on here? The facts you can make up. It really doesn't matter whether you paid six hundred and twenty-three dollars for the car, or five hundred and eighty-seven dollars. It depends on what rhyme you need there.

That's, basically, what I think creativity is, taking something from a dreamy little concept, and being able to figure out how to succinctly put it forth. It's a big idea in a three- or four-minute song.

Talk about the role of the subconscious mind in songwriting.

I think it comes into play more for some writers than others, and I'm probably in the middle. I know writers who, everything they create comes from that subconscious mind. They're writing words down, they don't know what they mean. You have to drag them kicking and screaming to the analytical party. I probably lean a little more heavily towards that side of it, so I have subconscious thoughts that just come out, and I'll write something. But I'm immediately kind of, "What the heck does that mean? Okay, what can I do with that?"

I've never had a whole song come to me, like some people, in a dream. I'll have a line, or a thought. I think writing is a conscious effort, for me, more than for other writers I know. I'm a fairly literal writer. That's why I was talking about figuring out who you are.

When you listen to most of my songs, like them or not, you know what I'm talking about, kind of the common man's language. I always go back to what Mark Twain said when they asked him, "Do you consider your writing like fine wine?" He said, "Well, not really. My writing's a little more like water." Then he paused and said, "Everybody drinks water." You know, there's something to that. I think it's more of a conscious thing, for me, but I definitely get thoughts, and things that come to me. A lot of it is just being aware.

Randy Newman said this, and it's always stuck with me: "You're the grand observer, and you also are the commentator on the era that you live in. You have a historical responsibility to reflect what's going on in the time you live in." When you think of songs, they really do.

So my ears are always open, my eyes are open. I'm having a conversation with somebody, and I'm listening to them, but I'm just waiting for them to say something I can turn into a song. I think the writer's job is to take something that somebody says, and put it in a completely different context.

Are there activities that help you contact the muse?

Yeah, walking is good. One of my favorite books on songwriting is called *If You Want to Write*. Mike Reid turned me on to that book. It's not a songwriting book, that's what I like about it. I tend to like books that are about writing. I've read all of them, or most of them, from Natalie Goldberg books like *Writing Down the Bones* and *Wild Mind*, to *Bird by Bird*, by Anne Lamott, and *The Artist's Way*, by Julia Cameron. I like to read books that get me in touch with my soul and my inner workings.

In *If You Want to Write*, she [author Brenda Ueland] talks about walking a little further than you need to for exercise. There's a phrase, "Clear your mind and something will come to it." I think we walk around, a lot of times, and our minds are cluttered with a million things. How could you create?

Walking is good. Reading is great. I don't read as much as I want to, but it's been a great endeavor for me when I do, in terms of my songwriting.

Once a year, I go up to this place called the VCCA. It's an artist colony, Virginia Center for the Creative Arts. We go up there for two weeks, five or six of us. They give you a place to stay, three meals a day, and a studio to write in. And, for two weeks, you're a writer and nothing else. You don't have to worry about anything. There are no phones. You disconnect from your world, as you know it, and you just write.

Every year when I go there, what happens to me, is that I get into a zone. It takes three days to decompress, and then I get into a zone like I can't get into anywhere else. A lot more subconscious things come to me. I'm just on a walk somewhere, looking at the birds, and flowers, and the trees, and something will occur to me.

Do you write songs while you're there, or just get lots of ideas?

Both. In the years I've gone there, I've written anywhere from five to ten songs in the two weeks. I go through periods where I'll write an amazing amount. I wrote three songs in the last four days. Then, I'll have a month where I don't write anything.

I don't believe in writer's block. It's like a faucet. There are times when it's flowing, and there are times when it's not. There are times when you are meant to be living. Go live, and then you'll surely write about it. Trust that the faucet will come back on again. It always has for me.

How many songs might you be working on, at any point in time? Do you like to keep that limited in any way?

I do not work on a lot of songs at one time. Probably the most I've worked on is three or four, in the course of co-writing, in a week. In some of the co-write sessions that I do when I come to Nashville, we'll almost always write a song in a day or two. Some people are faster than others. I can be fast, but I prefer to be slow.

For example, Allen Shamblin and I wrote "Don't Laugh at Me" in about four or five hours, no rewrites. It just felt right. We wrote "Cactus in a Coffee Can" in over six months, over eighty hours.

Now, one might ask, "Why did you spend that long on it?" Well, because we couldn't get it right. We have a standard that we're trying to achieve. One of the good things about a good co-writing situation is that you don't disagree too often on the standard

"When I declare a song done, I do not think, for a second, that everyone I'm going to play it for is going to love it."

I think one of the ways you become a great writer is to be willing to do the work, and to realize it's not a race. There's not somebody waiting outside your door for this song. You have to serve the song, and you owe it to yourself, and that song, and to the listeners who will eventually hear that song, to polish it and work on it till at least you think it's right. The buck starts with you.

When I declare a song done, I do not think, for a second, that everyone I'm going to play it for is going to love it. However, if I declare it done, *I* love it. I love every note and every word. If I don't, if I can admit to myself, "I don't really like that line," then, what the heck am I calling it done for?

When I play a song for an A&R person, or a producer, and they go, "Nah, what else you got?" they bring a lot of baggage to that table. They're not saying that song is not good. When that happens, I don't feel like I need to go home and rewrite the song because so and so at MCA records didn't like it. They are just looking for songs for a particular artist. Talk about a round hole/square peg. It's a very specific thing they're looking for. My job is to walk out of there respectfully and say, "Thank you," and go take it to somebody else who thinks it's a brilliant piece of work.

I think a lot of young writers get swayed by people. They want so much to have feedback that they sometimes don't understand the subjective nature of this. You could play me any song that's in the Top 10 right now and I'd find a way to rewrite them better, in my way.

What I'm saying is, it's so important to keep growing and getting your own level of self-critic, and that's a great place to start. The nature of music is such that not everybody's supposed to like it. That's why there's something for everybody. You're not going to please every audience, but if you have passion, and you're true to what you do, there will be an audience for it, and you can find more people like that, that want to hear what it is you do.

Talk about the importance of opening lines.

I think opening lines are very important. In most cases, I think they ought to do quite a bit, in terms of introducing the characters, introducing emotion, setting the stage, for the whole thing. When you have "I'm a little boy with glasses, the one you call a geek," you don't know what that means, but it's all directed at "Don't laugh at me." It gives you a character.

Allen and I just finished a song, and the first line is "It was thirty-four to seven at the half." You don't know exactly where we're going, but you know it's a football game, instead of a baseball game. You know it, just by the virtue of the score. And it's halftime; it's not going to be a hockey game. It tells you a lot of information.

I think the job of a first line, as in any line in the song, is to keep you interested in hearing the next line. You want to constantly pique the listener's interest. The first line is the first chance you have with the listener.

The most potent lyrics, to me, are a combination of two things: emotion, heart, what makes you care about the character, and secondly, the imagery. They call it "furniture" in Nashville. Show me the movie. I always say, "Show me, don't tell me. Paint me a picture that makes me feel a certain way, as opposed to telling me how you feel."

I love that kind of writing, and I've got to say, that is one of the things that Nashville has taught me more than anything. Writing something like fifty songs with Allen Shamblin has taught me.

I'll tell you a little story. The first song Allen and I ever wrote was "Life's a Dance." We had set a date to get together and, the night before, I wrote the chorus to "Life's a Dance," music and lyric. I had always been really good at that. I think you have to spot what your strengths are as a writer, and my strength, lyrically, had always been the big picture, the emotion, the chorus, the heart, because that's where I came to my writing from.

My weak spot, back in 1990 (I'd like to think I've gotten way better now), was the pictures, the images. I remember sitting there going, "Life's a dance, you learn as you go," finishing that chorus and thinking, "Okay, now I'll write the verses." I was going to write it by myself, but I just wasn't getting anywhere that I liked. I thought, "You know, tomorrow, you're getting together with the guy that wrote, 'He wore a starched white shirt buttoned at the neck. He'd sit on the porch and watch the chickens peck. His teeth were all gone, but what the heck, I thought he walked on water.' Why don't you just go watch TV, or something, and wait?"

I'll never forget this, as long as I live. I walk in there to Hayes Street Music, and Allen and I talked about half an hour, and then I said, "You know, I've got this idea I started last night. See what you think: *Life's a dance.*" He said, "I really like that." We started the first verse, and I don't know who came up with what, but, "When I was fourteen I was falling fast for a blue-eyed girl in my homeroom class," and then I believe I said, "Trying to find the courage to ask her out." And I'm thinking it needed to say that it was a difficult, never going to happen, near impossible, kind of thing. And, out of Allen's mouth comes, "Trying to find the courage to ask her out was like trying to get oil from a water spout." I looked at him and said, "Now that's why I waited till today to write this song." I could've been a hundred years old, I never would've thought of that line.

What verse do you think is the hardest to write?

Sometimes, the start of the song is fairly easy for me because something has happened that's led me to write that song. There's an event, there's a seed, and so I have what I need to write about. Then, if you're a good writer, you can figure out how to put the words and the music together.

The second verse, though, you've got to make it up. Your inspiration is gone. It's time to fictionalize. When you write the second verse, you have to consider context. You can't just write it from the total dreamy place, because it's got to go with everything you've already written.

If I'm sitting there for hours, thinking, "Okay, what happens next," one of the things I've learned is to say, "Wait a minute. If I can't think of what happens next, maybe what happens next actually happened before the first verse. Maybe my jumping off point is not my jumping off point. Maybe that's not a great first verse. Maybe that's the second verse, and I need to write what happened before that." When I make that conceptual switch, the fountain's on again.

When we're having a real difficult time, we're just barking up the wrong tree. You can be stubborn about it, and it can take two days barking up the wrong tree, or you can realize it. I think, as you get to be a better writer, you realize a little more quickly.

"If the listener sees your work, you're dead. I think it has to end up looking like you didn't do any work at all."

If the listener sees your work, you're dead. I think it has to end up looking like you didn't do any work at all. Like it just came flowing out of you, just like that. Well, the truth is, you spent twenty hours pushing and pulling, but if that shows, if the listener feels manipulated, then, I think, you lose.

It's the same thing with that imagery/emotion thing. If you told me I could only choose one, not both, I'd take emotion every time because imagery without emotion means nothing. Your use of the language, and putting forth pictures and images, if they don't come to some emotional head, then they don't mean anything. Nobody's going to be impressed with your use of adjectives and colorful descriptions if they don't care about it, whereas you can get away with a lyric that doesn't have a lot of pictures in it, if you make me care about the characters. I always think the best songs combine the two.

What basic skills should we be developing as aspiring songwriters?

The ability to listen. The ability to observe is a good skill, to chronicle emotional events, even your own. I think one of the things that also happens to me, is that I try to draw from my whole life. I've been married for twenty-one years, but if I think of a hook for a song that's about heartbreak, I'm right back to my college girlfriend dumping me. And I'm going, "Oh, yeah, I remember how that felt. I can write this song." It doesn't matter that I'm happily married now. I think that's a skill one needs to develop, to call up, as an actor would. I think we are all very much like actors and actresses.

I think the other skill would be to, musically, have a basic knowledge of theory. You don't have to be able to read or play a piece of Mozart, if you don't want to. But you should have a basic knowledge of how chords go together, and a basic knowledge of prosody, how to put the right music with the right lyrics.

The whole process of songwriting consists of highs and a lot of lows, especially for young writers. Give us some advice on maintaining some stability and surviving that roller coaster ride.

It's important to have a belief that what you have to share with the world is important, and that you're good at it. That you'll keep doing it no matter what, and that, hopefully, somebody will recognize your genius in this business.

Again, I think it's important just to get joy out of the writing. The bottom line is, anybody that does this for a long period of time, does it because they can't help it. If I had never made a nickel at writing songs, I'd still be writing them. Don Schlitz says that all the success he's had, basically, means he gets to keep doing this without worrying about how he's going to pay his mortgage.

If you don't have that passion for it, you're not going to keep doing it. You don't enter this songwriting as a profession to go, "I think I'll go make some money, I'll write songs." I don't know what the percentage is, but it's something like 5 percent of ASCAP or BMI's writers who actually make more than twenty grand a year at songwriting. So, what does that tell you? It's hard, when you're talking about playing in that arena. It's very competitive.

The average artist looks at five hundred or so songs for an album of ten. A lot of those are darn good. So, if you're up against it, that better not be your only goal. The music should be your goal, making the music. And I believed that before I had any success, by the way.

11

ALLEN SHAMBLIN

With the tremendous popularity and critical acclaim of his song "He Walked On Water," songwriter Allen Shamblin has positioned himself among the great storytellers who have given country music its legacy and continuous popularity.

In August of 1987, Shamblin moved from Texas to Nashville, Tennessee, with fourteen completed songs. Upon his arrival, he held several jobs, including parking cars and working in a warehouse. It didn't take long, however, for industry insiders to catch on to Shamblin's talent and for his demo tapes to get passed around. In May of 1988, he signed as a staff writer at Hayes Street Music/Almo Music Corp.

Within nine months, Shamblin had songs recorded by Lee Greenwood, The Forester Sisters, and James House. However, it was Randy Travis's #1 version of "He Walked On Water" that brought Shamblin to the forefront of the Nashville songwriting community, seemingly overnight.

He has since had a hand in writing such #1 songs as "Walk On Faith," recorded by Mike Reid, "In This Life," recorded by Collin Raye, and "We Were In Love," recorded by Toby Keith. Other singles include "Life's a Dance," by John Michael Montgomery; "Thinkin' Problem," recorded by David Ball; "Man Of My Word," recorded by Collin Raye; "I Can't Make You Love Me," recorded by Bonnie Raitt; and Dove Award winner "In God's Hands Now," recorded by Anointed.

To date, Shamblin has had more than 50 million recordings of his songs by such artists as Wynonna, Patty Loveless, Willie Nelson, Kenny Rogers, Bette Midler, Ricky Van Shelton, Dolly Parton, Ricky Skaggs, John Berry, Kathy Mattea, Susan Ashton, Prince, and others.

www.allenshamblin.com

Give us an overview of how you became a songwriter.

I graduated from Sam Houston State, in Texas, in December of 1982 with a degree in marketing. I moved to Houston and I was loading airplanes for Continental Airlines for a while, and then I got into real estate appraisal. I had taken a couple of real estate courses in college.

I went down to visit my brother and sister in San Marcos, Texas, and I loved it down there. I picked up an Austin paper and saw a job opening for a real estate appraiser in Austin, so I circled that ad with a red pencil and I told my sister, "There's the next place I'm going to work." She said, "Did you already interview?" I said, "No, I just know I'm going to get that job." I drove down there. They offered me the job, and I was living in Austin two weeks later.

A big part of the reason I wanted to be in Austin was that I wanted to be around the music. I had started playing the guitar my junior year in high school, when I came down with mononucleosis. I was bedridden for about six weeks, and had to stay away from everybody. My dad had an old Gibson guitar, and a couple of songbooks, so I'd sit there all day trying to learn how to play chords. All through college, I was learning the guitar on the side, and having fun with it, but I hadn't written any songs at that point.

I got down to Austin, started appraising real estate, and I just hated it. I started thinking about who I was and what I could be passionate about. What was I passionate about? The only answer I had was music. I knew three or four chords on the guitar, not a whole lot. But I remember distinctly the night it all intersected. I was going for a walk; it was one of these real starry nights in Austin. I looked up and I said a prayer. I said, "God, I've never asked you this before, but if it's your will, will you help me be a songwriter?" Something that simple. And instantly, I didn't hear a voice or anything, but I had a sense that that's what I was supposed to do.

So I started coming home from work every day, and I'd eat, take a nap, and get up and write. I was very disciplined about it. And then, after about six months, still no songs. But I remembered back to that night, and that prayer, and I think I even said another prayer like, "I'm still thanking you ahead of time for the songs I know you're going to send me." And literally the next week, songs started coming together. All of a sudden, I had six songs. A chorus I had been working on would fit with a verse. Things I had been working on for about six months just came together.

When I finished the sixth song (why that number even matters I don't know), I was in Wyatt's Cafeteria in Austin, talking to my buddy, Tim Janecek. I pulled a lyric out of my back pocket and I was reading him the lyric. We were laughing, because it was a silly song. A lady standing right beside me, said, "Did you write that song?" I said, "Yes ma'am." Then she asked, "Are you a songwriter?" Again, I said, "Yes ma'am." She asked if I was any good and I told her that I thought so, but she'd have to judge for herself. And she said, "Well, why don't you come over and play me your songs, and if I like them, I might be able to help you." She gave me a phone number. End of conversation.

I didn't know anything about her, but I had this sense that that was part of an answer to that prayer I had prayed six months earlier. I called her the next day. She said, "Why don't you come over tomorrow, or sometime, and play me your songs?" I went over and played her the six songs I'd written, and when I finished she said, "I'm going to try to help you. My best friend is Martha Sharp, who's executive vice president of Warner Brothers Records, in Nashville. And my brother in law is Johnny Gimble, who has played with Bob Wills and the Texas Playboys, and on George Strait and Merle Haggard albums."

Her name is Linda Orsak, by the way, and she has since become a dear friend. She said, "Go write some more songs." So, the next week I wrote four more, 'cause I was just so inspired. Now I had ten songs to my name.

So, she took me over to Johnny Gimble's house. He had a little stereo system, not your typical recording setup. We did all ten songs. I played guitar and he played fiddle, and we sent that off to Martha Sharp in Nashville.

I didn't hear a thing for three months. I called up Linda one day and asked, "Have you heard from Martha?" She said, "No, but you can call her if you'd like," so she gave me the number for Warner Brothers Records. I called and the receptionist said that Martha was out. I gave her my name and number and asked her to have Martha give me a call. I hung up, and I remember, I turned around and there was an office full of guys, real estate appraisers, and I said, "Man, I just called Warner Brothers records in Nashville."

About that time, the phone rang. Our receptionist was out to lunch, so I reached over and grabbed it and went, "Heelllllo!!" The voice said, "Yes, this is Martha Sharp calling to speak to Allen Shamblin." I swallowed hard and said, "That's me, and I was calling to see if you liked my songs." She said, "Yeah, I do, and I like your voice too. Do you perform?" I said, "Yeah," even though I had only performed one time in my life, at a writer's night. She said, "Barry Beckett and I are going to San Antonio to see a guy we're about to sign, named Randy Travis. Then we're going to rent a car and drive to Austin and see you."

I hung up the phone and asked if anybody had ever heard of Randy Travis. Nobody had. In my mind, I'm thinking, "Poor dude, he's a struggling singer songwriter, but I'm fixing to be famous." Ha!

Linda called Don's Depot, and asked the performer there if I could sit in during his break so Martha and Barry could hear me sing. I'd practiced, and rehearsed, and practiced, and rehearsed. Of the ten songs I'd written, I practiced the five songs I thought were my best all afternoon for weeks leading up to their visit. So, finally, the night comes, and it's almost time for the singers' break, and they're not there yet. He called me up on stage anyway, and I did the five songs that I *hadn't* practiced. I came off the stage and, unbeknownst to me, they had walked in during my first song.

I came off stage and there was Martha and Barry. They were smiling, big as day. They both encouraged me, and later on Martha said, "Hey I really liked that. I think you need to move to Nashville and you need to keep writing songs."

Well, that so overwhelmed me. The first few songs I had ever written, and within months I'm sitting' down with Martha Sharp and Barry Beckett, who's produced Bob Dylan. I wrote four more songs, then nothing. I tried every day as hard as I could, and I did not write another song for more than a year. Suddenly, I was self-conscious and I was trying to impress, and I was just not using my voice and having fun.

So, one day I'm in the same office appraising real estate, and my same buddy, Tim Janecek, goes, "Hey Allen, do you ever think about moving to Nashville? Do you think you'll still go?" I told him that I was praying about it. We went to lunch, and when we came back there was a message on my desk from a publisher in Nashville.

I called them and they said they understood Martha Sharp had been interested in me, and wanted to let me know that if I ever moved to Nashville, they would let me write with their writers. Said they couldn't offer me any money or a deal, but they'd let me come in and hang out with their writers.

I walked right in and said, "Tim, I got my answer, I'm moving to Nashville." I gave my two weeks' notice. In two weeks, I was living in

Nashville. I got a job loading trucks. I did that for a while, and then I started parking cars down there, at Centennial Baptist Hospital, in the section where the pregnant ladies would come in.

Were you writing during the day?

Yeah, when I could. I was meeting with writers, and co-writing a little bit. I eventually picked up the yellow pages and started calling publishers. I got through to a guy named Al Cooley, at MCA Publishing. I told him who I was, and told him Martha Sharp had been interested. I was using her name any way I could. Thanks, Martha!

Al invited me to come in and play him some songs. He really liked them, but he said, "We're just not looking for that right now." He had me call an attorney named Ken Levitan. He thought Ken would like my music. So I called Ken, and gave him my tape and, within days, I was sitting down across from Don Schlitz.

Don Schlitz had just opened a publishing company. I was in my car parking uniform when I went to meet him. In fact, I think the first time that Don and I wrote together, I was wearing my car parking uniform. Don was incredible. We wrote a couple songs together, and then they said they'd like to sign me as a writer. And that's where I started, at Hayes Street Music, with Don Schlitz and Pat Halper.

You know there's no doubt that you were meant to be a songwriter.

"I don't want to over-spiritualize this, but at the same time, I recognize that this is my calling. God opened the doors and I walked on through."

There's absolutely no doubt. I don't want to over-spiritualize this, but at the same time, I recognize that this is my calling. God opened the doors and I walked on through. After I signed at Hayes Street Music, I wrote for six months, every day and night. I was so glad to not be parking cars.

After six months, Pat Halper called me into her office and said, "You know, Allen, there's just something missing in your songs. We're not hearing, in these songs you've just written, what we heard in those songs you wrote while you were still in Texas. Why don't you go back down to Texas and reconnect with your roots, and then come back to Nashville and write by yourself?"

I hadn't written by myself in over two years, at that point, but it was almost a relief. I thought, I guess we're all fixing to find out if I really am a songwriter. So I flew back to Austin, because that's where a lot of my friends were. While I was there, Don Schlitz called me and said, "Hey, I'm down here in Austin, and I'm fixing to do Austin City Limits Saturday night with Mike Reid, Harlan Howard, Kye Fleming, Janis Ian, and Mark Wright. You want to come hang out?" I said, "Man I would love to."

So I went to watch them do their sound check. This big guy comes walking by, sits down right beside me and started talking. It was Mike Reid. Mike puts people at ease that way. I just opened up and said, "Mike, I thought I was supposed to be a songwriter, so I moved to Nashville. I've been writing as hard as I can for six months, and I've written a lot of songs. But my publisher's not really happy with them and, to be honest, I'm not really happy with them." He said, "Well good." I asked what he meant, and he said, "You've learned a lot about the craft; now when you go back to Nashville, write about something that matters to you. Write about something that's important to you."

We left there, went over to a Mexican food restaurant, and Harlan Howard was sitting there talking. He said, "If you want to advance your career five years faster than anybody else, write by yourself. If a song was written with one name on it, then there's no wondering, 'Is this person a songwriter or not?'" I was getting all these affirmations, and promptings, to write by myself.

That night, I went to the show, and I heard all these great songs. I had an epiphany there that night, which was that every line counted; there were no weak lines. They didn't write a verse, chorus, and a last verse and, in the last half of the last line, slough it off.

In fact, it seemed like the first verse would be excellent, the chorus would be better, the second verse would be even better, and the last line would be great. They went uphill. It started strong, and just kept getting better, till the end.

What a great opportunity, to be in the room with that many of the songwriting greats.

It was! So, Sunday I got on a plane, and flew back to Nashville. I got up Monday morning, and I walked over and turned on the TV. I had my back to the TV, and as it came on, it was an early morning televangelist. These were the first words out of his mouth: "There's somebody out there fixing to give up on a dream." And I turned around, just like that, and he was pointing right at me [laughs]. He said, "Don't give up. The race always gets toughest right before you cross the finish line." And I thought, "All right."

An hour and a half later, I'm in my car, I pull up at a red light, and the lines, "He wore starched white shirts, buttoned at the neck. He'd sit in the shade and watch the chickens peck. His teeth were gone, but what the heck," literally came out of nowhere. I didn't even know what it was about, who it was about. All I know is, I grabbed my pencil, and I scratched them down as fast as I could, and I drove on into the office.

I remember thinking, "Neck, peck, and heck, that's kind of corny, but I'll take it." I sat down at my desk and I wrote those lines out pretty neat, and then I got up and walked around the room, and about halfway around in a little circle, the words, "I thought he walked on water," literally fell out of my mouth. I got chills that ran up my arms and back, all the way up to the top of my head.

I remembered then, sitting down with my great grandfather when I was four years old. My mother went and picked him up, and brought him over to the house to spend some time with me, so we could get to know each other.

The song just came. I wrote it all verses, with no choruses. When I played it for Pat, she said, "Well, it needs some kind of a lift in there somewhere." So I went back to my apartment and the chorus came, literally, just as fast as I could write it. I went back and played it for her, and she goes, "Yeah, that's more like what we were thinking about."

I remember feeling like you could have taken a baseball bat and tried to hit me, but there was a force field around me. Not because I had written a song that would go on and make money, and become a number one hit, but because I felt like I'd done my first really honest piece of writing since moving to Nashville, and everything else was irrelevant. I'd forgotten about it, and then two weeks later, Pat called me and said, "What about that song you played me? Why don't you go over to Almo Irving and put it down on tape?" There was a split publishing deal between Hayes Street and Almo Irving. They had a little eight-track studio at the time.

You hadn't thought about recording a demo before that?

I loved it, and I was playing it for my friends, but I was still trying to learn it. So I went over and put it down. Chris Oglesby and James

House were behind the glass, and I played and sang it live. That was it. When I came back into the control room, I think they had tears in their eyes. They said, "Boy, Allen, that's a really good song."

I took it back to Pat Halper and she ran it over to Warner Brothers, to Martha Sharp. That week, Martha called and said that Randy Travis liked it, and wanted to record it. Within just a few months it was a number one.

At that point, my writing changed a lot. Because at that point, I stopped looking out there for ideas, and the answers, and I started going in here, and writing about things I knew about and was passionate about. It was such a relief for me. Things that mattered to me, that's what I needed to be writing about.

Not that I've done that every song since, but usually, when the writing is not going well, it's because I'm not hoeing in my own garden. So, that's kind of how I got into the business.

How much of your encouragement comes from within?

I believe one of the most important questions writers need to ask themselves is, "Why am I writing?" If you can answer that question, you can weather some awfully bad storms.

I write because I believe that's what I was born to do. I believe everything that led up to this point was preparation for me being a songwriter. I've had affirmation along the way, that it was God's plan for my life. So, when times got really bleak, and I was low on money, or not writing the kind of songs I thought were in me, I still always believed that this was my calling. And whatever that requires me to endure, I'm going to endure it for as long as I believe that I'm supposed to do it.

There might come a day when God whispers down, "That's it," and then, hopefully, I'll have the grace to let go and try something else. But as long as I believe that's what I'm put here to do, then that's where I get my drive.

Did family or friends encourage you in the early days of your writing career?

My sister was like an angel, in that from the time I was very young, she was a positive voice about the writing. She was always saying, "Allen, you have a way with words. You should do something with that."

Actually I left out a story earlier, that's just as wild as the other one. My sister came to Austin to visit me. She was going to Southwest

Texas, in San Marcos. I told her that I was going to run to the grocery store, and that I'd be back in a little while. She was going to hang out all day, so I took my time shopping. When I got back, she had been in my closet, in my box of lyrics, that I'd carried around for like ten years. It was my private thing I didn't want anybody in the world to know about.

She had a legal pad, and was spread all over the floor with a red pencil, and was circling things saying, "You need to finish this, you need to finish that, and you need to finish that."

At first I was irate. I felt violated. She said, "Allen, you have a million dollars in that box." I said, "I do?" And so, that was kind of the beginning. At that point I had not completed a song. That night I picked one of those ideas and started working on it.

My parents were like a lot of parents: "You went to college, and got a marketing degree, and now you're what?" That's understandable. I have no ill will towards them. My dad told me if I moved to Nashville, and ran out of money, I shouldn't expect him to help me financially. And when I got to Nashville I quickly ran out of money.

My mom called me one night, and she asked, "What'd you have for supper tonight?" I told her I had cornbread and beans. She said, "That sounds good. What'd you have last night?" I said, "Cornbread and beans." Then she asked, "How much money do you have?" I told her I had a five-dollar bill and some change. She said, "I'm going to send you some money, but don't tell your dad."

She told my dad that I wasn't doing too good. He called me up the next day and said, "Look, I'm going to send you some money, but don't tell your mom." I got like three hundred dollars that week. They were great. When the rubber hit the road, they were there to help me out.

Are you aware of the cycles of creativity?

Yes, but I try to work at it every day. I don't try to write a song every day, but I show up every day. I make myself available every day, whether that's listening to music, or writing in my journal, or writing a song. When I'm not in one of those periods where I'm writing a lot of songs, I'm still sharpening those tools for when those cycles come back around.

What is your workweek like?

It's pretty much five days a week, ten to five. But I'm really on the clock twenty-four hours a day.

I have a song on Bonnie Raitt's new CD called "Valley of Pain," which I co-wrote with my friend Rob Mathes. The lyric came one night while I was checking my e-mail. The phrase, "valley of pain," just flashed in front of my face. I was printing out an e-mail, so I turned it over and wrote, almost first word to last word, as fast as it came.

I don't typically write fast, so I just thought, "Well, this must not be anything." I held it over the trash can for about two seconds, and then I moved it to the left, and I laid it down right there on the ground. It sat in our bonus room, by the trash can, for two weeks. My wife knows not to throw anything away with lyrics on it.

Rob came in from Connecticut to write, and we stared at each other for a day. I went home that night and I thought, "What can I take him?" I went upstairs and there was that lyric. I walked in the next day and said, "Rob, this is all I've got to show you." He looked at it and said, "I love that. Get out of here, leave me alone."

So I went downstairs to my office, and maybe thirty minutes later, he called me up here, played it for me, and I loved it. That's a long way around to say, I'm disciplined, and I'm on the clock all the time.

Talk about the role of your subconscious mind in songwriting.

I really trust that the subconscious mind is going to deliver and, in a way, I try to work around the conscious mind because, when we're writing, and *thinking* about it, we're filtering so much. So, when I write, I try to bypass my conscious mind as much as possible, especially when I'm writing by myself. I'll pick up the guitar and start singing nonsense.

I trust that when I'm working on a lyric, I might work all day on a line or a verse and get nothing, but I don't believe that time is wasted. Because, time and again, I've found that, after a good night's sleep, my subconscious works it out. I come back the next day and it's solved. I believe the subconscious plays a huge part in the creative process of writing songs.

What about dreams?

I've dreamed scenes. I wrote a song last year called "The New Good Old Days." The first verse is the scene I saw in a dream. I had no idea on earth how to approach the subject matter that I was writing about. I worked on it Monday, Tuesday, and maybe Wednesday, and nothing. Then, Wednesday night, I had a dream that I was back down there in Huffman, Texas, in our living room. I came in the next day, and that's where the song started. "Last night, in a dream, I traveled down to Texas, to the living room of the house where I was raised. My dad was young and healthy and my mom was smiling. She said, 'Son, welcome back to the good old days.'"

That was my way into that song. It doesn't happen a lot, but I think it probably would happen more if I paid attention to that more. Or, maybe if I kept a notebook by my bed, for just documenting dreams, I might get more out of that.

Have you ever experienced a period when the flow of your creativity seemed endless?

Probably the most creative time for me was about the third or fourth year that I was in Nashville. I was still single at the time, and that's all I was doing, writing songs. It gathered steam and momentum, because I was in such a rhythm of working every day. Every song seemed to come with two more song ideas. It's like the more you draw from the well, the deeper it gets.

I think that was a good time, but I don't think, for your whole career, you could always write with that intensity. You would burn out. Now I'm more balanced about it. I'm not saying all those songs were wonderful either, but I was definitely in the "just letting it rip" mode. I still let it rip, but I do take time to recharge my batteries.

Do you feel like you want to move back to Texas and write from there?

Yeah, I don't know if that is in God's plan for me, but I'd like to try it.

I've gone back through my catalog to see how well the songs I've written right after coming back have done. "He Walked On Water," "We Were In Love"—that was a number one song for Toby Keith—a song called "Don't Laugh At Me" for Mark Wills; all three of those songs were written the week after I came back from Texas.

You have an idea for something you want to say in a song. What process do you go through to develop the story?

I sit with it, I digest it, I brood over it, and I look at it. I'm talking about when I write by myself. That's my process.

It's two different processes. If I were co-writing, I would take the idea in and it'd be more like volleyball. It'd be like, "Here's the idea, what do you think?" And they would grab it and throw it back to me. It would be more bouncing it back and forth until we came up on something that inspired us both, gave us both energy to think, "Well, that's a fresh way to look at this idea."

When I'm writing by myself, I just start studying on it. I'll take an idea and write it out longhand, like I'm writing a short story. Just start writing. This is what I'm trying to write, in free-flow thoughts, no critiquing, no changing, no spelling, and no rhyming. Just as fast as my hand can go, trying to open up the subconscious, get as much of the emotion as I can and get to the heart of the idea. See if the heart spills out.

It's like turning on the water faucet, and the water's coming through, but you're hoping and praying that a nugget of gold would come out of there too. I've found, many times, if I just start with free-flow writing, and just lose myself in the idea, then the heart of what I'm trying to get to will fall out on the page.

> "I've found, many times, if I just start with free-flow writing, and just lose myself in the idea, then the heart of what I'm trying to get to will fall out on the page."

Do you like to read?

I've read almost everything that John Steinbeck has written. For years after college, mostly what I read was from the classic section. Right now, by my bed, are probably fifteen books stacked on the floor. I don't tend to read just a book. I have several going, and I see what strikes me that day, and read a while. I've got a book right now, on creativity in the second half of life, by my bed. I still read a lot of classic fiction, and I'm drawn to the spiritual classics. I try to read something from the Bible every day. There's no one subject.

Louis Lamour's book, *The Education Of A Wandering Man*, is about his process for writing. He made a lot of sense. He said, "Read about wherever your passion takes you." For example, if you're feeling really passionate about butterflies, read about them. It'll amaze you because, down the road, you'll need a verse or something about butterflies and you'll have that knowledge to draw from.

Do you think of yourself as disciplined?

Yeah, but I'm going through a time when I'm really working on balance. I think you can be over-disciplined, to the point where you are squeezing the juice out of your life. So, yes, I am disciplined, but I'm trying to be disciplined and awake at the same time.

If I encounter something that used to upset me, like a phone call right in the middle of writing, now I try to open up and embrace it. Maybe there's a reason for this, and I'll take it. Or I'll stop working and talk to somebody who might pull up outside, when it used to be that I would've hid out and just kept writing. I am disciplined, but I'm trying to be awake too.

How important is the opening line?

I think it's very important. The first line sets the tone, and sets the stage. Especially if it's a story song, that first line is like part of a movie, when the scene opens up, you're in a place.

I try to have the first line open up the scene in a place where the listener wants to be, or that looks interesting, or intriguing enough to want to find out how the rest of the song goes. It's more of a gut thing. I don't sit around and sweat or worry over the first line. When I'm writing, it usually reveals itself.

How important is imagery in songwriting?

Imagery in songwriting is important to me, because that's probably one of the strengths of my gift. I like to write visually. The reason I do is because, as far back as I can remember, I liked songs that I could see while I was listening to them.

"I liked songs that I could see while I was listening to them."

I think one of the reasons I like songs that are visual is because, long after I might have forgotten the words, I can still see the movie and remember it. I like to give the listener something they can see, and hang onto, while they're listening to the song.

Do you see the video sometimes as you're writing?

That's one of the main ways I write. I see a picture. I let myself daydream, see the movie, and start describing it.

What is the hardest part about writing a song?

For me, the hardest part about writing a song is the period between songs, when you're waiting, and digging, and hoping, and praying for the next idea that inspires you enough to invest your life into it. I'm at a point now, where the idea has to come with enough inspiration to keep me interested.

What are the basic skills a songwriter should try to develop?

Learn an instrument. Learn about song structure and rhyme. I don't know if this is a skill, but fall in love with words. I'm in love with the sound of words.

Reading. I read with a pencil behind my ear and, every time I see a phrase I like, I underline it. Most of my books are underlined all through. But that's not a skill, though.

Let's take the word skill out, and replace it with "traits." Does that help?

Yeah, discipline, but not over the top with it. Show up every day. And that does not, necessarily, mean write a song every day. If that happens, though, don't stop it, don't hinder it, take it and be happy about it. If a writer will show up, even thirty minutes a day, at the end of the year they'll see a growth in their writing. That'll be the most important thing. And listening, that's a skill that can be sharpened, or become stronger. Tune your ear, every day, into conversations and what people are saying.

What are the advantages to co-writing? What are the disadvantages?

The advantage of co-writing is that if you have a glaring weakness, you can work with someone who, that's their strength. For me, I'm drawn to great melody people. But, in Nashville, most writers who are good with melody are great lyricists too, so that's twice the fun.

It doesn't mean it's better, but you have instant feedback. When I'm writing by myself, I might have a line, and wait for three days to bounce it off someone. But, in co-writing, you've got that instant thing going, and that's a benefit of co-writing. And it's a whole lot less lonely to co-write. You have someone in the room with you.

The downside of co-writing is that your gift, over time, can diminish. You can actually lose touch with your voice as a writer, and forget that voice, what it sounds like. I believe that to be true, only from experience. I'm not preaching to anybody. That's just my own experience of co-writing.

I've found that, give me a couple of weeks in there by myself, and, slowly, I get back in touch with it. Now I try not to get too far from it. When I sense I'm drifting, I'll clean my schedule for whatever time it takes.

The reason I believe it's important to be in touch with your voice as a writer, and your gifts and your strengths, is that, that way, you're really contributing. If both writers are contributing their strengths and their gifts, then you're going to get a third thing, that can be better than both these writers. That's what I'm striving for. If I'm sitting there co-writing and I catch myself thinking, "Well, maybe they'll come up with that line in a second," that's when I clear my schedule. I need a break. I've got to go back in and sharpen my tools.

What about that "editor voice" that we all have in our head?

I think, when I was down in Austin, Texas, developing as a writer, that critic was not so prominent. But when you move to Nashville, and make your living as a songwriter, the critic becomes something to contend with. I'm well aware of it, and I rebel against it.

But let me say this, the critic plays an important part in the process. It's just a matter of making sure the critic doesn't overstep his bounds and become stronger than the creator. I look at the creative part: Say, if there is a creator and a critic in my mind, I see the creator being like nine feet tall, and the critic being two feet tall. And as long as it stays like that, then they keep each other in check. Because you do need to go back and be ruthless sometimes, and say, "You know, that line just does not work. That line could be better." I'll re-write, and I'll write twenty verses to get one sometimes. I don't want the critic to get so loud that I'm not being creative, and not writing from a place of joy, and passion, and fun. You know, when the critic gets too strong, it's almost like working for a taskmaster or something.

How important is fun in songwriting?

When I'm co-writing, I catch myself laughing a lot. When we're laughing and cutting up, all the channels of creativity are open. I don't always have to be laughing; I don't mean to give that impression. But, for me, laughter is a big part of co-writing and having fun, even on serious songs.

Define "writer's block."

Fear.

Have you ever experienced writer's block, and if so, what did you do about it?

Yeah. That was right after Martha Sharp and Barry Beckett came down to Austin, and heard me do those few songs I'd written.

I think I was able to squeeze out four songs after they came down, and they weren't anything like the first ten. After that, I just locked down tighter than a drum, and it was simply just my being afraid of not impressing them.

Have you had it since?

No, I've had fallow periods, but I'm learning to understand the rhythms of all this, and it doesn't freak me out. It's not a block; it's just that I need to rest.

I came out of the workaday world, where if I'm not working, I feel guilty. So going to work's not been a problem for me. Slowing down and having balance has been my problem. But I've learned, after writing, writing, writing, to exhaustion, it's okay to learn to relax and take some time off. And I've only been able to do that the last four or five years.

During that time in Austin, I read a lot of books. I researched it. I went to the library, and researched writer's block. I read that Tom T. Hall wrote "Harper Valley PTA" after a year of writer's block. I read that Kris Kristofferson had writer's block. I read that Hank Williams Sr. had writer's block.

What I took away from it was, they all wrote their best stuff after their first bout with writer's block. I took comfort in that, a lot of comfort in that. Actually, the first song I wrote by myself after writer's block was "He Walked On Water."

What's the most intimidating thing about songwriting?

The blank page. For me, writing a song, each time is like the first time. Even though I've been a part of, or written, several hundred songs, there are still those butterflies. It's not like computer science, where you learn the buttons to press and then it happens.

You know, the people who chase tornadoes. Those people see, in a year, maybe twenty, because they know how to put themselves into position to see a tornado. And that's about it. I can't create the tornado, but I know how to position myself to be there when it happens. That's the way I view it. My process is to try and be there in that place.

Songwriting can be a real roller coaster ride. Do you have any tips on how to survive?

If, early on, you can answer the question, "Why am I doing this?" then the bumps and bruises, and ups and downs are easier to tolerate.

After it became clear to me that this was my calling, there was not an option to do something else really. Once I found my way into Nashville, parking cars and loading boxes, it was the happiest I'd ever been.

Although we need money to survive, that's not what drives me. That question was answered for me a long time ago. The reward is in the work. It's in getting up and being able to do this one more day. I'm not impervious to discouragement, but regardless of what the business is doing, I feel like this is what I was born to do. I've been given this gift, and the only thing I have control over is using that gift, and trying to improve that gift. Everything else is not really in my hands.

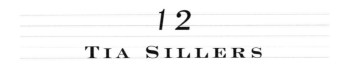

12

TIA SILLERS

As a Nashville teenager, Sillers had the good fortune to live next door to Dave Innis, a former member of Restless Heart. Through Innis, she had the opportunity to pick the brains of several great songwriters, including Dave Loggins, Don Schlitz, Bill LaBounty, and Becky Foster. The love of songwriting soon became a major part of Siller's life.

Her song, "I Hope You Dance," struck an emotional chord with listeners by capturing the essence of life experiences. The song received national exposure with articles in USA Today and Billboard magazine, as well as being an inspiration for the Florida Gators football team. The song earned 2000 CMA Song of the Year and Single of the Year. Sillers has had many cuts by other artists including the Dixie Chicks ("There's Your Trouble"), Pam Tillis ("Land of the Living"), George Ducas ("Lipstick Promises"), and Kenny Wayne Shepard ("Last Goodbye" and "Blue on Black"). Not only did "Blue on Black" have the honor of holding the number one spot on the rock charts for seventeen weeks, but it was also the 1998 Billboard Rock Song of the Year. Other artist to have recorded Siller's songs include Martina McBride, Trisha Yearwood, Diamond Rio, Wynonna, Patty Loveless, Suzy Bogguss, Kim Richey, Tammy Cochran, and Alan Jackson.

www.rutledgehillpress.com/store

Tia, how did you become a songwriter?

I'm one of the only songwriters in the world from Nashville, besides Matraca Berg. I grew up hating country music, being embarrassed of the music industry in general. I mean, the bug man was a songwriter. The gutter installer was a producer. Every single waiter and waitress was a future country star. So I grew up with a real disdain for it, not wanting to have anything to do with it. I just grew up waiting to be able to get out of this town.

I went away to college. I was always a real creative person. I was in plays, and I wrote. There were several bands that were the big thing on campus. I thought they were okay, but I also thought they could be better. I didn't quite know how they could be better, but I remember I went out and got one of their albums and wrote their lyrics down and thought, "Oh, that could be better, and this could be better, and that's a stupid chord, why did they go to there?" That is what started the whole thing.

And then, I was over for an exchange program in England, where I was working with the BBC. I was basically a coffee girl. They were making a documentary on Irish, British, and Scottish folk music. I just got completely sucked into it. I thought I definitely wanted to move to Europe.

But, when I came home to visit my family, my mom took me to the Bluebird Cafe to see Don Schlitz, "Don For a Dollar," and that was that. She had it all planned. She really wanted me to move back, and that did it.

Where do you find ideas?

I think you can find ideas everywhere, but I think one of the problems with our day and age now, is that there are too many options, and when there are too many options, you can't focus. Ideas don't come to you when there are too many things, or an idea will come to you, but something will distract you just as quickly.

I like to create, or seek out, environments that don't have that many options. If I'm going to go to the beach, for example, I don't want to go to Daytona Beach, or even Destin. I

> **"I like to feel the starkness of my humanity and be reminded that I'm just a speck."**

want to go to Apalachicola, St. George Island, population 380, where it's just me and a bunch of seagulls. I like to feel the starkness of my humanity and be reminded that I'm just a speck. Or I want to go to the mountains. But sometimes it's important to go to a city, or an exotic place where you are reminded of the whole of humanity.

We just got a TV. We haven't had a TV for years. But we don't have cable. It's downstairs in the basement and it gets terrible reception. We get channel five and eight, what more do you need? I don't even know how to work the remote control. It's just a distraction. My environment is very important. It has to be very simple.

Who are your biggest influences?

I just got married to a guy named Mark Selby, who's an amazing performer and writer. He has noted so many interesting things about me. One thing is that the people I idealize, I don't write like at all. And the people I end up writing like, or sounding like, I've never even listened to. A lot of people think I do vocal licks and certain melodies like Joni Mitchell. I don't even know what Joni Mitchell sounds like. I've never bought a Joni Mitchell record.

I think Paul Simon is one of the greatest songwriters in the history of mankind. I think Bruce Springsteen is also.

When I first moved back to Nashville, one of the first songs that was a hit was "Independence Day," which was written by Gretchen Peters. It made me look into, and investigate, a whole side of writers that I might not be hearing on the radio. And then, Gretchen had a couple of solo projects that were just absolutely great. She had a song called "Waiting For The Light To Turn Green." All of those songs opened me up to other singer songwriters.

And literature, in and of itself. I try to write like Willa Cather. You can't really beat Dr. Seuss. *Oh, The Places We Go*, is one of the most fantastic, sublimely simple books, with wonderful rhyme and wacky meter. And it continues to touch people, so there has to be something said for that. You can't compete with him, rhyme-wise! Shel Silverstein is sort of the same way, as far as his sparseness of language, and his sense of humor and orneriness. I love ornery writing.

> **"Creativity is not waiting for the muse. Creativity is actually a work ethic."**

What do you think creativity is?

I'm going to have to quote Stephen King. I can't quote him exactly, but, "Creativity is not waiting for the muse. Creativity is actually a work ethic."

It's really 99 percent perspiration and 1 percent inspiration. Stephen Spielberg says that the muse is not some pretty winged woman swabbed in silk. The muse is sort of like a Danny DeVito character with a green night shade and a cigar that says, "What, you're not working? Okay, I'm not coming back!" And he leaves.

But, if every time he knocks on the door, sticks his head in, you're there typing away, then he stays. I think truthfully that a real aspect of creativity is work ethic.

Do you have a writing room or special place where you like to write?

Mark, my husband, says one of the biggest secrets to my creativity, and his creativity, is that we are so protective of our time. We are like secret police to each other. We'll flat out lie to people for each other, and go, "Oh no, he's double-booked that day." And he's not! The truth is that he needs to go downstairs in his little writer's room and play with his speakers and his guitars for ten hours, and come out triumphant. That's the same with me.

To quote Lucinda Williams, you have to have "pens that don't run out of ink, cool quiet and time to think." Pens can run out of ink, that's fine as long as I've got plenty of pens. But time to think—you just do not get enough time to think.

I can write a lot in spurts, with other people, and have a real organized schedule, but then I have to disappear. So, maybe I could bust my butt and write with thirty-five people in two months, but then, that's it for two months. I'm just washed.

We're going to Costa Rica for vacation. We're going to a place without telephones and TV. I think that's the only way you come up with real ideas.

And you have to read so much. Reading is something you have to do solitarily. I mean, you don't do reading in a group, you don't read at a mall.

Are you aware of the cycles of creativity?

The highs are awesome. The lows are terrible because you are convinced it's over. The lows make you do stupid things. I've found that when I'm in the lows, I've just got to make myself get out of bed, exercise, and stumble through it. I have to be very militant about it.

I hate it when I go through a period where I'm not writing good songs, and there's this voice inside me, and it goes, "Well that's that; you're a has-been."

There hasn't been a year since I've started, that at least twice a year, I haven't woken up, got the newspaper and gone through the want ads to start looking for another job. Most people can't believe this, but I won a Grammy in February and basically quit in March.

Why?

Because everybody wanted me to write another "I Hope You Dance." Or my publisher will say, "Well, that's a good song, but it's no 'I Hope You Dance.'" I thought, "Just kill me now."

That's hard. I hate being defined. I mean, I'm so grateful for that song. I understand that I wrote one of the most timeless songs in the world, I understand that. But, all things being equal, I would have rather done it at forty or fifty. But that's me being ungrateful.

Talk about the role of your subconscious mind in songwriting.

Who said you can only listen to the subconscious in silence? That just goes back to being protective of my time and limiting my choices. If I have too many choices, and am not being protective of my time, then I don't hear my subconscious.

In the middle of writing songs, I definitely have a little voice going, "This isn't right, that isn't right, don't do this." Sometimes that voice has been wrong. And that's one of the reasons I love to co-write. Co-writing can shut up that voice. In co-writing, you can egg each other on. So many times I would have walked away, or gone downstairs, walked outside and planted in my garden. But, because somebody else was in the room, I kept shoving it away. And that's a very valid reason.

Do you meditate?

No, I don't meditate. I weed. I love to weed. It's amazing. I go for long walks. I live in a really neat neighborhood. We have all sorts of public areas and medians in the yards. I'll be out for a walk, and I'll stop and just sit down in the median, and I'll start to weed. Thirty minutes will go by and the whole place will be weeded. And I've just had this kind of excellent communal thing.

I'm building a stone patio. Every day I go out and it's like a puzzle because you have to make all the pieces fit. I'm dealing with random flagstones. I come out every night, and spend about thirty minutes, maybe. I just get seven or eight stones down. But I come back, real clear-minded.

Is there a certain time of day that you feel more creative?

I like to have ritual, or consistency, order. So, if I'm writing at my house, it has to be clean, or else I will sit there and go, "I should really change the dishwasher. I should really sweep this floor." And it will really nip my creativity.

I love it when I get up in the morning, go exercise, come home, and have this peaceful Zen latte, with a cat on my lap. I have this clock in my head; right about 10:30 or 11:00, I'm ready to write.

Nighttime, I tend to think more melodically, not as much words. My husband is an amazing musician. And we'll just sit in the house and play.

So, I guess the day is more actively working on writing a song, and evenings are more actively or passively creating new material.

When you and a co-writer have an idea for something you want to say in a song, what process do you go through to develop the story?

Typically, I've been the idea person. I don't know why. Nothing spurs my creativity better than somebody sitting in a room playing the guitar to a groove or rhythm you've never thought of before. Things just tend to flow out.

For some reason, I'm really gifted with opening lines. The song just starts at the beginning. The problem with that is, a lot of times it doesn't have a hook. The writers I seek out are able to work around that.

Many times we'll start writing an idea, and we'll realize that the way we're suppose to do it is naturally revealed to us, or we'll start writing a story one way, and halfway through it we'll go, "We are writing in the wrong person, it shouldn't be *I*, it should be *she*." Or, "It shouldn't be in the future, it should be now." So that changes everything. Unlike a house, in which you would want blueprints, and all the contractors, and estimates, and everything ahead of time, sometimes with a song it's best to just have a picture of a house and just change the plan as you go.

How many songs might you generally be working on at any point in time?

I tend to work better if I don't have too many songs working. The reason being that, if I'm not careful, I'll unintentionally rob Peter to pay Paul. It gets me in a little trouble. I try to finish what I start.

Typically, when I'm writing with somebody, I like to have two appointments within the week, or within a five- or ten-day period. If you can't finish a song in two full days, it might not be a worthwhile song. I'm talking about two fully constructive days.

Do you keep notebooks or idea books?

I started keeping journals about seven or eight years ago. They're my favorite way of organization. On the inside cover, and the first blank page, and the first several pages after that, I put nothing but quotes and funny things that happen all year long. And then, after several pages of that, I start my index, which are my song titles, who I wrote it with, and the date I wrote it. About four pages later is when I start writing the songs, finished in order.

That's the front part of the book. The back part of the book is all my ideas, and notions, and thoughts. Eventually, the pages just meet and, when they meet, it's time to get a new book. It ends up becoming a weird sort of amalgamation of the statement of everything I am for that year.

Have you ever had a song pour out of you, almost in its entirety?

I have a song called "Ticket Out Of Kansas" that completely poured out of me. My song "Some Days Are Better Than Others," which was on Trisha Yearwood's *Real Live Woman* record, was such a strange thing. I was writing it with my then-friend Mark (now my husband), and he had mentioned, a week or so before, that he'd like to write a song called "Some Days Are Better Than Others." All I could think of was the Miller Lite beer commercial, which was "Some days are better than others," and I thought to myself, "I don't know."

When we got ready to write two or three weeks later, and he was playing this melody, I assumed it was for "Some Days Are

Better Than Others." It went perfectly. I just looked at him and said, "If you see dark skies in these green eyes, it just means that I can't find no cover, these ghosts that haunt me, they get me when they want me, and some days are better than others." I just did the rest of the verse. He just looked at me and he said, "Go get a pen." That was such a spooky thing.

Did it scare you?

Yeah, and it was such a rush. God, when you're high you feel sexy, and immortal, and creative, godlike. The muse isn't with me; I *am* the muse. Oh, God that's great.

The other thing I love in "I Hope You Dance" is the part that goes, "Time is a wheel in constant motion, always rolling us along. Tell me who wants to look back on their years and wonder where their years have gone." It came out exactly like that, with the exact same melody, driving back from lunch. I said to Mark D. Sanders, "But that's for another song, we can't put that in this one." And he said, "Oh, yes we can!" He already had it all figured out.

> "God, when you're high you feel sexy, and immortal, and creative, godlike. The muse isn't with me; I *am* the muse."

A blank sheet of paper—now what?

Nothing more intimidating than a blank sheet of paper. Actually, the blank book is more intimidating. If you have to flip over five or six pages because the first five or six have songs on them, it's okay. But a brand new one, that has no notion that it's about to become a song notebook, that's depressing.

One of my biggest pet peeves of songwriters is when you get together, they've got a blank sheet of paper, and they want to know the title first. The title, that goes on the top, and they start writing the first line, and it goes in ink, where it should be.

Do you ever feel like everything has already been said?

For every fifty-year-old that says, "There's nothing new under the sun," or every thirty-year-old that says, "There's nothing new under the sun," there's some twenty-year-old that's experiencing it for the first time. The problem with "There's nothing new under the sun," is that it only works if everybody is born and dies at the same time. We have this birth/death, life/birth, death/life thing going all the time. So that means somebody's just figuring it out.

Somebody, right now, is just about to get his or her heart broken for the first time. Somebody, right now, is just about to kiss somebody for the first time. Somebody, right now, is about to get his or her first kitten. This is new stuff. Somebody, about a month from now, is about to walk to school for the first time. Somebody, right now, is about to become a mother. That mother wants to hear a song about hope and joy for her, and the future of her child. She doesn't mind if it's been sung a million times before, but it needs to be a new song for her time, and her perspective.

Do you think of yourself as disciplined?

No, although everybody says I'm one of the most disciplined people.

But you don't see yourself that way?

I read a great article on competence that was very comforting to me. You could replace the word competent with anything: disciplined, focused, honest, whatever. Competent people, because they're so aware, and they have insight, and they're operating from being organized and competent, tend to underestimate their competence. They think, "Well I could be doing a better job." That's because they're aware that, yes, indeed, they could.

Incompetent people, on the other hand, think they're kickin' ass. They think they're fantastic. They think they are Muhammad Ali in the ring. That's because they don't have a clue.

I would rather be incompetent and think I was great, but that's the short run. In the long run, being competent, I think I suck. I think my songs suck. I think my work ethic sucks. I am frustrated with myself. I am very hard on myself, and I think I could be working harder.

But you do enjoy what you are doing?

I do, and I actually don't like to call what I do "work." It's not always really good to tell other people how much fun your life is, because it just breeds animosity. I have a brother who works seventy-eight hours per week and I don't want to tell him, but the truth is, my time's my own until 10:30 every morning. If I want to work, I do.

Does writing on a different instrument alter your writing style?

I hate to admit it, but I'm a terrible musician. But people tell me that I'm an excellent musical person, in that I have tremendous sense of melodic arrangement. I have a real gift for knowing where to take things.

That's one of those things that have bugged me, made me feel like I'm less good than I might be. I've taken guitar lessons. I've taken piano lessons. I've taken music theory. Some people just aren't wired that way.

How important is the opening line?

"The night was sultry." "It was the best of times, it was the worst of times." "Call me Ishmael." Literature should say it all right there.

I just wrote a song, which I think has one of the neatest opening lines: "I found a rock in the shape of a heart on the banks of a slow moving river and, of course, I thought of you."

That says a lot!

It does. I'm alluding that your heart is a rock or a stone but then, also, that I can't even get away from you on the banks of a river.

Which verse do you think is hardest to write?

The first verse you write might end up being the second verse, that's the easy one. You've got the juices flowing. It's daunting when you realize that the first verse isn't the first verse, it's better as a second verse, and that you really need a first verse. That's very hard. The second verse is very hard because, many times, you've already said the really meaningful stuff.

And then, the bridge is a pet peeve of mine. I have a love/hate relationship with bridges, because a bridge either means you haven't said what you've needed to say yet, or it means I don't really have anything else to say here, but I want the music to go some place else. I feel like a lot of times the bridge is completely unnecessary, although many times the bridge can completely, brilliantly sum it up. But, the bridge has to be the most organic part of the song, or I just don't put it in there. It has to come to you so naturally that it just feels that it's just got to go to here, and it just sort of spills out of you. Otherwise, most of my bridges sound fake.

Do you think imagery is important in songwriting?

The best piece of advice I've ever gotten is from the guy I call my high school principal. He's not, but he was like a high school principal, always sending me to detention. That was Tom Collins, my old publisher. Tom produced Ronnie Milsap and Barbara Mandrell. He was an ornery old cuss, who was really smart and right on the ball. Boy, did he give me the best advice; it wasn't advice at the time, it was like orders. He said that every song has got to have furniture in it. Furniture. You wouldn't have a room in a house without furniture. Every song has got to have furniture in it, an actual concrete image, whether it's a red-tailed hawk flying across the sky, or a tiny diamond ring on my left hand, or I'm sitting on the sofa watching TV. It's got to have furniture. Even with "I Hope You Dance," I have an ocean, I have mountains as concrete things. "Give the heavens above more than just a passing glance." That's a definite action that somebody would do.

What is the hardest part about writing a song?

Being original. Not repeating yourself, not repeating what has been said. Not feeling like you have to emulate what's out there because, if you emulate what's out there, you're always going to be behind the curve, as opposed to ahead of the curve.

Feeling like you have to rhyme is dangerous. Feeling like it has to meter out, that's dangerous. There are some songs that require metering out, or a rhyme. You have to know when it's necessary and when it's not.

Bob DiPiero says the secret to Mark Sanders's success is that he knows when it is time to go to lunch. I think that's one of the hardest things in a song, knowing when to stop beating a dead horse.

I don't ascribe to this, because I don't like to think I'm writing songs so they will be hits. But Bob DiPiero also said, "The difference between a good song a great song is a hundred thousand dollars." The truth is, in many cases that is the truth, although there are many terrible songs that still make the big bucks.

There are certain basic skills a person needs to develop for any career. What are the basic skills we need to develop as songwriters?

First of all, if you love words, you're a better lyric writer. If you love melody, you're a better melody writer. If you're a better musician, you're a better music writer. If you have an affinity for alliteration, if you have a fiction, if you tend to fix on flare, if you are drawn to description, if you have a love for lyric, well, you're probably a lyric writer.

My husband cannot walk past a guitar and not pick it up. I think that says something.

How do you choose a co-writer?

First of all, I don't usually. That's one of those things I have no self-confidence in. I think people do not want to write with me. I have to be really struck with what I've heard from them. Then I have to find out how they operate.

For example, if somebody is purely a lyricist, I think we're going to get in trouble because I'm not sure I can carry the total musical weight, to give it the attention it needs. If I find someone who's purely a melody writer, who merely wants words, that's not really that much fun, because that's sort of forcing the words to fit, or forcing the music to fit, and that's not as organic as it should be.

It's kind of like growing the plant. If you're trying to grow the plant by having it rain for thirty days, and be sunny for thirty days, that doesn't really work. It needs to be a little bit of both.

In the past, though, I've become friends with people slowly. It takes me a year, or six months, or two years of observing someone and then, finally, I can bring up the writing thing.

Right now I have a new publisher, here at Famous Music, who just took over, and he's telling me, "I want to shake things up. What are your strengths, what are your weaknesses, and I'll go from there." So, he's putting me with some very commercial writers, who I would not normally seek out.

I've always said that if I could find one or two new writers per year that I click with, that's a real successful thing. Because the odds are, one or two of my favorite, older writers will fall out. Either they'll stop writing as much, or they'll move away. Like, Mark Sanders doesn't write nearly as much now. He's been writing for like thirty years and, at this point, he only wants to write if he's really inspired.

What are the advantages and disadvantages to co-writing?

You have to compromise. That is a disadvantage and an advantage. You have to be on better behavior. That is a disadvantage and advantage. You have to be malleable. That is a disadvantage and an advantage. You have to be willing to be surprised. You have to be willing to embarrass yourself. That is an advantage and a disadvantage. There's no clear advantage or disadvantage. Everything is a double-edged sword

How do you get charge of that "editor voice" that we all have in our head?

I don't have charge of that voice. That's why I co-write, because the voice is very loud, and very opinionated and smug sounding, a real know it all voice in my head. I defer to it way too much.

What advice can you give on dealing with the fear of failure?

There's not just a fear of failure that holds people back, there's also a fear of success. I think fear of success has held back just as many people. I have met some people who have been incredibly talented and focused, and they would do things to sabotage themselves, to keep themselves from having to reckon with success. Fear of failure operates in probably a similar light, in that it makes you desperate. That works for some people, it doesn't work for others.

I have met so many men who have written hits, who have gotten married, or been married. His wife quits her job. They have four kids and they get this fear of failure. This fear of, "Oh, my God, I have this big house, and these cars, and these people to support." They become desperate, and they start writing drivel. They start writing stupid, positive, up-tempo songs over and over again, until they just become reasonable facsimiles of good stuff.

There's a desperateness that comes in any songwriter I know, who does succeed, and goes out and buys the house and the car. Because I, for one, don't think you can be creative in a mansion. You can't be creative with a maid. We're like farmers. It's only going to come from sowing seeds, hard work. You can't be creative if you join a country club, and you have a wife that plays tennis every day, and when you get home goes, "Honey, the child needs more money for his lacrosse practice." That's so un-country music. That has nothing to do with country music. It's dissonant.

I think there are two kinds of fear of failure; fear of failure initially like, "Will I ever get that hit to begin with?" I have the fear of a failure now of, "Is this as good as I get? Is this it?" I have that fear. It's not like it ever goes away.

But you have to do things that protect you. You have enough doubts in your life. You have to do things to protect you from becoming desperate, or compromising your creativity. And having a maid or a butler will compromise your creativity. It might give you more free time, in which you would feel like you have to write more commercial songs, so you can make more money to pay for the butler.

Define "writer's block."

It's this impossible-ness. It's this impossible amount of blank space on a piece of paper, this lack of words out of my mouth. It's not one original note. Writer's block is when I feel like there is nothing new under the sun, and I'm afraid that might be true.

What do you do about it?

I go play, and I don't mean play a gig, I mean play. I'll go to the garden store, get some plants, go weed, go plant plants, play with my cat, play with my husband, read a book, imagine going on a trip somewhere, go out and get a travel book and plan something. Do other things, make phone calls, pitch songs, and hope it passes.

Do you have any "low point in the career" stories you'd like to share?

I've had a series of low points. I got a cut by Randy Travis, one of my very favorite songs, called "Dogs and Tattoos." I would run into people and they would go, "Oh, my God, it's the best song." It was my first cut, Randy Travis. Oh, my God, this was so amazing! It's a song that means so much to me.

My boyfriend at the time, who worked at Warner Brothers Records, brought home the tape of it. He said, "Check this out." I listened to it and I cried, and jumped up and down, and I was so excited. Then he said, "But it didn't make the record."

That's the cruelest thing anybody's ever done. He should have told me it didn't make the record, but do you want to hear the rough? I cried inconsolably for three days. I went out and got the want ads, looked through, thought about becoming a dental hygienist. I went, "Forget it." It hurt that much, that heartache of coming that close. I'm choked up right now just thinking about it. It hurts too much.

It took a couple years for me to stop taking it so personally and go, "All I can do is love the song, and I don't want to hear that it's on hold, I don't want to hear if it gets cut. If you want to hand me the CD when it comes out, that's fine, but I'm not taking it personally up until then." I know I can't take it personally because it is a business. It's the music business.

The other, really terrible, low point in my life was that I was married and I got divorced. That just sucked. That was just crippling, emotionally. Ironically, I wrote some great songs. I wrote "I Hope You Dance" at that time.

I was writing for me, saying, "I hope you can come out of this environment, this life, this time, this world, this sadness." That was terrible. It changed me, and my writing, forever. It made me have to rework my opinions and my beliefs. I've never felt charmed since then. I've really felt like this is probably a fleeting gift and I'm grateful.

What's the most intimidating thing about songwriting?

That somebody is in the next room doing the same thing you are. And that me, and somebody in the next room, and the four other people in this office then, have to write a song, and then we have to take it into a studio and demo it. And that demo has to be brilliant, as brilliant as we hear it in our head. And we have to have the right person to sing it, and somehow it's got to be perfect. Then, we've got to take it to our plugger, and our plugger has to have woken up on the right side of the bed, and had their coffee and their vitamins that day, and just want to hear that voice and that type of song that day, and think it's wonderful. And that plugger has to put their heart behind it, and then take it around this whole town, and everybody they play it for has to have gotten up on the right side of the bed, and had their coffee, and had a fight with their spouse, or not had a fight with their spouse, whatever it takes. Whatever heartbreak, or love, it takes for them to love that song.

And then, they have to play it for the artist, and the producer, and those same people have to feel the same way. Then it has to get cut, then put on the record. And then the radio record promoters have to think it's cool, and radio has to like it, and then the consumer has to like it in order for somebody to think I wrote a hit! It's intimidating.

Are there words, phrases, or subjects that you consciously avoid using in your writing?

I used to never use the words "daddy, mamma, flame, baby, hot." Unless it was literal, like "The woods are on fire," or "The flame in that candle is just about to burn out," or "It's a hundred and three degrees outside. I can't believe how hot it is." I use the word burn. I still haven't used "fire" or "candy."

Why did you avoid those words?

I avoid words that seem hypersensitive, overzealous, and fake. I have a friend who wrote this song, "Let's Make Love All Night Long." I am one of the most passionate women I know, but I know in the realities of love, and passion, and comfort, and tenderness, that is over-exaggerating!

I don't like to exaggerate human relationships, but I do like to talk about the times in human relationships when you feel like you're immortal. When you feel like you are flying, but you aren't. I like to make that distinction in the song. Like, "Oh, my God, I can't believe this is happening. I wonder how long it will last. I know it won't last forever." I like things to be tempered with reality.

There are a lot of ups and downs in the music business; do you have any tips on how to survive?

Don't pay attention too much to the business. Hide out. Don't be influenced by too many people. Don't let people do you favors. Do it for yourself. Protect yourself. Try to keep that joy, that wonder, that awe.

And, if you're a woman, for God's sakes, if you're starting off as a songwriter, don't get married and get pregnant. Actually, if you're a guy, don't do it. If you can come to this town with no strings attached, all the better. Maybe one string, because no matter how much somebody loves you, it takes an extraordinary person to not start to think that what you're doing might be crazy, after a couple years.

Especially when you're a younger person. No matter what it is, if you've made certain financial sacrifices to get here, and you have your friends and your peers start to make money and live in their nice, little house because they are salespeople, or bankers, or mechanics, or have their own businesses, somewhere along the way, a spouse, no matter how much they believe in you, might start to wonder, "Why can't we be more like the rest of the world?" There are obviously exceptions to the rule, but I think you have to be unattached for a while.

13
CRAIG WISEMAN

Hailing from the college town of Hattiesburg in Southern Mississippi, Craig began playing music at age twelve in the school band. After several years of playing drums professionally, he decided to move to Nashville in 1985 to chase his dream of becoming a professional songwriter.

After a few more years of playing clubs every night to make ends meet, Craig had his first success as a writer at age twenty-four with a song on Roy Orbison's Mystery Girl *album, "The Only One."*

Craig signed with Almo/Irving publishing in 1990 and went on to have over 170 songs recorded and over 50 charted singles. He recently signed a long-term publishing deal with BMG Music Publishing. He has been named one of Billboard *magazine's top twenty-five writers each year from 1994 to 1999. He was also named* Music Row *magazine's Writer Of The Year for 1997 and the Nashville Songwriters Association International's 1997 Writer of The Year. Wiseman has also been nominated as songwriter/composer of the year for the 1999 Leadership Music's Fifth Annual Nashville Music Awards. Craig also serves on the Executive Board of the Nashville Songwriters Association International and ASCAP's Advisory Board.*

Craig has had songs recorded by many of country's biggest acts, including Diamond Rio, Tim McGraw, Faith Hill, Lonestar, Phil Vassar, Joe Diffie, Kenny Rogers, Tracy Lawrence, Deana Carter, Randy Travis, Aaron Tippin, Lee Roy Parnell, Tracy Byrd, and Trisha Yearwood, just to name a few. He has penned twelve number one country singles, including "Walkin' Away" (Diamond Rio), "A Little Bit Of You" (Lee Roy Parnell), "If The Good Die Young" (Tracy Lawrence), "Everywhere" (Tim McGraw), "She's Got It All" (Kenny Chesney), "Where The Green Grass Grows" (Tim McGraw), which topped the Billboard *chart for four weeks in the fall of 1998; "Just Another Day In Paradise" (Phil Vassar),"Tell Her" (Lonestar), "The Cowboy In Me" (Tim McGraw), "Young" and "The Good Stuff" (Kenny Chesney), and the current Phil Vassar single, "American Child."*

Craig's success reaches beyond the country music community. He currently has a massive radio hit on BBC Radio 1, "Shoulda, Woulda, Coulda" (Beverly Knight).

How did you get into songwriting?

My mom said I was drawn to music as a kid. By the time I got to my early teens, I started playing drums in a band in Hattiesburg, Mississippi, where I'm from.

There was one summer when everything kind of fell into place. My brother, who was a huge country music fan, had gotten a guitar, and I was learning how to play guitar. So we would sit around and play songs. Also, I was playing guitar at church camp, doing all the standard camp songs. That was really cool. I figured out, after messing with all those church camp songs, that with three or four chords I could play a million songs.

Then I wrote a song, and I thought, "With three or four chords I can write a million songs." That was so incredible, just like discovering something that had been in the middle of your table, for half your life. How amazing that you could write songs.

I would stay up all night long and write. I had one of those little tabletop cassette recorders. I'm sure it was horrible then, because I was still much more of a lyricist than a melody guy. But, I think because I was a drummer, I liked the rhythm of stuff. But man, I would write four or five songs a night, just vomiting stuff out. I never had any regard for what the end was going to be.

I took a few trap set lessons, and the guy from the music store gave some band my name. I went and played at the VFW one night and made fifty bucks. I was fifteen, and got fifty bucks for two hours of playing music. I thought, "Man, this is great!" The band would just start a song and I would figure out the beat. It was one of my first run-ins with real country music too, because here I was, and here comes this Porter Wagoner wannabe. I started learning more about writing songs, because I just had to be the Don Henley of the band.

I traveled with my mom, and played in the honkytonks in the summertime when I wasn't going to school. About the time Alabama broke, our band got a money-backer. I was nineteen or twenty, and had been in and out of college. This money guy wanted to sign me, and the lead singer, to a big contract. I knew enough to know that I didn't need to sign anything without a lawyer. So, my mom was coming up here to Nashville, working on her doctorate, and I hitched a ride with her. I talked my way into Ken Levitan's office. He actually looked at my contract that day and laughed. He said, "These people want to own you, and your firstborn son, forever."

I went to the Grand Old Opry that night with a friend, and we got in backstage. I met the guy who ended up being my roommate for the first three years I was here. He was playing drums for one of the groups. I told him I was thinking about moving to town, and he thought I should do it. So I moved here on May 21, 1985.

I finally got my first Nashville gig, playing drums. After being in Mississippi and making four or five hundred dollars a week, I was making twenty-five dollars a night, six hours a night, seven nights a week. I was putting in my forty hours a week, but it was playing music. This gig was just relentless, but it was one of the best things ever.

I never sang with the band in Mississippi, but when you were in a band like this one, and somebody got sick, you had to fill in. I was the songwriter, so I knew all the lyrics to all the songs. So, as horrible as it was, I started singing. I realized the audience didn't really care. They just wanted somebody up there croaking whatever version.

We ended up playing that gig for seven months, and then a guy came up and hired us away, a private club, much better gig, six nights a week and thirty-five dollars a night. So we got a night off and a ten-dollar-a-night raise. I had time to start seeing the other music in town.

You've got to remember, the whole time I was playing the seven-nights-a-week gig, I was trying to write songs and meet publishers. The gig would be over at three, and you had to wait till four, till they cleared the register and paid you. Then it was a thirty- to forty-minute drive home. I'd get home at 4:45, sleep for a few hours, get up take a shower, be dressed to go to the gig that night. If I was meeting somebody, it was pointless for me to drive all the way back home just to turn around to drive all the way back.

Were you doing a lot of co-writing then?

No, not at all, just a lot of meetings, with people telling me I sucked. I had twenty songs that I'd demoed. I'd gotten a little list of publishers, and Ed Bruce was one of them. So I called and they told me to just drop a tape. I said, "I really want to be told I suck in person. That's what I'm really after." There's nothing else that has that kind of effect.

Bobby Cottell gave me a twenty-minute meeting. I ended up being there an hour and a half and we met again the following week. One thing led to another, and I ended up with a writing deal, but they didn't want to pay for demos.

Bobby Rymer, my publisher, was the first of several that were in my face about writing. He was always asking, "What do you mean by that?" Or, "I don't know what in the hell you're trying to say here." Or, "You're really missing the ball here. A song is pictures, a song is images, a song is now. You can't have line after line that paints nothing."

He was really big on images. I finally got to the point where I was thinking, "I'll give you images." So, all of a sudden, I started turning the corner and writing a lot more visceral. Everybody went from saying, "I don't understand what you're saying" to, "You can't say that."

I asked them, "What's the matter? Can't you tell what I'm trying to say?" And they said, "Yeah, I can't get it out of my head."

A few years later, I ended up writing for Almo Irving Music. Chris Oglesby kept in that same tradition of being in my face over lyrics, and making me write it right.

I think all those days of no demos was great training. I couldn't hide my stuff behind anything. It had to survive me singing and me playing it. I wasn't going to be a great singer or a great guitar player, so I just kept trying to improve the one part that seemed willing to grow.

Are there specific places or things that inspire you?

I'm really big on debunking all that stuff. I am not into the precious artist thing at all. This is your job.

Are there specific activities that are catalysts for creativity?

I used to get into all that steering myself to feeding the muse, but I really find that I don't worry about that anymore. I read voraciously, always have. Try to see movies and, if I can't think of anything to write about, I just go to the mall and sit down and watch life go by.

I did a question-and-answer panel and they were talking about how many songs I wrote in a year. One of the other panelist said, "Craig, he's still writing his life."

Well, I have written my life. I've written a song about growing up, and about getting married, and about getting laid. I've written dozens of those. Life is going on here. If you don't write it for you, write it for somebody else.

I really got into this, when I first came to Nashville, trying to watch for things that kept me from writing. For example, when I first started to co-write, this guy came to my house one day at ten o'clock in the morning. He said, "Have you ever read Arabian Nights?" I said, "Yeah, I've read that." He said, "Remember the opening line of that book, 'The last camel died at noon?' They were on the way to that French foreign legion thing. And they were in that sandstorm, and the camels were dying. What a great opening line! I want to write a song that has that kind of opening line."

We sat there, and we sat there, till six o'clock that night. All that was in my notebook was just a line or two. Finally I told him, "Get the hell out of my house. Just leave. Take your damn pissed-off look, and your plaid shirt, and your star-spangled guitar, and get your ass out of my house."

I have started paying attention to these ruts that you can get in. Do I sit down and not write more than I sit down and write? A lot of people say, "Don't co-write too much because you'll never write by yourself again," but I've spent years training myself to co-write. I happen to like co-writing. I like the social-ness of it. When you're writing by yourself, there's a whole lot of running around in your robe, unshaven, novelist kind of a vibe. Writing alone is a more introspective journey.

What are some other things you've found out along the way, that have stopped you from writing?

You can only wear one hat at a time. You can't be a writer and a critic at the same time. Your talent as a critic is going to grow so much faster than your talent as a writer. We can all be world-class critics in days, and the writing thing might take a little longer than that.

And then, there's the whole self-awareness thing. Self-awareness is what God gave us after we fell from the Garden of Eden; you know, shame. It doesn't come from a good place. If there is a metaphor from that story, that is one of them: self-awareness, where it came from and where it gets you.

My wife has a great book called The Grace of Great Things. It talks about Charles Darwin when he was just a naturalist. He was out one day and, on a tree, he saw a bug he had never seen before. He grabs it and has it in his hand. Then he sees another new bug, grabs it, and has it in his other hand. Then he sees a third bug and, without thinking, he pops the first bug into his mouth, to grab the third bug. Then, of course, the first bug spews something in his mouth and he spits it out.

The point is that he was so lost in his passion that he had no concept of how he was coming off. If he had had a moment of self-awareness, he would have never popped the bug in his mouth. Get to the point when you can just pop the bug in your mouth. I think being a critic is to look at yourself from the outside, and see how you are coming off.

You also ought to write what you know. Some housewife in North Dakota writing songs about being a high seas captain doesn't work. A lot of people don't feel equipped enough. Only you know what it is like to look into your lover's eyes. Only you know how those Monday mornings feel.

If you ever find yourself in a rut, how do you shake things up?

I keep moving. One of the things that keeps me out of a rut, is co-writing. Co-writing is hard. It's like finding a best friend, or a girl-friend. It's a very intimate relationship.

I could be very comfortable, and just co-write with people I've had all my hits with. We all have friends who do that. They wrote those couple of Alabama hits back in 1986, and they still write with those same buddies. And everything they write sounds like it belongs in 1986. All they want to do is sit around and bitch about how lucky Craig Wiseman has been. I had a guy I wrote with in 1986 too, but I don't write with him anymore, and that's not a bad thing.

One of the reasons I came to BMG Music was that there are a lot of young writers here. There are more young people to mix it up with. For me, it's about keeping yourself out of a comfort zone. I've sort of got comfortable with being out of the comfort zone. I'm always trying to push myself.

Do you have a certain time of day that you feel you write better?

I used to. It was a weird thing. I'd get out of my gig at midnight, and I'd write all night long. But when you first get to Nashville, and somebody you've heard of wants to write at 10:30 in the morning, I found I could write in morning.

I don't like starting at two or three in the afternoon. If I have to write at that time, I'll book something before that. If I wait that long to write my head gets all that business crap in it. All the blood goes to the wrong side of the brain.

I write at ten in the morning now, then I'll write again in the evenings. My wife will normally conk out about nine or ten o'clock, and I'll write some more then.

I'm not convinced that you are really writing, when you have to wait for inspiration to beat you over the head. Like your grandma dying, you're only going to have two of those events, so you need to start finding other wells to draw from. I'm a big believer that you've got to embrace what you've got. If you've got nothing to write about, then write about having nothing to write about.

Do you keep idea books?

I had legal pads that looked like somebody hit them with a weed whacker. I learned to just turn about ten pages in, with the legal pads, and start there, because by the time I got to the end of it, I had beat off the front pages. The coffee stains, the cigarette burns, and the tire tracks. I recently started getting those bound books, just for durability.

> **"I'm a big believer that you've got to embrace what you've got. If you've got nothing to write about, then write about having nothing to write about."**

I've got a friend who keeps this quote with him: "The more your mind is there as a writer, the better off you are."

I know when Mark D. Sanders reads books he has a yellow highlighter. He highlights parts that he likes. So, the more your mind is on it, the better. It's learnable, and you can get better at doing this.

Do you set aside a day that is only business, no writing?

No, for the most part, it's all about writing. I've had to constantly remind myself, "I don't make money in the stock market; I am a songwriter." So, if you're a songwriter, have yourself a business card made that says your name and the word "Songwriter" under it.

You're a songwriter, so write songs. If you're in love, you should be writing songs. If you're divorced, you should definitely be writing songs, because you've got to pay for the divorce.

I haven't brought an idea to a writing session in, I don't know how long. A lot of times it's just, "Let's get a cup of coffee and talk," and pretty quick, we'll hit on something. It's, "Man, I went to school with a guy like that." The next thing you know, you find the life of it. That's all I'm looking for anyway, is just an honest take on life.

Do you like to read? What kind of books?

I like to read, and go to movies, and to be around other people who create well. To be around good work. You want to be around that. You want to expose yourself to that. I think every creator should go to Paris, to be around that, to feel yourself. And to feel yourself as miniscule is also great. You're just this one guy in this whole river of stuff. That takes a load off.

So many people are looking for that "last camel died at noon" shit. I think that's why I write a lot, because I take it easy on myself. I'm just writing a song today. Every day I'm not going to write "Everywhere" or "The Good Stuff," and I don't want it to be like that. It would suck if it were. I wrote a song yesterday, and I'll write a song today, and another song tomorrow.

Is traveling good for you, as a writer?

Yeah, sure. I started traveling to the castle, in Europe. Miles Copeland has this big, old castle, and he invites writers from all over the world to come write. I was heating up, as a writer, in 1997 or 1998, but I was writing for this market. In the U.S. anyway, we tend to believe it's just us. We are the ballgame.

But writing with these guys from Europe, I began to realize how poor I was at writing. So, after I started having some success here, I started spending more time in Europe. It was totally good for me to not be anybody, to not have any notoriety. You're only as good as what you come up with today.

My understanding of the castle is you go for two or three weeks, and that's all you do, songwriting, and playing, and demoing.

Yeah, you go there for eight days, and every morning at breakfast they whisper, "Craig, today you're with an Irish folk singer and an Israeli pop star. Good luck." You're totally trying to be light on your feet and write a song. And then you have to go record it. It's very intense. That's why it lasts for eight days.

I started realizing I wanted to be able to write on a larger scale than just where I'm at here, so I started making trips to Europe. I've had a pop hit, and a Top 5 hit, over there. Got a couple of album cuts. All that is working quite well.

Talk about developing an idea and making it into a song.

What you're talking about is when you have a linear story idea. There's a fine line you draw. I can't stand it when people make shit up.

I got so mad at a co-writer when I realized how different we were. We were talking about growing up, and he was telling me about this pool hall where he grew up. He'd go there after school and hang with the older guys. Also, the back parking lot was a good place to go park with your girlfriend. It was kind of one of those coming-of-age kind of things. It was a cool thing, and I thought that would make a great song.

So we started writing a "looking back" kind of thing. "I go home now and I walk downtown, and it's not even a town along the railroad track, and it's just all boarded up. I can look in the windows and I still see the tables all covered up."

I thought, "Wow, that's really cool." When we got to that part of the song where I was saying, "I'm looking back through the dust and I see the tables." He said, "We shouldn't say that in the song. We should say it's been torn down and there's something else built there."

I said, "Oh, is there something else there?" He said, "No it's still there." And I thought, "What's wrong with you? This is real. This is your life. You are freaking me out. You'd rather make up some shit than talk about real life."

The general public—they are not dumb. They have an extremely sophisticated bullshit meter. I think that's where a lot of songwriters really fail. They just want to make shit up. It's your life, talk about it.

"One of the greatest insights I ever made was getting humble enough to realize I'm not special. I'm just an average guy, and if I feel it, and I think it, and I do it, then I'm virtually guaranteed that everybody has felt the same thing."

One of the greatest insights I ever made was getting humble enough to realize I'm not special. I'm just an average guy, and if I feel it, and I think it, and I do it, then I'm virtually guaranteed that everybody has felt the same thing. Therefore, I don't have to put it in esoteric terms.

But, I can speak of some very esoteric things. People actually do respond to that. You look at Pulitzer-winning novels; time and time again, it's somebody telling their story, in their language, in their way. They're not trying to modify it.

I remember reading this story about one of these forty-something adrenaline junkies, and thinking, "This guy's an idiot." He decided he wanted to spend a winter up in the Arctic. So he bought this metal boat and he took his wife along. It turned out his wife's father found that he had terminal cancer, and they came and flew her out at the last possible moment before they were iced in. They were going to come back and forcibly take him. They hadn't known those idiots were up there. But the weather closed in before the helicopter could back for him. Here's this guy in a forty-foot sailboat with only a little cabin. Almost killed himself with carbon monoxide poisoning.

Here I am, a guy from south Mississippi, reading about him. I'm far from an adrenaline junkie. This guy is about as polar-opposite from me as you can get, but I was enthralled by him. This guy's search for self was all it was. There's something about the people who are willing to go so deep, and reveal something about themselves, that allows you to find yourself in there.

We're all on a spiritual journey, and somebody telling of their journey helps you with yours. I don't understand why there are so many songwriters that just want to make stuff up.

We did a BMG writer's retreat where we brought in people from all the offices. Just really to meet each other and sniff butts. It wasn't so much about whether you write a song or not. The last day of this retreat is when we wrote "Young." It was me, Naoise Sheridan, and Steve McEwan. They started playing guitar.

I'd been getting these letters about my twenty-year class reunion, and David and I had been talking about all these high school stories. We started throwing stuff out: "Look at me now, makes me laugh." We had the chorus and the first verse all in place. Steve had a really good rock and roll voice, so he was singing it, and he added the vocal part that goes, "Whoo, whoo, whoooo." I told him, "Steve, you just came up with the best lyric of the song."

But, in those first verses, I had been telling David how we used to go to this place to swim called the Rapids, and how you had to carry your beer over this railroad trestle. We went there because the cops would never go there, since you had to go up over this trestle and down. He said we should put that in the song, but I thought it was too esoteric. I thought it came out of nowhere. And, you know, more people have said that they love that trestle part. That they used to go to a place like that. I almost didn't put it in there.

Should a songwriter know how to play an instrument?

I've always had guitars and basses around, and stuff for recording purposes. It's always good to mess around with those things. Nowadays, you can buy a battery-powered keyboard you could throw a hundred yards, and that will play a bass line into a drumbeat. It's a little cheesy, but it's enough for you to hear.

I remember being at songwriting camps, and somebody would say, "I don't really play, but I'm thinking about buying a guitar." And then you see them, the next year or the year after, and they say, "I'm thinking about buying a guitar." I tell them, "If you'd gotten that guitar or keyboard last time we talked, this would be you playing on this tape, accompanying yourself."

Somebody, just the other day, was telling me about how they were trying to be a lyricist. I said, "Trying to be a lyricist is like trying to be a chef that never cooks anything." It's understanding what happens whenever that heat comes on. It's that chemistry and that interplay of things.

There's only so much you can do by making cold salads. But, when it's all said and done, any chef needs to cook. He needs to apply heat. And, to be a songwriter, you have to either find a co-writer for music, or you should seriously spend some time trying to learn an instrument.

Do you place a lot of importance on the opening line?

Not really, I don't try to look at it like that. But I am a stickler on the top of the song, making sure people know where you are. If it's a linear thing, try to let them understand what's happening.

Here's a person who is coming off heartache, let us know what their frame of mind is, or who they're talking to.

All that stuff is kind of second nature for me, I guess. I don't struggle over that, by any means. I do a lot of re-writing as I write, and a lot of times I'll throw away whole verses.

Which verse is hardest to write?

I like to write second verses better than the first verses. I like "The Good Stuff" because that's when the story really opens up.

Ralph Murphy does a great job at ASCAP talking to young writers. I've heard him say if you have a first verse and you don't know where to go with the second verse, maybe that verse is your second verse. If you can't write beyond where you're at, then maybe you need to be before where you're at.

Don't cop out. Don't think, "All I've got to do is get back to that great chorus." It's rarely easy. I sit here till dark a lot of times. At a lot of the companies I've been at, I'm the last one to leave the building. I'm the one who turns on the alarm a lot of times, because it isn't easy.

Being the Songwriter of the Year and being the Toyota Salesman of the Year are not dissimilar at all. Something tells me the Toyota Salesman of the Year is the first one there in the morning, and the last one to leave. I was talking to Chris Lindsey, and he pointed out something that is so true. He said, "Do you want to write a hit song, or do you want to have written a hit song?" Seems like a lot of people want to have written a hit song.

How important is imagery in songwriting?

I just try to tap into real life. I love the Joe Diffie song "Third Rock From The Sun." The audio version of that song beat the video. There was more imagery, and more story, in the song than they could capture in the video. That is writing. I consider the guitar a video camera.

It took about nine solid hours to write "The Good Stuff." We just kept going, trying to come up with something better. Anytime I got a line that I liked, I'd ask myself if I could do better. We'd push farther, until we found the lines that are great.

Like in the first chorus of that song, "The first long kiss on a second date." Or, the line, "Dropping the ring in the spaghetti plate, 'cause I'm shaking so much." That happened to me.

The next line is my favorite, "The way she looks with rice in her hair." The night my wife and I got married, everybody was out front with all the birdseed and stuff. She got in the car and I got in on my side. It was hot in there, and it was airtight after I shut the door. We'd just gone from all that screaming to that quiet. She looked over at me and there was birdseed and little grains of rice in her hair, and they were falling on the console.

I never even thought about that until I got into that song. But that says so much. I'm at this place, too, of letting the song work for itself, and letting songs speak for themselves, but not letting them over-speak. Instead of saying, "The night we got married," we used, "The way she looked with rice in her hair." What does that say? Of course, you just got married. It's

"I'm at this place, too, of letting the song work for itself, and letting songs speak for themselves, but not letting them over-speak."

obvious! One of my pet peeves is when somebody says, "When she calls me on the telephone." As opposed to what? The CB radio? Come on, man, you're bullshitting, you're wasting time.

What is the hardest part about writing a song?

I actually do take breaks. I took seven weeks off in the summer, and went to our river house. But, for the first couple weeks coming back from that, I'm like, "I'll never write again. I don't know how I ever wrote a song before, I'll never write again."

How long does it take you to get past that?

Couple of weeks or longer, I just go through the motions. I'm learning now. That's when I try to put a lot of young songwriters that I've never written with before in my schedule. I tend to be on my toes more, and their energy is really good.

Playing the game at this level is tough, and a little taxing, but it's not as tough as being a firefighter in New York was last year. It's not as tough as digging a ditch.

What are the basic songwriting skills we should develop?

Practice what you don't know. I came at this as a trained musician. I always worked on my guitar playing, and I always worked on trying to record. When I didn't know the first damned thing about recording, I went and bought stuff, took it home and started messing with it. Then I'd want to put a bass part with it. So, I'd get a bass from the pawnshop and learn how to play that.

All these things really helped me as a songwriter. I could go to a recording session and tell the bass player, "Man, I tried to do that walking bass part at my house, and you can probably walk a bass part so much better than me, but I just don't like it. It makes it feel too rushed. Let's just keep that bass part in 2/4 time." You're able to talk and communicate with the players. So many people can't do that.

Especially these days, you can buy a crappy digital eight-track recorder for about $400. You can get drum loops and all kinds of stuff. You can get a keyboard for $200 that will actually play whole band parts on it, you know. There are so few excuses. You don't even need all that stuff. Just get a guitar and a recorder.

Study the people who have come before you. Embrace whatever you have. If you can't play, then you can use that to your advantage.

What should we do to develop our lyrical skills?

I think a lot of that is just writing. Just continuously hooking words to music. You get to the point where you're not trying to write so much, you're just trying to tell. Writing can be so contrived. I just want to tell.

One of my favorite writers is former president Jimmy Carter. The way he writes, you feel like you're just sitting down at the kitchen table with him. In his new book, *An Hour Before Sun Up*, he just tells. He uses simple sentences, paints these things, and they are just amazing.

I find writing very humbling. When I write, it's revealing. I'm really trying to be honest, and it's humbling, and it's scary. "Another supper from a sack, a ninety-nine-cent heart attack." Yeah!

Do you try anymore to solo write?

Yeah, I've tried to do it again, even in the past couple months. My big criteria is, I do not compromise anything by co-writing. I do not walk away from the song where I've compromised anything. That song does everything, and more, than I can imagine. Therefore, I don't mind co-writing at all. There's no compromises in that. I enjoy co-writing.

I miss being in bands. I miss the camaraderie of that. I love being in this whole Nashville thing. I hate songwriters who really see things on a real competitive level. I can't even get that in my head. I cannot even figure out how to interpret this business in that spirit. It is so apples and oranges. The fact that Tim McGraw didn't cut your song— did that take that drumstick out of your baby's mouth?

Do you recommend that writers just write, write, write?

Yeah, to some extent, it's just like mastering an instrument. At first, you're just trying to jam things together. Then, you see your style starting to emerge. Eventually, you have an arsenal of licks, and you start trying to find out when it's appropriate to use those licks. So, it's very similar to mastering an instrument.

And it takes years. It's a way of life. You know, I'm an extremely successful writer right now. I had thirty cuts last year. Going back a few years, I've had over two hundred cuts, and sixty singles. So, at the top of my game, I was getting one out of four songs cut, which is amazing.

Dolly Parton says her ratio is one out of a hundred. One out of twenty-five is good, that's a couple cuts a year. But, even if you are getting four of ten cut, with the vast majority of what you write, the only thing you're going to get is the pleasure of writing that song. To be a songwriter, your favorite song will probably not get cut; you'll go to your grave with the vast majority of your work never being heard or recorded.

What about that "editor voice" that we all have in our head?

Just don't bring that to the party. There's a time and place for that. I don't worry about that anymore, because I know it's not going to shut me down. But if it's shutting you down, you have to do something about it.

My wife has a good story about that. This lady was a pretty good painter. She and her husband were very creative. They both had gotten into some bad ruts. There wasn't much joy in their relationship, or their work. One of them said, "You remember what we use to do in college? We'd just put on the record player and we'd make stuff up." So one night, they put on their sixties records, and they started cutting up paper, and doing decoupage. And they ended up switching projects, and having a lot of fun. Eventually, it became a regular Thursday night thing. After a few months, both of them had really opened up.

No matter how many deep songs I've written, I want to go to my grave always knowing I can write. That's why I'm thrilled to have that Jameson Clark cut "You Da Man." I want to always be able to write something that's just fun. I want to be able to look back over a year, and see three or four of those kinds of songs.

So many people are so serious. You want to know my professional secret? The reason I have half the cuts I have, is I write tempo. Plain and simple. I write tempo that's more than just fluff. That's all there is to it. I learned to think tempo. I just started writing songs I would love to play drums to. Like "Forever And Ever, Amen" was a rocking thing. It's the playfulness of it. It's not the melancholy. It's the underlying playfulness of that song that makes it work.

I use to write a lot of the ballads. When I got to this town, I started trying to imitate what I heard on the radio. That is not the barometer you need go to at all. But I was trying to imitate people who were trying to imitate people that were writing for George Strait, and it was horrible. My publisher was unimpressed; nobody liked it.

I was dating this girl at that time. Her driver's license was on the table and I saw her full name. She was going by her middle name. I said, "Hey, your first name is Ellen?" She said, "Don't call me Ellen. My family called me Ellen and I hate that name." So I told her, "I'm going to write a song called 'Ellen,' and I'm going to say Ellen as many times as I can."

That's just me. I was like, "Cool. Now that I'm having sex, let's see if we can screw that up." So, I wrote this song called "Ellen." Ellen was a fun word to rhyme with. I demoed that thing, and I got more response to it. It was just that freshness.

It was a light bulb, wasn't it?

Yeah, it was. All of a sudden, all these people were wanting a copy. I asked my publisher, "Somebody wants to cut it?" He said, "No, they just want to listen to it." So I thought I needed to write more things like that. I just lightened up, and wasn't trying to chase the ball so much. Many songs are not going to get cut. That song did not get cut, but that song chronicled and captured a moment in my life, a whole summer of my life.

What's the average time between when you write a song and when it appears on the radio?

With "Walking Away" by Diamond Rio, it was seven weeks. Annie Roboff and I wrote that on a Friday. I demoed it that Monday. Diamond Rio heard it on Wednesday, and cut it on Thursday. They cut it six days after we wrote it.

I was in Oklahoma for Christmas, and a couple weeks later, I heard it on the radio. That is as fast as humanly possible. Average though, for me, and around Nashville, is about two to five years.

Define "writer's block."

I think that's nonsense. If you got writer's block, then you're having life block, heart block. A lot of times you're just taking yourself too serious. If your life is going on and it's not moving you enough to write about it, then you're not a songwriter. Do something to shake yourself out of your rut. Go down to the children's hospital and burp some babies. Go down to Habitat and build some houses. That does it for me. Do some church stuff.

A writer who has writer's block is not a writer. If you call yourself a writer, then write. If something were stopping you from breathing, you would try to find out what was wrong immediately, would you not? The definition of insanity is doing the same thing over and over and expecting a different outcome.

Songwriting can be a real roller coaster ride. Do you have any tips on how to survive?

This is how I keep myself sane these days. I've got a song in the top five that Phil Vassar and I wrote, "American Child." When people ask me, "Where's your song at?" I tell them I don't know.

It's the old adage of, "Be careful not to give power to things that you have no control over." I think that's where you really need to ask, "Do I want to write a hit song, or do I want to have written a hit song?" Try to be careful what you attach your expectations to, what you're going to give power over you.

INDEX

Books from Allworth Press

The Art of Writing Love Songs
by Pamela Phillips Oland (paperback, 6 x 9, 240 pages, $19.95)

The Art of Writing Great Lyrics
by Pamela Philips Oland (paperback, 6 x 9, 272 pages, $18.95)

How to Pitch and Promote Your Songs, Third Edition,
by Fred Koller (paperback, 6 x 9, 208 pages, $19.95)

The Songwriter's and Musician's Guide to Nashville, Revised Edition
by Sherry Bond (paperback, 6 x 9, 256 pages, $18.95)

Gigging: A Practical Guide for Musicians
by Patricia Shih (paperback, 6 x 9, 256 pages, $19.95)

The Quotable Musician: From Bach to Tupac
by Sheila E. Anderson (hardcover, 7 1/2 x 7 1/2, 224 pages, $19.95)

**Managing Artists in Pop Music: What Every Artist and Manager Must Know
to Succeed**
by Mitch Weiss and Perri Gaffney (paperback, 6 x 9, 256 pages, $19.95)

**Making It in the Music Business: The Business and Legal Guide for Songwriters and
Performers, Third Edition**
by Lee Wilson (paperback, 6 x 9, 256 pages, $19.95)

**Making and Marketing Music: The Musician's Guide to Financing, Distributing, and
Promoting Albums**
by Jodi Summers (paperback, 6 x 9, 240 pages, $18.95)

Profiting from Your Music and Sound Project Studio
by Jeffrey P. Fisher (paperback, 6 x 9, 288 pages, $18.95)

Moving Up in the Music Business
by Jodi Summers (paperback, 6 x 9, 224 pages, $18.95)

Career Solutions for Creative People
by Dr. Ronda Ormont (paperback, 320 pages, 6 x 9, $19.95)

Creative Careers in Music
by Josquin des Pres and Mark Landsman (paperback, 6 x 9, 224 pages, $18.95)

Rock Star 101: A Rock Star's Guide to Survival and Success in the Music Business
by Marc Ferrari (paperback, 5 1/2 x 8 1/2, 176 pages, 14.95)

Booking and Tour Management for the Performing Arts, Third Edition
by Rena Shagan (paperback, 6 x 9, 288 pages, $19.95)

Please write to request our free catalog. To order by credit card, call 1-800-491-2808 or send a check or money order to Allworth Press, 10 East 23rd Street, Suite 510, New York, NY 10010. Include $5 for shipping and handling for the first book ordered and $1 for each additional book. Ten dollars plus $1 for each additional book if ordering from Canada. New York State residents must add sales tax.

see our complete catalog on the World Wide Web, or to order online, you can find us at *llworth.com.*